Conducting Meaningful
Interpretation

A Field Guide for Success

Conducting Meaningful Interpretation

A Field Guide for Success

Carolyn Widner Ward and Alan E. Wilkinson

Fulcrum Publishing
Golden, Colorado

Library of Congress Cataloging-in-Publication Data

Ward, Carolyn Widner.
  Conducting meaningful interpretation : a field guide for success /
Carolyn Widner Ward, Alan E. Wilkinson.
     p. cm.
  Includes index.
  ISBN-13: 978-1-55591-530-8 (pbk.)
  ISBN-10: 1-55591-530-2
  1. Communication--Audio-visual aids. 2. Visitors' centers. I.
Wilkinson, Alan E. II. Title.
  P93.5.W37 2006
  302.202'08--dc22

                                                          2006017899

Printed in the United States of America
by Thompson-Shore, Inc.
0 9 8 7 6 5 4 3 2 1

Design: Patty Maher
Cover images courtesy of (clockwise from top): Humboldt State University;
California State Parks, Cahill; Carolyn Widner Ward; and
Oregon Caves N.M., NPS

Fulcrum Publishing
16100 Table Mountain Parkway, Suite 300
Golden, Colorado 80403
(800) 992-2908 • (303) 277-1623
www.fulcrumbooks.com

Contents

Foreword

I have always believed that the foundation of any profession is its advancement of knowledge about the activity it embraces. Any professional you can think of—whether plumber, chef, electrician, auto mechanic, physician, accountant, politician, teacher, preacher, winemaker, sign maker—is defined first and foremost by their profession's intelligent applications of a body of *knowledge*. Knowledge about a practical activity, such as interpretation, springs from many sources: personal observation, trial and error, anecdotes, and systematic research, to name a few. But until that knowledge is coalesced into explanations for what actually occurs (and how things turn out), it remains as isolated opinion, and practitioners have little guidance in how to apply it outside the situations in which the knowledge was first acquired.

To me, explanations are the stuff of *principle*. While I am tempted here to launch into my own opinions about the necessity of theory in growing practical knowledge, I can summarize it more easily by referring to it simply as "principle." To a face-to-face interpreter, a principle is advice based on an accumulated body of knowledge about interpretation, not just rhetoric. It is not simply made up by the person offering it, and it is not simply the advice-giver's subjective opinion. It is an evidence-based conclusion about what has "worked." If a principle is sound, it is enduring and resilient over many situations, not just one; and it is verifiable by those who wish to test it out, expand, or extend it. Whenever we extract a principle from our knowledge about interpretation, we have made a professional leap forward. I

believe that Dr. Carolyn Widner Ward and Alan E. Wilkinson have taken such a leap in *Conducting Meaningful Interpretation: A Field Guide for Success*.

The growing number of published texts on interpretation is evidence enough of the subject's popularity. This is good news. Access to a wide universe of ideas and ways of thinking about interpretation benefits us all. As they have from the 1950s, opinions abound on what interpretation encompasses and how to do it. Scattered among these "opinions," I have found mainly two kinds of advice. Happily, some of it is principle based, drawing on evidence derived from substantiated theory, research, or the authors' systematic observations and explanations of what "works." Many published opinions, however, reflect mainly the authors' subjective experience of what has seemed to "work" for them and appear more as the authors' personal style–based preferences than they do a thoughtful analysis from which principles can be extracted and widely applied by readers. I do not mean to say that published accounts of personal successes (and shortcomings) cannot be good teachers; clearly, they can be. But they are far more useful when accompanied by principled explanations of *why* things "worked."

In *Conducting Meaningful Interpretation: A Field Guide for Success*, Ward and Wilkinson produced what I consider to be one of the most important principle-based analyses of personal interpretation to hit the streets since the early 1990s. Their approach is fresh and original, and it is based on reasoning that draws on an impressive body of theory and research, underscored generously with their own experiences as practicing interpreters and many years as interpretive trainers. What strikes me most about the fourteen chapters contained within these pages is Ward and Wilkinson's ability to draw on such a deep theoretical foundation in such a practical way. Put simply, they have put into practice what the book itself preaches: principle-based interpretation.

Many volumes these days can be classified as a "he said/she said" repackaging of previously published interpretation principles that seem to offer little in the way of original thinking or advancement of new applications. "Rehashings" sometimes have value in that they make the original works available in different forms and formats, but a distinction of *Conducting Meaningful Interpretation* is that it doesn't simply "pass on" what Mills or Tilden or Lewis or Ham or Cable or Beck or Larsen or Carter or Pastorelli have already said. It makes something new and different from them and offers a practical point of view about planning and delivering personal interpretation that is original and is, in its own right, a bona fide advancement of the interpretation profession. Readers will find in these pages not simply a rehash of what is already known about personal interpretation, but rather a contemporary integration and synthesis of seminal thinking that is, in turn, woven into the authors' own ideas and practical experience. The result is a fresh and original synthesis, scholarly in the way it is treated yet practical in the way it is presented. *Conducting Meaningful Interpretation* is a most welcome contribution to the literature on interpretation, and one I believe will be central to advancing our profession.

Ward and Wilkinson refer to this book as a "field guide," and perhaps that's what it mainly is. But it is a comprehensive field guide. The fourteen chapters offer not only careful explanations of principles for thinking through the preparation and presentation of the most common interpretive activities,

such as talks, walks, campfire programs, children's activities, and audiovisual presentations, but they provide colorful discussions of founding interpretation principles and outline a detailed history of interpretation's historical evolution in the United States. I have found their discussions insightful, carefully reasoned, and engaging. Readers who turn these pages will be treated to an "interpretation of interpretation." Explanations are both instructive and fun, and each chapter is chock-full of examples, illustrations, and analogies that really teach. It is no wonder that years of work have gone into the manuscript.

Having taught interpreters in nearly 50 countries, I can attest to the international relevance of this volume and hope that readers in Europe, Asia, Australia, Canada, and elsewhere in the Americas will appreciate the authors' need to focus the history chapter on their own country. Ward, Wilkinson, and I discussed this focus in an early draft of the manuscript, and they considered attempting a more global historical analysis. Fortunately, we recognized the enormous effort a world history of interpretation would engender. Although such a volume must someday be written, a satisfactory historical treatment of interpretation worldwide would be a mammoth undertaking requiring in-depth historical analyses in dozens of countries. This simply was not the time or place for it. Notwithstanding the historical analysis, however, non–U.S. readers will find the remainder of this book centrally relevant to virtually every aspect of their work. The principles it espouses and the evidence on which they are based are defined not by political boundaries, but rather by a passion about connecting human hearts and minds to the world's special places and what those places represent. That, in a nutshell, is what this book is all about.

In Chapter 14 (Professionalism), Ward and Wilkinson sum up their hopes about the impacts this book might have:

The future of the profession is up to *you*, the practicing interpreter. The role you play in the development of the discipline is significant. ... Ask questions, contribute, grow, change, challenge, and discover. The profession begins to die when the members become complacent and stop learning.

I have enjoyed my role as executive editor of every book in Fulcrum's acclaimed Applied Communication Series. But rarely have I been as optimistic about the potential impact of a single volume as I am about the promise of *Conducting Meaningful*

Interpretation. As Ward and Wilkinson remind us, interpretation is a noble profession deserving of critical analysis, hard questions, and reasoned answers. And that is precisely what their book delivers. When the world history of interpretation is finally written, I believe this volume will be singled out as having kick-started a new phase of growth in the interpretation profession: a long-awaited updating and extension of seminal ideas and founding principles. Interpretation in the world will be better, stronger, and more successful because of it.

Sam H. Ham, Ph.D.
Professor and Director
Center for International Training and Outreach
Department of Conservation Social Sciences
University of Idaho, U.S.A.

Deputy Director
Tourism Research Unit
Monash University, Australia

Preface

As students of natural and cultural history, we know the value of good field guides. They are essential for helping to identify, understand, and appreciate the subject being conveyed. It is through the pages of field guides that a love and passion for the subject is formalized into a lifelong dedicated study.

It was with this in mind that we wrote *Conducting Meaningful Interpretation: A Field Guide for Success*. Although this field guide is especially designed for the novice first-time practitioner of interpretation, it can also be used as a reference guide for the more advanced student of the field. There are 14 chapters taking the reader from the history of the practice to the future of the profession.

Chapters 1 through 4 review the history, theory, and founding principles of interpretation. Chapter 1 guides the reader through the historical evolution of the field from the past to the present. It reviews the significant people and organizations in the field. Chapter 2 discusses the basics of conducting meaningful interpretation. From connecting the visitor to the resource to accomplishing other management goals and objectives, this chapter encourages the reader to consider carefully the purposes underlying all interpretive efforts. Chapter 3 outlines the foundation of interpretation: communication. Understanding the steps of the basic communication process and covering persuasive techniques, Chapter 3 is an essential guide to communication. Chapter 4 discusses the elements of planning for successful interpretation. It covers research methods, identification of target messages, strategies for developing interpretive opportunities, and evaluation.

Chapters 5 through 10 guide the reader through conducting the basic forms of interpretive programs, including an in-depth examination of strategies, mechanics, and tools for success. Chapter 5 outlines the foundational structure of all interpretive programs. Chapter 6 reviews the essential elements of conducting an interpretive talk from the preparation to the closing. Chapter 7 discusses techniques specific to providing interpretive walks, including a large section covering detailed aspects of moving a group through a resource. For conducting interpretation in the dark, including traditional campfire programs and high-tech audiovisual presentations, Chapter 8 provides you with the tools you need to be successful. Providing interpretive opportunities for children is the topic of Chapter 9. Chapter 10 outlines the skills involved with taking the message to the visitor through roving.

Chapters 11 through 13 review tools and strategies useful in any type of interpretive program. Chapter 11 outlines some extra essentials, including conducting programs with "special groups," dealing with emergencies, and techniques for publicizing programs. Operating and maintaining audiovisual equipment is covered in Chapter 12, and Chapter 13 outlines the essential principles and methods of evaluating programs.

Chapter 14 leaves the reader with a discussion of the profession of interpretation and our responsibilities as practicing interpreters to the resources we represent, the disciplines we practice, and the publics whom we serve.

Together, these chapters form the essential components of personal interpretation. We hope this guide will help lead you through the basics of practicing one of the most rewarding and pleasurable professions: that of being a guide for others ... being an interpreter.

Acknowledgments

In most endeavors—and certainly in this one—there is a great deal of collaboration, research, decision making, soul searching, and love. Our more than 40 years of combined experience in presenting, teaching, and evaluating interpretive programs, conducting research, and interacting with visitors provided us with a strong foundation for developing this book. This field guide reflects the generosity, patience, and shared expertise of colleagues, experts, family, friends, and the diverse audiences who we interact with for assistance.

A very special thank you goes to our spouses, Alan Ward, teacher, and artist Barbara Dolan-Wilkinson, for their enduring encouragement. They provided reviews of the art and science requirements of personal interpretation presentations. Their patience and input is much appreciated and was crucial to the quality of the field guide.

In researching and writing, we were fortunate to receive mentoring, technical guidance, and heartfelt assistance from many. We would particularly like to acknowledge Dr. Sam H. Ham, who edited this work for accuracy and relevance.

The genesis of this field guide originated with our development of a comprehensive, standardized Basic Interpretation Learning System (BILS) for California's Department of Parks and Recreation. This system, consisting of the *Basic Interpretation Handbook*, a *Student Workbook*, an *Instructor's Guide*, and a *Field Training Officer's Guide*, is used to train ranger and lifeguard cadets. It also serves as a stand-alone resource for all California State Park interpreters. In the development of BILS, many park personnel were involved. A special thank you to Mott Training Center manager Broc Stenman (ret.) for program oversight and Donna Pozzi, chief of interpretation and education division, and her staff for review and assistance.

We are deeply appreciative of Patricia Widner, Chris Beresford, and Buzz and Judy Webb for their manuscript reviews, proofreading, and critical comments. Additionally, we wish to thank Roger Brandt, Brian and Joanie Cahill, Jennifer Graves, Bob Wick, Kara Murtey, Steve Martin, Alan Ward, and the staff at Humboldt State University, Crater Lake National Park, Oregon Caves National Monument, and the Bureau of Land Management at the Arcata field office for their assistance with providing photographs.

Chapter 1

Interpretation from Past to Present

Interpretation builds visitors' connections to the resource. Courtesy of Carolyn Widner Ward

Knowing the historical evolution of interpretation helps build a foundation of understanding.

Main Points

Communication is the process of transferring meaning from one source to another. Sometimes, due to barriers in communication, an interpreter is necessary to complete the communication process. Interpretation is the translation of language or information from one source to another in order to facilitate comprehension and understanding.

Environmental, natural history, heritage, and cultural interpretation are no different. These types of interpretation involve the translation of the language of the scientist, the voices of the past, and the significances of the place to create meanings and connections with the people of the present. Throughout this text, the term "interpretation"

refers to and incorporates both cultural and natural resource interpretation.

Interpretation's overall goal is to connect people to a resource and direct that connection within management mandates. The resources can be physical objects, places, people, or even ideas. Interpretation assumes a short, usually one-time exposure to a message. It addresses the modern reality of an audience that is easily distracted, time-constrained, and free to pay as much or as little attention to a message as the communicator inspires.

Although there are numerous definitions of interpretation, they all center on the idea of translating information from the scientist, the historian, and the manager to the visitor or the layperson. Over time, how interpretation has been defined and delivered has changed and evolved. Chapter 1 provides an overview of this historical development in the United States, summarizing the primary foundations of interpretation, presenting some of the currently accepted definitions of interpretation, and reviewing the primary types of interpretive services.

Defining Interpretation

Interpretation is an artful form of communication that stresses ideas and relationships, not simply isolated facts and figures. This is most frequently done through the use of

In·ter·pre·ta·tion (noun)

: the act of the result of interpreting: explanation
: a particular adaptation or version of work, method, or style
: a teaching technique that combines factual with stimulating explanatory information

—*Merriam-Webster's Online Dictionary*, 2006

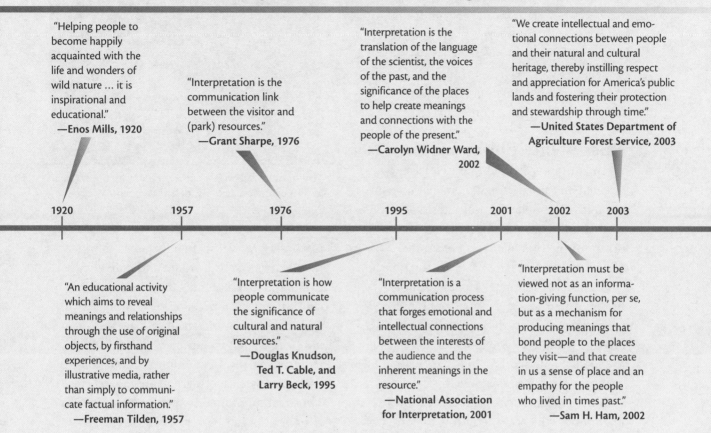

Interpretation Definitions through Time

"Helping people to become happily acquainted with the life and wonders of wild nature … it is inspirational and educational."
—Enos Mills, 1920

"Interpretation is the communication link between the visitor and (park) resources."
—Grant Sharpe, 1976

"Interpretation is the translation of the language of the scientist, the voices of the past, and the significance of the places to help create meanings and connections with the people of the present."
—Carolyn Widner Ward, 2002

"We create intellectual and emotional connections between people and their natural and cultural heritage, thereby instilling respect and appreciation for America's public lands and fostering their protection and stewardship through time."
—United States Department of Agriculture Forest Service, 2003

1920   1957   1976   1995   2001   2002   2003

"An educational activity which aims to reveal meanings and relationships through the use of original objects, by firsthand experiences, and by illustrative media, rather than simply to communicate factual information."
—Freeman Tilden, 1957

"Interpretation is how people communicate the significance of cultural and natural resources."
—Douglas Knudson, Ted T. Cable, and Larry Beck, 1995

"Interpretation is a communication process that forges emotional and intellectual connections between the interests of the audience and the inherent meanings in the resource."
—National Association for Interpretation, 2001

"Interpretation must be viewed not as an information-giving function, per se, but as a mechanism for producing meanings that bond people to the places they visit—and that create in us a sense of place and an empathy for the people who lived in times past."
—Sam H. Ham, 2002

hands-on approaches, firsthand experiences, and/or the use of physical objects. Interpretation communicates the science of the natural world, the stories of cultural heritage, and the excitement of recreational opportunities. Interpretation is provocative, inspirational, and stimulates an audience to discover more.

Although typically used in reference to services provided by park rangers in parks, interpretation is also used in many forms by public relations personnel, educators, salespeople, or anyone who desires to increase the effectiveness of his or her communication. Interpretation is a technique or form of communication. Used correctly, interpretation functions as the preferred light-handed management tool increasing an individual's connection to park resources and as an effective strategy to manage and protect that connection.

There are numerous definitions of interpretation. In fact, Freeman Tilden (1957) said good interpreters will come up with their own definition. But tell anyone outside

Linking the visitor to the resource through firsthand experience is a critical component of successful interpretation. Courtesy of Oregon Caves N.M., NPS

of the discipline that you are an interpreter and they will ask what language you speak. In a way, they are right in their understanding of the word: to interpret is to translate. Just as the discipline itself has evolved and changed, as you progress through this book and your career, think about how your definition of interpretation evolves.

Types of Interpretation

Interpretation is divided into two basic types: personal and nonpersonal. Personal interpretation involves some type of physical interaction between the interpreter (communicator of the message) and the visitor (receiver of the message). This is the typical picture of the interpreter leading visitors through the resource. Nonpersonal interpretive services involve the communication of a message without physical interaction or discourse. Signs and brochures are classic examples of nonpersonal services.

Nonpersonal services are nonlinear. In other words, the visitor controls the order of information received. For example, when visitors pick up a brochure, they can read whatever parts may interest them. Personal interpretive services, on the other hand, are linear, with the interpreter controlling the order of information.

There are positive and negative aspects to each approach. Although this text focuses primarily on personal services, the following section briefly describes each approach and its accompanying qualities and characteristics.

Nonpersonal

Nonpersonal interpretation typically includes any informational, orientational, and educational written, audio, or visual messages provided for visitors without the use of direct personal contact. Nonpersonal services include brochures, pamphlets, newspapers, signs, exhibits, videos, computers, and audiovisual programs (see table 1.1).

Trail signs enable visitors to connect with the resource at their own paces. Courtesy of Carolyn Widner Ward

Nonpersonal interpretation typically reaches more visitors than personal interpretation, allows visitor freedom and individual exploration, and often is the first line of contact; however, because visitors can pick and choose what they read or view, they may not be receiving the primary message intended by management. In addition, it is difficult to determine what messages, if any, are received. The creation of quality nonpersonal interpretive services can be very expensive, time-consuming, and requires expertise and equipment often not readily available.

A great deal of thought and planning should go into the creation, placement, and selection of nonpersonal interpretive services. Due to the high front-end cost, most nonpersonal interpretive services are used for years. Too many or inappropriately placed nonpersonal interpretive services can result in a negative image for the agency. Care and attention should be used to ensure that nonpersonal interpretation is up-to-date and in good condition. If it isn't, it should be replaced or removed.

Personal

The focus of this book is on personal interpretive services. This involves direct person-to-person contact with the visitor. Personal services include walks, talks, demonstrations, children's programs, roving, audiovisual programs, casual interactions, and

Table 1.1 Common Nonpersonal Interpretive Services

Brochures/pamphlets/maps—Paper publications conveying information, orientation, or educational messages. These are portable messages and the most common form of nonpersonal services used in parks. Brochures are often the first contact a visitor receives. Brochures also provide a take-home souvenir that is highly valued.

Audiovisual—Videos or DVDs are usually used as the introduction/welcome to the resource and are shown in visitor or information centers. They may be available for purchase as souvenirs and promotional tools. Videos and DVDs are increasingly being shown on either television or Web sites to reach an off-site public.

Signs—Freestanding, affixed messages provided at specific locations. Signs are usually two-dimensional, include graphics, and may be interactive. Made of numerous material types, including wood, metal, porcelain enamel, and fiberglass embedment, signs are highly valued because they are accessible on the site at all times.

Exhibits—Three-dimensional, object, or artifact-based displays. Exhibits are often interactive and can include written, visual, kinesthetic, and auditory methods of communication. There are numerous types of exhibits, from dioramas and relief maps to interactive and hands-on exhibits. Due to the interactive and dynamic nature of exhibits, they are generally inside visitor centers and museums.

Wayside exhibits—A sign or exhibit that is located along a road or trail. Wayside exhibits allow an increasingly mobile visitor population to receive important messages.

Self-guided or interpretive trails—Through the use of brochures, signs, and/or audio mediums of communication, self-guided trails allow visitors to explore the resource at their own pace, whenever they desire, and reading or listening to only the messages they are interested in receiving.

Newspapers—Guide that is usually developed annually or seasonally for the resource or the region. Newspapers often include more in-depth information than is provided on signs, exhibits, or brochures, including rules and regulations, activities, and general information.

Computers—Interactive method for visitors to receive specific information. As a modern interactive exhibit, computers are often found in visitor centers and include a touch screen, keypad, mouse, and monitors. Computers, through Web sites, are also increasing the parks' ability to reach visitors. Computers can allow visitors to virtually "visit" a site that may be too fragile, dangerous, or remote to visit in reality.

Radio transmissions—Low-frequency radio transmissions that reach visitors' car radios. Radio transmissions provide the mobile visitor population important visitor orientation or informational messages. Signs along roadsides indicate where passersby can tune for more information.

providing information at the entrance station or front desk. The linear nature of personal interpretation generally allows the interpreter to control the order of information presented.

There are many benefits of providing personal interpretive services. The primary benefit is that you may have the greatest control over what messages the visitor receives. In addition, you have a chance to interact with the visitor and answer questions or clear up misunderstandings. Most visitors

like knowing that a real person is available. In this day and age of computerized phones and automated services, personal experiences can be very rewarding and satisfying. Personal contact with visitors also provides management with a better understanding of what problems and concerns visitors have before the issues become critical.

The term "authenticity" has also been used to distinguish personal from nonpersonal services (Knudson, Cable, and Beck

Personal interpretation allows visitors to connect with resources through interactive discovery with an interpreter. Courtesy of Humboldt State University

1995). The interpreter has a better chance of physically engaging visitors in the resource and creating a more authentic experience with the resources than through the use of nonpersonal secondhand illustrative media. With many agencies' primary mandates to protect resources and provide for visitor enjoyment of those resources, personal contact with visitors affords one of the best opportunities to meet those goals.

There are negative aspects to providing personal services. Many point to the cost per person contacted for interpreter-led programs. On average, most estimates conclude that only 20 percent of visitors attend interpreter-led programs (Knudson, Cable, and Beck 1995). In addition, each interpreter can only be in one place at a time, thus reducing both the overall visibility and the number of visitors contacted throughout the resource. Poorly conducted interpreter-led programs may also reduce visitors' feelings of freedom and discovery. As with nonpersonal services, poor training, preparation, and presentation can leave negative impressions on visitors.

The History

When reviewing the history of the interpretive profession, certain names—such as Enos Mills, John Muir, and Freeman Tilden—consistently appear. Many parks and agencies have also played a key role in the development of the discipline. Interpretation in the United States began as a private endeavor and was soon adopted by public agencies and organizations. As the country and its people changed and evolved, so did the discipline of interpretation.

The People

Enos Mills (1870–1922)

Considered one of the founders of the interpretive profession, Enos Mills started interpreting in 1889 in what later became Rocky Mountain National Park. Mills had an insatiable thirst for knowledge about the resource and believed a nature guide must "have a wide range of knowledge and to be capable of tactfully imparting this directly and indirectly" (Mills 1920, 110). During the span of his career, Mills led more than 250 groups to the summit of Longs Peak, always encouraging their connection to the resource that he loved so dearly. Mills was one of the first to make use of the relationship between how much visitors know and care about a resource to how much they want to protect that resource.

He influenced the evolution of park protection, started one of the first programs in the country to train interpreters, and authored more than 15 books about the art and science of interpreting. His book *The Adventures of a Nature Guide*, written in 1920, paints a wonderful historical picture of interpretation early in its professional development. "This new occupation is likely to be far-reaching in its influences; it is inspirational and educational. Anyone who has a vacation or an outing in contact with nature will have from the great outdoors its higher values as well as a livelier enjoyment if accompanied by a nature guide" (Mills 1920, 154). Mills's thoughts and observations regarding the

I developed nature guiding, that is, helping people to become happily acquainted with the life and wonders of wild nature.

—Enos Mills, 1920

Enos Mills was central in developing the art and theory of interpretation. Many of his founding principles form the basic building blocks of interpretive services provided today. Courtesy of Enos Mills Cabin Collection

impact on the field of interpretation as Tilden's *Interpreting Our Heritage*.

Tilden developed basic principles of interpretation that are still used in one form or another today. (See table 3.1.) He said all interpretation must relate to the visitor, reveal relationships, not just facts and figures, address the needs of the whole person, use artful means to communicate, and address the needs of specific audiences, especially children.

John Muir (1838–1914)

Although John Muir's role in the development of interpretation is less obvious than Mills's or Tilden's, it is no less important. Muir has been credited with being the first to use the term "interpret" in reference to nature when he said, "I'll interpret the rocks, learn the language of the flood, storm and avalanche. I'll acquaint myself with the glaciers and wild gardens, and get as near the heart of the world as I can."

Although Tilden studied the discipline of interpretation and contributed to the development of its practice, Muir's work embodied the *essence* of interpretation. He used his communication about the natural world to encourage people to protect and preserve the topics of his stories. Muir was seminal in the establishment of Yosemite as a national park and was the founder of the Sierra Club. Through his writings and presentations, Muir interpreted much of the American West to the nation and the world.

profession form the foundation of interpretive theory and practice still used today.

Freeman Tilden (1883–1980)

Freeman Tilden's influence and impact on the field of interpretation is one of the most strongly felt today. Many consider him to be the father of modern interpretation. Unlike Mills, he was not a naturalist or an interpreter but instead a writer and a reporter. He was hired by the National Park Service to tour the parks, observe all he could, and write about the interpretive services provided. His book *Interpreting Our Heritage* is one of the most widely accepted reviews of the philosophy of interpretation. Tilden wrote many other books and continued his work for more than 20 years. His books are still found on the shelves of most parks and interpretive centers around the world. No modern literary work has had the same

Stephen Mather (1867–1930)

Stephen Mather's influence and impact on interpretation was driven by his innate passion, dedication, and commitment to the environment he loved. His concern for the deteriorating Yosemite National Park pushed

I'll interpret the rocks, learn the language of the flood, storm and avalanche. I'll acquaint myself with the glaciers and wild gardens, and get as near the heart of the world as I can.

—John Muir, 1838–1914

Mather out of retirement to accept the position as the first director of the National Park Service in 1916.

In 1919, Mather was traveling in the Tahoe area when he saw a captivated crowd gathered around Loye Miller and Harold Bryant at Fallen Leaf Lodge. Miller was a paleo-ornithologist and Bryant was the educational director of the California Fish and Game Commission. Both were adept at educating audiences with entertaining presentations.

Mather, charged with protecting the national parks, recognized that this was exactly what he was seeking "in order to counteract those persons who would selfishly destroy park values" (Sharpe 1976, 31). After several months of discourse, he succeeded in convincing Miller and Bryant, who were involved at Tahoe, to come to Yosemite National Park. Mather was so sure that nature guiding was essential to the successful management of the parks that he personally financed the early work in Yosemite for several years.

William Penn Mott Jr. (1909–1992)

William Penn Mott influenced the practice and existence of interpretation on all levels, including local, regional, state, and national. Perhaps Mott was best known for his long-range vision of what parks and interpretation could be.

Mott was always concerned about educating the public in order to help facilitate the protection of the environment. For example, on a regional level, in 17 years as the superintendent of parks for Oakland in California,

Mott broke new ground by appointing the first municipal park department naturalist (Butler 1999). Mott moved from this position to serve as the California State Parks director, where he added 24 new park units during his tenure. Before taking over as director of the National Park Service in 1985, Mott served as director of a local park and the CEO and president of the California Parks Foundation, a nonprofit parks association he started. During his tenure as director of the National Park Service from 1985 to 1989, 17 new parks were established.

Modern interpretation is shaped by the work and dedication of numerous individuals. The field has become more specialized as trainings and certifications, research programs, and academic disciplines have been developed across the country. Authors such as Ted Cable, Sam H. Ham, and Ron Zimmerman are writing books on interpretation, while others, such as David Larsen and Tim Merriman, are marking their own places in the history of interpretation by developing the profession through training practitioners in the field and fostering a professional organization. Research supporting the development of relevant theory and practice is helping to direct the growth of the field. Educational programs, such as those at Humboldt State University in California, University of Idaho, and University of Wisconsin at Stevens Point, all have strong academic programs in

Interpretation should be taken out of the realm of entertainment. It must become the serious business of education. I am not suggesting that we eliminate entertainment, but all too often interpretive programs have as their primary objective entertaining people. Entertainment should not be the end product, but it can be a means toward the end product, which should be education.

—William Penn Mott Jr., 1909–1992

interpretation turning out the next generation of interpreters. These people and places continue the tradition of growth and development of the theories, approaches, and skills in interpretation began so long ago by those such as Mills and Tilden.

Federal Agencies

Interpretation, in one form or another, is used by all major natural resource management agencies today. Whether used by the information officer, public relations expert, naturalist, or an actual interpreter, the skills and strategies of interpretation can make all communications more effective. Although interpretation is used in a number of capacities, the primary function of interpretation in agencies has always been as a management tool.

National Park Service

When thinking of agencies or groups that provide interpretive services, the National Park Service (NPS) often comes to mind first. The NPS was established in 1916 out of a desire to protect and preserve some of the country's precious natural resources. Only three years after the establishment of the NPS, the first paid park interpreters were hired. Soon after, interpreters or naturalists were working in several national parks. These first interpreters were brought in to try to achieve the management goals of appreciation and protection of park resources.

NPS is a leader in the development of both personal and nonpersonal interpretive services provided in areas of natural and cultural resources. Yellowstone, the first national park, and Yosemite were both leaders in the development of interpretation. By the early 1920s, Yosemite, Yellowstone, Mesa Verde, and Lassen Volcanic National Parks were all in varying stages of providing museum services for the public.

Currently, NPS oversees a variety of park areas, including parks, rivers, parkways, lakeshores, historic areas, scenic trails,

reserves, military parks, and historic battlefields. The NPS manages more than 78 million acres of land, much of which is interpreted to the public in one form or another. With more than 2,000 paid interpreters and 200,000 docents and volunteers working across the country, the NPS is the largest federal agency providing personal interpretive services for the public.

The NPS is not only the largest, but also one of the leaders in the field working to develop standards, competencies, and benchmarks of performance and quality. Their Interpretation Development Program provides curriculum, standards, certifications, trainings, and accountability measures for interpreters. Having developed and evolved over time, the NPS's current philosophy on interpretation is that "people will care for what they first care about."

United States Department of Agriculture Forest Service

The United States Department of Agriculture Forest Service (USFS) manages 155 national forests, more than 100 national scenic byways, and approximately 70 visitor centers across the country. The agency began to

The National Park Service has a long and distinguished history of providing a variety of interpretive services for the public. Courtesy of Oregon Caves N.M., NPS

develop its own version of interpretive services when it created the branch of Visitor Information Services in 1961 to help explain to the public the complex policies set forth in the Multiple Use–Sustained Yield Act of 1960. The USFS was shifting its focus for the management of the public's resources, and it was clear that the public needed to be educated about the changes.

Since formally offering the first interpretive services in 1961, USFS has had a tumultuous history of providing interpretation. In 1980, USFS changed the name of its interpretive program from Visitor Information Services to Interpretive Services, the focus being to orient, inform, and interpret to visitors.

USFS has developed an Interpretive Services Strategy, which is a "guide for better delivery of interpretive experiences through our services and facilities, and for providing exceptional service to the public both on and off the national forests and grasslands" (USDA Forest Service 2003, 2). Employees in the USFS are asked to perform many duties. There are currently approximately 500 employees participating in providing some form of interpretive services (Nelson 2004); however, more than half of those conducting interpretation are only focusing about 20 to 50 percent of their time on interpretation (Prell 2002).

United States Fish and Wildlife Service

The United States Fish and Wildlife Service (FWS) also began providing interpretive services in response to management concerns. Early in its inception, hunters and fishermen, through the purchase of licenses and equipment, provided much of the funding for the agency. The 1980s saw a decline in the sale of licenses and an increase in a new population of users. These nonconsumptive users were not interested in shooting the wildlife with a gun, but with a camera. Terms such as "watchable

wildlife" surfaced, and new management issues occurred. In fact, one of the most popular recreation activities today is bird-watching, and birders flock to lands managed by the FWS.

As one of the largest land managers of public lands, with 88 million acres, the FWS provides interpretive services to millions of visitors across the country. One of FWS's current goals is to provide the public with a better understanding and appreciation of fish and wildlife ecology.

Bureau of Land Management

The Bureau of Land Management (BLM), much like the FWS, has a relatively young history in interpretation. With the largest public land base in the country at more than 264 million acres, the BLM has great potential for increasing its interpretive efforts. Like the USFS, the BLM began offering interpretive services in response to a legislated change in management mandate. In 1976, the Federal Land Policy and Management Act was passed, requiring that the BLM manage its land for multiple uses, including recreation. Increased use combined with fragile arid environments resulted in the agency providing more interpretive services in an effort to protect resources and provide for the mandated multiple uses.

There are currently more than 20 types of land designations used by the BLM, ranging from national monuments to herd-management areas. The variability of site classifications influences the types of visitor services offered by the agency. Today, several BLM sites around the country, such as Coos Bay in Oregon and the Lost Coast in California, are providing more traditional personal interpretive services; however, the focus of interpretation for the BLM, as with the USFS, is nonpersonal.

United States Army Corps of Engineers

The United States Army Corps of Engineers (USACE) provides the largest water-based recreation opportunities in the country. Although the agency began in 1936, it did not start providing recreation services until the mid-1940s. In the early 1980s, the USACE began to establish a Visitor Perception and Interpretive Services Program. The goal of the program is to educate and enlighten the public regarding the purpose and concept of the USACE, the operation of their water projects, and the historical and natural features of the area (Propst and Roggenbuck 1981).

In addition to providing many of the same interpretive services as the other federal agencies, the USACE also provides many unique opportunities in interpretation, such as self-guided water trails and interpreter-led boat tours. Although today there are many water-based interpretive opportunities provided by other organizations and agencies, the USACE was one of the first to provide such services for the public. The USACE also conducts research to demonstrate the effectiveness of interpretation in meeting agency goals and objectives.

State Agencies

There are a plethora of specific state agencies and departments that provide interpretation services for recreational, historical, or cultural resources. These may include, but are certainly not limited to, parks, natural resources, soil and water conservation service, fish and game/wildlife, extension service, historic or preservation areas, state farms, and virtually any other agency that serves to interface with the public through communication. There are some states with large, well-developed interpretation programs. For example, California, Oregon, and Illinois have comprehensive interpretation programs offering the more "traditional" interpretive services, such as ranger-led talks and campfire programs. There are more than 3,000 state parks in the United States offering varying degrees of visitor services, including personal and nonpersonal interpretation. There is, of course, an inherent

variability in what services are offered, the manner in which they are provided, and who provides the services.

Local Agencies

Many towns, cities, districts, regions, and counties have parks, recreational facilities, and public-participation programs that provide interpretive services for the public. Many museums, cultural sites, and zoos are provided, managed, and interpreted by local governments. As with state agencies, there is large variability within local organizations in terms of their interpretive offerings, training, personnel, and services provided. For example, Santa Clara County Department of Parks and Recreation in California provides interpretive programs for thousands of visitors annually. They offer extensive training for interpreters and provide quality oversight and direction for program development. On the other hand, many counties across the country may offer little or no formal interpretive programs for the public.

Private Agencies

Nongovernmental organizations that provide interpretive services and opportunities can be classified into two groups: for-profit and nonprofit.

For-Profit

For-profit organizations are similar to those that gave rise to the profession of interpretation. For example, the early work of Mills and Miller was conducted for a fee. Today, this for-profit work has transformed from a few individuals conducting programs for a minimal fee (and maybe food and lodging) to a multimillion-dollar-a-year business. Ecotourism is one of the fastest growing areas in recreation (Doyle 1999). Tour companies, cruise lines, motels, and travel organizations often hire interpreters to help visitors have meaningful and enjoyable experiences, thus ensuring customer satisfaction and return

Events in the History of Interpretation

1864—Yosemite officially made the first state park in the nation

1866—Galen Clark appointed as "guardian" of Yosemite

1872—Yellowstone established as the first national park

1889—Enos Mills began leading trips as a "nature guide"

1891—Forest Reserve Act created the National Forest System

1897—Forest Management Act established reserves

1905—One of the first "displays/exhibits" created in the Arizona Territory of prehistoric artifacts

1916—National Park Service Act passed

1918—National Park Service Education committee established

1920—Steven Mather hired the first paid "interpreter" in the national parks

—Yosemite Museum Association created

—Enos Mills published *The Adventures of a Nature Guide*

1927—California State Park system created

1938—Yosemite established the first Junior Naturalist Program

1957—Freeman Tilden published *Interpreting Our Heritage*

1960—Multiple-Use Sustained Yield Act passed

1961—The United States Department of Agriculture Forest Service created the branch of Visitor Information Services

1964—Wilderness Act passed

1976—Federal Land Policy and Management Act passed

1980—United States Army Corps of Engineers established Visitor Perception and Interpretive Services Program

1988—National Association of Interpretation established

1992—Sam H. Ham's book *Environmental Interpretation* released

1995—National Park Service began the Interpretive Development Program

2003—United States Department of Agriculture Forest Service created the Interpretive Services Strategy

business. Many individuals also make their living providing contractual interpretive services and training for outfitters and guides.

Nonprofit

There are thousands of nonprofit organizations throughout the country that provide interpretive services to the public. Organizations such as the National Audubon Society, the Nature Conservancy, the National Parks and Conservation Association, and the Sierra Club are a few well-known nonprofit organizations. These organizations each have their own mission, vision, and agendas for their cause or area of concern.

For many state and national parks, there are also nonprofit cooperating associations that assist in fund-raising to support interpretive efforts in the parks. These organizations work in cooperation with existing parks to help meet park missions and objectives. Some of the most visible services that are provided by cooperating associations are often in the sales and services provided in visitor centers and bookstores.

In the Next Chapter ...

Now that we have an understanding of the foundations of interpretation, the next chapter begins to discuss the purposes and values of conducting interpretive programs. Creating and delivering meaningful programs that are driven by clear goals and objectives should be at the heart of our programming. Chapter 2 introduces some of the primary goals and objectives that underlie most interpretive services provided, regardless of the specific agency or resource involved.

Review

1. Communication is transferring meaning from one source to another.

2. Interpretation is an artful form of communication stressing ideas and relationships to help build connections between resources and people.

3. There are two basic types of interpretive services: personal and nonpersonal.

4. Nonpersonal interpretation focuses on communication methods without using direct face-to-face contact between the sender and receiver of the message.

5. Nonpersonal visitor contact typically reaches more people than personal interpretive services, allows more visitor freedom, and is generally the first line of contact visitors receive.

6. Personal interpretive services are often more meaningful forms of providing information. They allow for interaction between communication participants and assist in achieving many management goals and objectives.

7. Enos Mills is considered one of the first practitioners and founders of interpretation.

8. Freeman Tilden wrote one of the premier and most widely used books on interpretation, *Interpreting Our Heritage*.

9. John Muir was one of the first to use the term "interpret" in reference to resource interpretation. His work personified the essence of interpretation.

10. Stephen Mather was the first director of the National Park Service and an avid supporter of interpretation services in parks.

11. William Penn Mott influenced the practice of interpretation on a local, state, and national level.

12. There are five primary federal agencies that provide interpretive services for the public: the National Park Service, the United States Department of Agriculture Forest Service, the United States Fish and Wildlife Service, the Bureau of Land Management, and the United States Army Corps of Engineers

13. The National Park Service is the largest of the federal agencies providing interpretive services for the public.

14. There are more than 3,000 state parks across the United States providing varying degrees of interpretive services.

15. Interpretation is offered by both for-profit and nonprofit groups.

Questions and Exercises

1. Compare and contrast personal interpretive services with nonpersonal ones.

2. What is the historical evolution of interpretation in your state?

3. Are personal or nonpersonal interpretive services more effective? Why?

4. What was the historic function of interpretation? Has that changed today?

References
Books
Butler, Mary Ellen. 1999. *Prophet of the Parks: The Story of William Penn Mott, Jr.* Ashburn, Va.: National Recreation and Parks Association.

Doyle, Kevin, ed. 1999. *The Complete Guide to Environmental Careers in the 21st Century.* Washington, D.C.: Island Press.

Gross, Michael P. and Ron P. Zimmerman. 2002. *Interpretive Centers: The History, Design, and Development of Nature and Visitors Centers.* Stevens Point, Wisc.: UW-SP Foundation Press.

Ham, Sam H. 1992. *Environmental Interpretation: A Practical Guide for People with Big Ideas and Small Budgets.* Golden, Colo.: Fulcrum Publishing.

Knudson, Douglas, Ted T. Cable, and Larry Beck. 1995. *Interpretation of Cultural and Natural Resources.* State College, Pa.: Venture Publishing.

Lewis, William J. 1981. *Interpreting for Park Visitors.* Philadelphia, Pa.: Eastern Acorn Press.

Loewen, James W. 1999. *Lies Across America: What Our Historic Sites Get Wrong.* New York: Simon & Schuster, Inc.

Mackintosh, Barry. 1986. *Interpretation in the National Park Service: A Historical Perspective.* Washington, D.C.: History Division, National Park Service, Department of the Interior.

Mills, Enos. 1920. *The Adventures of a Nature Guide.* Garden City, N.Y.: Doubleday, Page, & Company.

Muir, John. 1912. *The Yosemite.* Garden City, N.Y.: Doubleday, Page, & Company.

Sharpe, Grant. 1976. *Interpreting the Environment.* New York: John Wiley and Sons, Inc.

Sirch, Willow Ann. 1996. *Eco-Women: Protectors of the Earth.* Golden, Colo.: Fulcrum Publishing.

Tilden, Freeman. 1957. *Interpreting Our Heritage.* Chapel Hill: University of North Carolina Press.

Manuscripts and Papers
Ham, Sam H. 2002. "Meaning Making—The Premise and Promise of Interpretation." Keynote presentation to Scotland's First National Conference on Interpretation, Royal Botanic Gardens, Edinburgh, April 4, 2002.

Propst, Dennis and Joseph Roggenbuck. 1981. "A Guide to Cultural and Environmental Interpretation in the U.S. Army Corps of Engineers." Instruction Report R-81-1.

Online
USDA Forest Service. 2003. *Interpretive Services Strategy.* Online training manual. http://www.fs.fed.us/im/directives/fsm/2300/2390.txt.

Organization
National Association for Interpretation, Fort Collins, Colorado.

Personal Communications
Nelson, Christian. 2004. Personal communication, August. USDA Forest Service.

Prell, Sharon. 2002. Personal communication, 16 July. USDA Forest Service.

Ward, Carolyn Widner. 2002. Personal definition used in coursework. Humboldt State University.

Chapter 2

Conducting Meaningful Interpretation

Meaningful interpretation connects visitors to the resource, encourages resource protection, and promotes the agency's goals/mission. Courtesy of Carolyn Widner Ward

Meaningful interpretation
is based on management needs,
visitor desires, and the
benefits produced.

There are countless values and benefits of interpretive programs for both management and the visitors. The key for success in meeting the needs of both groups is a well-thought-out program that is meaningfully conducted with clear goals and objectives. Most interpretation began from a need to fulfill a management goal. Whether that goal was to garner public support, to control visitor behavior, to protect the resource, or to increase visitor enjoyment, it was clear that interpretive efforts were meaningful to management and driven by the benefits produced.

The purposes and values of interpretation today can be divided into similar categories: benefits directly associated with the visitor and those more closely aligned with management. Although we will make categorical distinctions between various types of benefits, they are all related and impact each other in varying degrees. For example, increasing visitor enjoyment of the resource is clearly a visitor-based benefit that has management implications. We have essentially two goals with our interpretive programs: to connect the visitor to the resource and to protect and manage that connection within management mandates.

Connecting the Visitor to the Resource

Connecting visitors to the resource has been a goal of interpretive efforts since Enos Mills began leading groups up Longs Peak. From John Muir and Steven Mather to today's modern interpretive programs, building visitor connections with the resource is a primary focus. There are three basic ways through which interpreters can connect visitors to the resource. The first and most common method is by providing information and orientation services to visitors. A second method is by providing educational programs and opportunities. Creating inspirational and spiritual connections is the third method that interpreters use to build connections between the resource and the visitor.

Before we can hope to connect visitors to the resource, enhance their recreational enjoyment, or promote park messages, we must understand the basic needs of our visitors. Psychologist Abraham Maslow (1954) developed a hierarchy (figure 2.1)

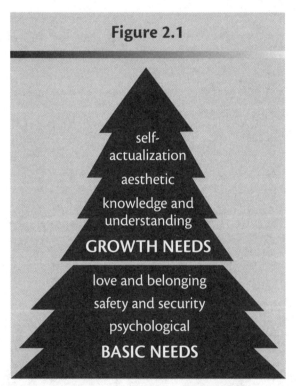

Figure 2.1

Figure 2.1 Adapted from Abraham Maslow's (1954) Hierarchy of Needs

A well-developed bulletin board is an effective and economical tool that meets many visitors' informational needs. Courtesy of Alan E. Wilkinson

that helps us understand the nature of human needs. A person's most basic requirements must usually be met before his or her growth can be enhanced. Recognizing and understanding which level of need a visitor has is key to providing successful interpretive services. For example, a visitor may not be receptive to educational opportunities if she is frightened or lost. In the following sections, we'll explore how interpretation can be used to meet visitors' needs and establish connections to the resource by providing

information and orientation, education, and, finally, inspirational interpretation.

Information and Orientation Services

One of the first needs a visitor has is for basic orientation and information about the resource. The most common method of connecting visitors to the resource is by providing this information and orientation service. *Where is the restroom?* and *What are the poisonous plants in the area?* may be visitor expressions of these basic needs. From face-to-face contacts (or personal contacts) to providing information boards, interpretation is used in several ways to help connect visitors to the resource by meeting these basic needs.

Off-Site

Much of the visitor information services are not conducted on the site with face-to-face contact, but instead through long-distance means, such as the telephone, electronic mail, and regular mail. These methods of communication are the first line of contact for many visitors. Think about the last special location

Field Tips for Providing Off-Site Information and Orientation Services

Answer the phone when possible. Automated phone-answering systems don't allow for personal interaction and can be frustrating for the caller. If using a computerized phone answering system, be sure that all information is updated daily, especially if it includes a weather report.

Smile while you're on the phone. Smiling while talking changes the inflection and tone in your voice. People can hear a smile, even though they may not see it.

Treat visitors on the phone as you would in person. For example, have you ever put a person on hold who is standing in front of you?

Provide the requested information. Do not just send out the "standard" packet of information.

Answer the phone with a greeting that reflects the name of your agency and your name: *Hello, my name is Carolyn. Thanks for calling Montezuma Castle National Monument. How may I help you?*

Have phone numbers and other commonly requested information at your fingertips, ready for callers.

Develop a standard protocol for responding to regular and e-mail contacts in a timely manner. Include a personal note in each request for information thanking them for their interest in the resource.

Keep the Web site up-to-date.

you visited. Did you call first, visit a Web site, or request brochures before actually visiting? Many first-time visitors and those traveling long distances are likely to seek out this type of information and orientation service before arriving at the park. For many, this may help determine which location they visit.

Meeting information and orientation needs for potential visitors is very similar to the on-site in-person contacts; however, there are a couple of special things to consider. Be sure that you respond to requests for information in a timely manner, especially those e-mail and regular mail contacts. Try to personalize all contacts as much as possible. For example, don't just stuff the standard bunch of brochures in an envelope and send it. Give people what they request and include a signed note thanking them for their interest and saying that you hope to see them when they visit. This personalized attention to detail means a great deal to visitors and functions as a great public relations tool for your agency. These "extra" touches help forge visitor connections to the resource before their arrival.

On-Site
PERSONAL

The most common place for providing information and orientation to visitors on-site is at the entrance station or behind the desk in the visitor center. Visitors who come to these locations are usually seeking to meet their basic physiological and safety/security needs. *Where is the bathroom?* and *What kind of snakes are here?* are common types of questions that represent information and orientation needs.

There are several methods that you can use to help facilitate meeting these needs. Be prepared to provide clear, concise, and accurate information. Begin keeping track of what information visitors seek when interacting with you. The list of questions will evolve and grow and with it; so will your ability to respond to those needs. At first, you may not know many answers, but, as time passes, the number of questions that you hear for the first time will dwindle. Once you have created a rather lengthy list, categorize them into meaningful subgroupings, such as flora, or the rules, and so on. Once you have made categories, you can create (if

Visitors often seek information from interpreters in visitor centers. Know the resource and be well prepared to answer the most common questions. Courtesy of Carolyn Widner Ward

Providing accurate and timely information on bulletin boards helps meet many of the basic needs of visitors. Courtesy of Carolyn Widner Ward

they don't currently exist) several books of commonly asked questions that you can leave on the front desk for visitors to peruse. These will be available even when you are not, and thus reach even more visitors. Make the book as meaningful as possible. For example, if the book is on flora, try to have pictures of the plants and the locations that they might be found.

Hearing that same question over and over can get tiresome. There is not an interpreter in the world who cannot sympathize with you; however, keep two things in mind: 1.) it is the *first* time the person standing in front of you has asked the question, and 2.) he or she had to get up a lot of nerve to approach you. For many visitors, it takes a lot of curiosity, fear, uncertainty, and so on, to spur them to ask a question. Take advantage of that. As you will learn in Chapter 10, these spontaneous interactions with visitors are often the most meaningful and they can affect the overall impression an individual has of the entire location and your agency. Remember, to the visitor, you are a public servant.

NONPERSONAL

Another avenue for providing information and orientation services to visitors is through the use of bulletin boards and information kiosks. These nonpersonal methods don't require the physical presence of staff, and they possess many of the qualities discussed in Chapter 1 regarding nonpersonal interpretation.

Although nonpersonal information and orientation can be provided through the use of brochures and signs, bulletin boards and kiosks are primarily used to convey the basic what, where, when, and why answers. Bulletin boards are probably one of the more underutilized communication media. The main reason for this is that people don't read very much. On average, most visitors read about 20 to 30 seconds' worth of material. That's about 60 to 70 words (Serrell 1996;

Field Tips for Providing Personal On-Site Information and Orientation Services

Always have trail, facility, local, and highway maps available. Maps assist the visitors to spatially orient themselves. Place maps where visitors have easy access. The front desk can get crowded and may not be the best place for large maps.

Provide scratch paper for note taking. Providing scratch paper helps you reuse resources and allows visitors to record their desired information.

Anticipate questions. Provide books or binders of commonly asked questions and their associated answers. Categorizing these questions into several books also helps visitors quickly find answers, i.e., a book of plants, animals, historic sites, lodging, etc.

Provide interpretive answers. Don't just give facts; tell stories!

Have common field guides and reference materials handy. Resources and guides allow visitors to find their own answers. They can also be used to promote items sold in the gift shop.

Ward et al. 2003). Writing in a short, concise, and clear manner is more difficult, but more effective, than lengthy pieces of information. As Mark Twain said, "I would have written you a shorter letter but I didn't have the time." Maximize the effectiveness of bulletin boards by using a few simple pointers provided in the field tips on page 20.

Education

Once Maslow's basic needs for information and orientation are met, a visitor is more likely to be receptive to educational messages. A second method of connecting visitors to the resource is through educating them about that resource. Education was probably one of the first types of interpretive messages given to the public. The hope is

Field Tips for Providing Nonpersonal On-Site Information and Orientation Services

Use color to catch attention. Black print on white paper is boring.

Keep everything up-to-date. Have at least one section of the board that is updated weekly.

Pictures are worth a thousand words. Include photographs of resource attractions with captions that tell a story. Connect information to the tangibles visitors have around them.

Minimize detail. Keep it simple and short.

Organize information into meaningful categories and subcategories. Titles and subtitles help visitors quickly find needed information.

Include emergency contact information: after-hours phone numbers, location to the nearest phone, hospital, etc.

Tell stories; don't just give facts. Include at least one interpretive story on the board.

Use variability in size, shape, color, etc. of graphics, text blocks, and column lengths. Reading ease increases with varied appearance of information.

that through education, the public will come to understand and appreciate the resource more and therefore support protecting that resource. The following section reviews basic types of educational messages and discusses methods and techniques used to increase the effectiveness of educating the public.

The educational messages we deliver through interpretive opportunities are determined by the needs of the management, the site, and the visitor. We will review this in detail in Chapter 3. For now, it is important to understand that there are three primary types of messages that must be considered when determining what story to tell the visitors: the cultural, the natural, and the managerial. We will segment the types of messages provided to the public into these

three categories. Remember, we use these types of messages, in part, to increase visitor enjoyment of and connection to the resource, both of which serve to promote the overall experience.

Cultural

Every location, object, or person has a cultural history. For many resources, the cultural stories are a central feature of the resource. Most of the time, you will be asked to interpret a culture that is not yours. In addition, many visitors may be coming to your location to learn about their heritage and history from you. There are several techniques and strategies to help you succeed in this delicate process.

Become familiar with the history of the cultures in and around your resources and be sensitive to cultural diversity. Remember, the "rightness" of an act or a belief system is determined by the historical context in which it occurred. History is not a fact, but instead an interpretation of the people who recorded it, the time in which it occurred, and those who are listening to it today. James Loewen's (1999) book, *Lies across America*, provides an eye-opening view of this theory. Talking about sensitive or controversial aspects of culture and cultural history is something we should be doing, but you must remember that the appropriateness of your comments and actions will be judged by the audience of today. What may not be offensive to one will almost certainly offend someone else. Sensitivity, tact, accuracy, and common courtesy go a long way when conveying cultural messages.

Through interpretation, understanding; through understanding, appreciation; through appreciation, protection.
— *National Park Service Administration Manual*, 1953

Is It Education or Interpretation?

It is important to distinguish the purpose and value of interpretation from education. Although some of our programs strive to impart knowledge to visitors through our interpretive efforts, it is not the singular overall purpose. The purpose is to provoke the audience to want to learn more on its own. There are several characteristics used to distinguish education from interpretation. Motivations and the captive versus noncaptive nature of the audience are two such characteristics (Ham 1992).

The primary characteristic separating interpretation from education, even environmental education, is the time frame involved with the program. In education, there is typically a longer time frame and repeated exposure through which to build knowledge and learning. With interpretive programs, we usually have one opportunity to achieve our goal. Since we only have a short time, our greatest success is to inspire visitors to learn more on their own. The interpretive program is not an end unto itself, but instead should serve as a catalyst for learning. We are planting the seeds.

There are many perspectives from which to tell a story. Be sure that you are accurately reflecting the culture and not simply playing into stereotypes. If possible, seek out living members of the culture by conducting some firsthand research. Remember, this person only reflects *one* perspective of the culture and not *the* perspective. It is not possible to describe every perspective on a culture, nor is it an interpreter's responsibility to do so; however, it is your responsibility to convey which perspective you are representing and that it is one of many perspectives.

Conducting cultural programs helps create tolerance for others. Interpretation provides a wonderfully protected and neutral atmosphere through which visitors can come to know others different from themselves. It also provides opportunities for many to discover their own culture and history, which in today's melting pot can become lost. Cultural pride and tolerance for cultural diversity are both benefits of providing educational interpretive programs dealing with culture and cultural history.

Natural

Educational messages are also used to connect visitors to the natural resources. Deciding what to interpret to the visitors is dependent on many factors. It is important to note what the significant resources are and why the resources were protected. Consider what is special about the resources. In addition to interpreting the significant biological resources, you also want to draw visitors' attention to the details, the biological resources that are often overlooked. When thinking about your resource, remember that interpretation should illuminate the hidden elements of the biological and natural resource.

Successfully interpreting the resource stems from knowing the place. There is no shortcut. In fact, the longer you are in the resource, the more you will realize how little you know about it. Immersing yourself in the resource, talking with others more familiar with the resource, using field guides, listening to visitor questions and comments, researching the current science, and exploring

Perhaps we should hire poets instead of biologists to write our science textbooks! Undoubtedly, we must simplify our messages and express them in ways that assure more lasting effects.

—Steve Van Matre, 1983

Representing a rich cultural history, the Statue of Liberty provides thousands of stories to tell visitors. Courtesy of Carolyn Widner Ward

the local library will all assist you in successfully interpreting these natural resources.

Illuminating the resource for visitors has several benefits, including visitor and resource protection. Visitors are more likely to protect the resource and adhere to rules and regulations if they understand the resource-based reason for the rule. For example, knowing how fragile the cave animals are may result in less damage by the public. We know that visitors are more likely to do as requested if the request is connected not to the management, but to the resource or to the visitors (Oliver, Roggenbuck, and Watson 1985; Schwartzkopf 1984; Wallace 1990; Widner, and Roggenbuck 2000).

If (visitors) never learn to enjoy the diversity of their fellow-citizens' customs, styles, and attitudes, they may be intolerant of those who are "different" and therefore perceive them as "dangerous."

—Douglas Knudson, Ted T. Cable, and Larry Beck, 1995

A second key benefit from interpreting the science of the natural resources is that you are providing a public service by educating individuals about often confusing science. As interpreters, we serve as the link between the scientist and the general public. Educating the public about the importance of our natural resources translates into visitor support and protection of those resources.

History is not a fact, but instead an interpretation of the people who recorded it, the time in which it occurred, and those who are listening to it today.

Managerial

A third area to consider when creating educational interpretive opportunities for visitors is the managerial elements. Don't forget to educate visitors regarding the agency for which you work, the specific management perspectives of your facility, and any special management considerations. For example, there are usually critical issues that require special attention and management. Don't ignore the controversial and delicate issues, but instead use interpretation as a means to educate the public.

Try to develop a thorough knowledge of not only the rules and regulations, but why they are in place and what the overall management concern is for the rule. Talk with your supervisor, resource specialists, and managers about the overall messages they would like the public to take with them. Remember, the public often does not share the same perspectives regarding the resource and the management of the resource. These types of educational programs allow you to bridge those gaps and build a constituency.

Interpretation is meaning making.
—Sam H. Ham and
Betty Weiler, 2002

There are many benefits to providing educational messages regarding how the resource is managed. We will review those benefits later in the section on accomplishing management goals and objectives with our programs. Remember, the motives behind visitors' attendance to our interpretive programs are numerous and varied. The key to overall success is diversity of messages, programs, and opportunities.

Inspiration

Many of the philosophies of interpretation are written with words such as "passion," "spiritual," "whole," and "inspiration." This is the ultimate goal of interpretation: *to inspire others to want to explore further, to learn more on their own.* As an interpreter, the greatest gift that you can bestow is a path through which visitors can come to know. To create explorers out of followers is the function of inspiration and provocation. Because this type of connection is often an emotional one, it is one of the most powerful ways to connect a visitor to the resource. It is also the type of connection most likely to result in a behavioral change. Freeman Tilden spoke of this ability of interpretation to reach and change people when he said it occurs, " … not with the mere recitation of facts. Not with the names of things, but by exposing the soul of things—those truths that lie behind what you are showing your visitor. Nor yet by sermonizing; nor yet by lecturing; not by instruction but by provoca-tion"(1977, 38).

Inspiring visitors is not as straightforward as providing informational or educational messages. In fact, we probably can't give them peak experiences. What we can do is

set the stage by providing opportunities for the visitors to find these types of experiences on their own. We can "provide resources for independent exploration" (Knudson, Cable, and Beck 1995, 64). We can create programs that attempt to "light the spark" of curiosity and wonder. Helping visitors become familiar enough with an environment so that they want to forge their own path is the ultimate method of connecting them to the resource.

Accomplishing Management Goals and Objectives

The second major purpose and value of interpretation is meeting management goals and objectives. In fact, it is *the* primary

A nature guide is not a guide in the ordinary sense of the word, and is not a teacher. At all times, however, he has been rightfully associated with information and some form of education. But nature guiding, as we see it, is more inspirational than informational.

—Enos Mills, 1920

By making visitors feel connected to and comfortable in the resource, we can help facilitate them having their own inspirational experiences. Courtesy of Carolyn Widner Ward

Do not try to satisfy your vanity by teaching a great many things. Awaken people's curiosity. It is enough to open minds; do not overload them. Put there just a spark. If there is some good flammable stuff, it will catch fire.

—Anatole France, 1844–1924

reason interpretive efforts should be undertaken. If the interpretive program is not meeting a management goal, then why are you doing it? If interpretation is not purposefully done to somehow address the mission or goals of the place, it becomes simply entertainment. For example, even the previously discussed purpose of "connecting visitors to the resource" is done to meet management goals and objectives. Increasing visitor enjoyment, promoting recreational activities, and encouraging visitor education are all management goals. Like it or not, budgets often drive the ability to provide visitor services, and those services that can clearly show benefit are the most likely to be supported.

There are three categories of management goals and objectives that we must meet

Field Tips for Connecting Visitors to the Resources

Help visitors locate themselves within the context of the resource.

Provide information services that enable visitors to answer basic questions.

Support communications, both in nonpersonal and personal forms. Meet visitors' safety and security needs.

Provide opportunities for education and discovery.

Encourage visitors to make their own connections.

Provide cultural, natural, and managerial resource connection opportunities.

through our interpretive efforts: protect the resource, protect the visitor, and promote the agency. Programs should always consider these three goals. Through increasing visitors' enjoyment and connecting them with the resource, we hope that they will not only become stewards, but advocates and supporters for the agency. The next section briefly discusses each of these goals and objectives.

Protect the Resource

There are two ways to view protecting the resource. One is to focus on decreasing the amount and severity of depreciative visitor behavior: behavior that harms the resource. Carving on picnic tables, picking flowers, walking off trail, and leaving litter are all common forms of depreciative behavior. The second way to protect the resource is to increase compliance with rules and regulations. These two perspectives are similar and related. One method focuses on rules for behavior and the other on the outcomes from behavior. As we will see in Chapter 3, a combination of both approaches is best for overall success.

There are two methods through which we manage visitors: heavy-handed (direct) or light-handed (indirect) approaches. Heavy-handed approaches involve things such as law enforcement and direct manipulation of the site. Light-handed approaches include interpretive messages designed to promote visitor compliance while maintaining visitor freedom.

As interpreters, you are in a unique position to control visitor behavior through the *spirit of the law*. Many researchers and theorists contend that behavior controlled through interpretive means is the preferred method for several reasons (Christensen and Dustin 1989; Knudson, Cable, and Beck 1995; Vande Kamp, Johnson, and Swearingen 1994). A majority of depreciative behavior is thought to occur not out of malice but out of ignorance. In fact, estimates are that, on average, only about 2 to 4 percent of depreciative behavior is malicious (Vande Kamp,

Johnson, and Swearingen 1994; Widner 2000). If depreciative behavior occurs out of ignorance, then it would follow that interpretive methods of educating the visitor about the rules and regulations would be the most effective means of controlling that behavior.

A second reason to attempt to control behavior through interpretive means is that recreation areas and parks are considered one of the last places that humans can be free. To escape the rules and restrictions of society is one of the driving factors that push people into the out-of-doors (Knopf 1988). Our efforts to protect the resource must consider this motivating factor. If we manage and regulate people too closely, the experience itself, which we are also charged with protecting, will be lost. We must protect the resource, but not necessarily at the expense of the visitors' experience. Balance is the key to successfully meeting this dual mandate. *Interpretation provides a wonderful opportunity to both protect the resource and provide for its use and enjoyment.*

A third reason to control behavior through interpretive means is that we may have a better chance at influencing long-term behavioral change through interpretation rather than regulation. The presence of a uniformed officer probably serves as a discriminative stimulus preventing depreciative behavior from occurring only while in the presence of the officer (Vande Kamp, Johnson, and Swearingen 1994; Geller 1994). For example, speeders slow down temporarily when in the presence of a police car. This type of behavior modification may not result in any long-term effect. In other words, seeing one police car probably does not translate into driving slower all the time. In addition, getting a speeding ticket may only serve to make you angry and slow you down for a little while, but probably won't change your driving behavior over the long-term. Following this logic, many researchers contend that the best method to modify depreciative behavior is through

education and other light-handed management techniques (Eagly and Chaiken 1993; Petty and Cacioppo 1984; Latane and Darley 1975; Widner and Roggenbuck 2000).

Protect the Visitor

Another goal of interpretation is to protect the visitors. There are two elements to this protection: protection from each other and protection from hazards and dangers in the resource itself. As public servants, we are charged with increasing the visitors' safety while in the resource and minimizing the amount of visitor conflicts with each other while on the site.

One of the basic needs outlined by Maslow is safety and security. Until these needs are met, visitors are often unable to achieve higher needs and goals from the resource. Whether it is poisonous plants, dangerous undertows, steep steps, or venomous snakes, there are often elements within each site that, without proper consideration, pose a threat to visitors' safety. As stated previously, much of the danger comes from a lack of knowledge about the resource and not an intention to perform dangerous behaviors. Interpretation often serves as the most effective means to address the problem.

Although certain forms of recreation lend themselves to danger more than others (e.g., rock climbing as opposed to taking pictures), ignorance can make one as dangerous as the other (e.g., taking pictures too close to a 1,000-pound rutting elk). It is through interpretation that we educate visitors to the potential hazards in the resource and proper methods needed to protect themselves as much as possible.

Many sites are small and sustain an ever-increasing number of visitors pursuing a vast array of recreational activities, many of which are in fundamental opposition to each other. Visitors have the *right* to use the resource, but not the *right* to destroy other users' abilities to also enjoy the resource; however, the inherent characteristics of some users naturally cause more "disturbance" than others. A classic example is motorized users versus their human-powered counterparts (e.g., snowmobilers versus skiers; hikers versus off-road-vehicle users). These inherent qualities of some recreationists often make them the "target" for zoning and limits on use. This is not always the most equitable solution.

Managing these situations is a delicate task. Interpretation provides the opportunity to not only manage the problem, but to help visitors understand it as well. Sometimes the heavy-handed approaches of zoning or limiting use only serve to further alienate visitors and encourage more user conflict. Many times, the solution simply requires educating users about each other and pointing out how similar they really are to each other (Jacob and Scheryer 1980; Widner 1994). One of the best methods of accomplishing these objectives is by roving, as we will discuss in Chapter 10.

Promote the Agency

These management goals and objectives of interpretation can be viewed as immediate

and short-term. For example, we hope that while visitors are on-site, they take care of the resource, don't get into dangerous situations, get along with others, comply with rules and regulations, and become connected with the resource. Another goal of interpretation is to promote the agency. This goal stems from being successful in the short-term but is itself considered a long-term goal of interpretation. In other words, if we connect them with the resource, are successful in educating them about the need to care for the resource, and protect their experience while recreating, we are more likely to garner long-term support from the visitors for the agency's goals/mission.

These long-term effects are evidenced in voting behavior, legislative support, financial support, and constituency formation. This long-term goal demonstrates the interconnected nature of everything we do. From our friendly welcoming voice on the phone to our well-thought-out, relevant educational programs, everything we do makes an impression on the visitor and contributes to the overall image of the agency. This overall image and conception the public has regarding the purposes and values of our sites, resource areas, and interpretive program translates into money, votes, and overall support. In turn, this support results in our ability to do our jobs effectively and provide those publicly desired services and opportunities.

In the Next Chapter …

Now that we have a firm understanding of what interpretation is and why we conduct programs, let's turn to the foundation of every program: the basic communication process. Chapter 3 reviews the basic communication process and reveals *how* to create effective messages. This next chapter builds the basic foundation of all other communication forms and program types covered in this field guide to personal interpretation.

Interacting with visitors while in the resource encourages resource protection and helps build visitor appreciation for the agency that you represent. Courtesy of Carolyn Widner Ward

Review

1. Interpretation should be meaningfully conducted with clear goals and objectives.

2. Benefits of interpretation can be divided into two categories: those associated with the visitors and those more closely aligned with management.

3. Connecting visitors to the resource is a primary goal of interpretation.

4. Visitors can be connected to the resource through orientation, information, or educational messages.

5. Orientation services help visitors cognitively and spatially locate themselves in the resource.

6. Information helps connect visitors to the resource and meet their basic information needs.

7. Information and orientation services can be offered both on the site and off the site through long-distance mediums.

8. Educational messages are one of the most common methods of connecting visitors to the resource.

9. Educational messages should include natural resource, cultural resource, and management-based messages.

10. Inspirational connections to the resource often come after basic visitor needs have been met.

11. Accomplishing management goals and objectives is the second primary reason and benefit for providing interpretive services.

12. Protecting the visitor, protecting the resource, and promoting the agency are the three major management goals and objectives for interpretation.

Questions and Exercises

1. Is it more important to protect the resource or to provide for the enjoyment of the resource? Why?

2. You witness a visitor illegally gathering downed firewood for a campfire. Describe how you could interpretively manage the situation to educate her, protect the resource, and allow for the visitor to maintain her dignity.

3. Are there times when an interpretive approach to control visitor behavior would not be the option of choice? Explain your answer.

4. What do you think is the most important purpose of interpretation?

References

Articles

Christensen, Harriet H. and Daniel L. Dustin. 1989. "Reaching Recreationists at Different Levels of Moral Development." *Journal of Park and Recreation Administration* 7 (4): 72–80.

Ham, Sam H. and Betty Weiler. 2002. "Toward a Theory of Quality in Cruise-Based Interpretive Guiding." *Journal of Interpretation Research* 7 (2): 29–49.

Jacob, Gerald R. and Richard Scheryer. 1980. "Conflict in Outdoor Recreation: A Theoretical Perspective." *Journal of Leisure Research* 12: 368–380.

Knopf, Richard. 1988. "Human Experience of Wildlife: A Review of Needs and Policy." *Western Wildlands*: 2–7.

Oliver, S. S., Joseph W. Roggenbuck, and A. E. Watson. 1985. "Education to Reduce Impacts in Forest Campgrounds." *Journal of Forestry* 83 (4): 234–236.

Petty, Richard E. and John T. Cacioppo. 1984. "The Effects of Involvement on Responses to Argument Quantity and Quality: Central and Peripheral Routes to Persuasion." *Journal of Personality and Social Psychology* 46: 69–81.

Wallace, George. 1990. "Law Enforcement and the 'Authority of the Resource.'" *Legacy* 1 (2): 4–8.

Widner, Carolyn and Joseph Roggenbuck. 2000. "Reducing Theft of Petrified Wood at Petrified Forest National Park." *Journal of Interpretation Research* 5 (1): 1–18.

Books

Beck, Larry and Ted T. Cable. 2002. *Interpretation for the 21st Century, Second Edition.* Champaign, Ill.: Sagamore Publishing.

Eagly, Alice H. and Shelly Chaiken. 1993. *The Psychology of Attitudes.* Fort Worth, Tex.: Harcourt Brace Jovanovich College Publishers.

Fazio, James R. and Douglas L. Gilbert. 2000. *Public Relations and Communications for Natural Resource Managers, Third Edition.* Dubuque, Iowa: Kendall/Hunt Publishing Company.

Geller, E. S. 1994. "The Human Element in Integrated Environmental Management." In John Cairns Jr., Todd V. Crawford, and Hal Salwasser, eds., *Implementing Integrated Environmental Management.* Blacksburg, Va.: Virginia Polytechnic Institute and State University.

Ham, Sam H. 1992. *Environmental Interpretation: A Practical Guide for People with Big Ideas and Small Budgets.* Golden, Colo.: Fulcrum Publishing.

Knudson, Douglas, Ted T. Cable, and Larry Beck. 1995. *Interpretation of Cultural and Natural Resources.* State College, Pa.: Venture Publishing.

Latane, Bibb and John M. Darley. 1975. *Help in a Crisis: Bystander Response to an Emergency.* Morristown, N.J.: General Learning Press.

Loewen, James W. 1999. *Lies across America: What Our Historic Sites Get Wrong.* New York: Simon & Schuster, Inc.

Machlis, Gary E. and Donald R. Field, eds. 1984. *On Interpretation: Sociology for Interpreters of Natural and Cultural History.* Corvallis: Oregon State University Press.

Maslow, Abraham H. 1954. *Motivation and Personality.* New York: Harper & Row.

Mills, Enos. 1920. *The Adventures of a Nature Guide.* Garden City, N.Y.: Doubleday, Page, & Company.

Serrell, Beverly. 1996. *Exhibit Labels: An Interpretive Approach.* Walnut Creek, Calif.: Sage Publications, Alta Mira Press.

Strang, Carl. 1999. *Interpretive Undercurrents.* Fort Collins, Colo.: National Association for Interpretation.

Tilden, Freeman. (n.d.) *The Fifth Essence: An Invitation to Share in Our Eternal Heritage.* Washington, D.C.: The

National Park Trust Fund Board.

———. 1977. *Interpreting Our Heritage, Third Edition.* Chapel Hill: University of North Carolina Press.

Trapp, Suzanne, Michael Gross, and Ron Zimmerman. 1994. *Signs, Trails, and Wayside Exhibits: Connecting People and Places, Second Edition.* Stevens Point, Wisc.: UW-SP Foundation Press.

Van Matre, Steven. 1983. *The Earth Speaks.* Greenville, W.Va.: Institute for Earth Education.

Manuscripts and Papers

Schwartzkopf, S. Kent. 1984. "Feeding of Golden Mantled Ground Squirrels by Park Visitors at Crater Lake National Park." Res. CPSU/OSU 84-9. Corvallis, Oreg.: National Park Service Cooperative Park Studies Unit.

Vande Kamp, Mark, Darryll Johnson, and Thomas Swearingen. 1994. "Deterring Minor Acts of Noncompliance: A Literature Review." Tech Rep. NPS/PNRUN/NRTR-92/08. Seattle: Cooperative Park Studies Unit College of Forest Resources, AR-10, University of Washington.

Ward, Carolyn, Steven Martin, James Absher, Denise Newman, and Jennifer Tarlton. 2003. "Interpretation Effectiveness at Taylor Creek Visitor Center." RWU 4902 Technical Report. USDA Forest Service, Pacific Southwest Research Station.

Widner, Carolyn. 1994. "Conflict among Hikers and Horseback Riders in the Mount Rogers High Country of Virginia." Thesis. Blacksburg: Virginia Polytechnic Institute and State University.

Chapter 3

The Foundation of Interpretation: Communication

Communication is a process that begins with the interpreter. Courtesy of Carolyn Widner Ward

Communication is the essence of interpretation.

Main Points

- Communication Process
- Interpreter
  - Credibility
    - Message Content
    - Personal Style
    - Delivery
- Message
  - CREATES
    - Connects
    - Relevant
    - Enjoyable
    - Appropriate
    - Thematic
    - Engaging
    - Structured
  - Persuasive Techniques
    - Attitudes
    - Norms
    - Specific Requests
    - Positive Spin
    - Reasons Why
    - Moral Reasoning
    - Multiple Methods (Shotgun)
      - Approach
- Translation
- Visitor
- Filter
- Feedback
- Real World

Now that we have an understanding of the historical evolution of interpretation and why we conduct interpretive programs, let's review the basic foundation of all interpretation: communication. The principles covered in this chapter form the foundation of all communication, regardless of the mediums, the venues, the audiences, or the message types. Although these elements are certainly important, there is a basic theory and a process of communicating that set the stage for building specific types of programs.

Communication is the process of transferring meaning and understanding from one source to another with minimal distortion of the original message. Research suggests that, on average, only 10 percent of what is verbally communicated is retained by the receiver (Grater 1976). This is not a very encouraging statistic and suggests why an overall goal of interpretation needs to be to provoke visitors to learn more on their own, not just to retain specific content from the program.

Communication Process

With an understanding of the basic communication process, we can maximize the retention, comprehension, and understanding of our messages. Communication (figure 3.1) begins with a communicator, in our case, an *interpreter*. The *message* is the second step in the communication process. The interpreter then *translates* (third step) the message into the appropriate language or communication medium. After the actual communication of the message, the *visitor* receives the message (fourth step) and *filters* it (fifth step). After filtering, there is a *feedback* process (sixth step) for communication back to the interpreter. All of this occurs in a *real-world* setting, with its own set of characteristics that influences the entire process (Fazio and Gilbert 2000). Now, let's look at each individual step in more detail. It is through understanding the communication process that we can begin to improve the overall success of our communications.

Interpreter

The communication process begins with the sender of a message, the interpreter. The personal style and attributes of an interpreter that affect the overall reception of the message, such as appearance, voice, body

Words, like eyeglasses, obscure everything they do not make clear.

—Joseph Joubert, 1754–1824

language, and passion, are all linked to one quality: credibility.

Credibility

Many things impact a visitor's perception of your credibility. Remember, it does not matter how credible you actually are; all that matters is the *perception* that the visitor has of your credibility. For example, you may be the resident expert in a particular topic, but if you shuffle your feet and can't maintain eye contact, you will not appear very credible. Think about the last time you asked someone a question and he/she would not look you in the eye and answer. That person may have been telling the truth, but you were probably skeptical due to the lack of eye contact. It should also be mentioned that judgments of credibility vary depending on the target audience. In fact, all of the communication process is inextricably linked, and each step impacts and affects the other steps; however, we must discuss each one separately in order to establish the foundation of communication. The following is a brief review of the major elements that impact a visitor's perception of your credibility. These can be divided into characteristics inherent to the content of the message, the interpreter, or in the actual delivery of the message.

Uniforms and costumes are effective methods of establishing credibility. Visitors often perceive the "dressed" interpreter as an authority on the resource. Courtesy of Jennifer Graves

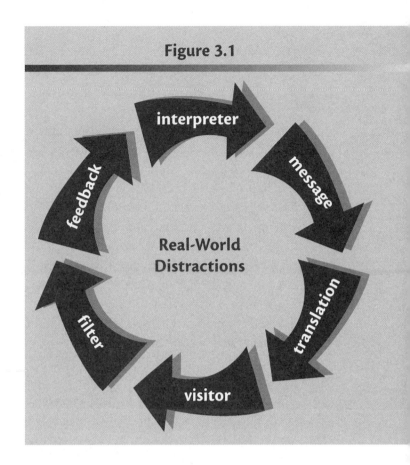

Figure 3.1

interpreter

message

translation

visitor

filter

feedback

Real-World Distractions

Message Content

The primary aspect that many think of when considering credibility is the actual message content. Does the person know what he or she is talking about? Again, we will discuss many things that affect this perception, but you must begin with truthful, accurate information when building the content of your message. There is nothing worse for your credibility than to be proven wrong during a talk. The judgment of being *trustworthy* will, in part, be influenced by whether or not visitors think you know what you are talking about. The key for success in this step is straightforward: do thorough research before presenting information.

This is not as easy as it seems on the surface. There are three basic types of messages that we interpret for the public: cultural, natural, and managerial. In each of these, it is important to present a fair, unbiased, and accurate picture of one whole story. Tilden (1957) points out there are many

> *The way to become boring is to say everything.*
> —Voltaire, 1694–1778

whole stories to tell regarding any one topic. The choice of which story to tell is driven by many factors that we will discuss in Chapter 4. The key for accuracy is to conduct honest, thorough, and unbiased research in an attempt to truly understand the concept, theory, story, or fact. When conducting research, you soon realize that you can never know "the truth" of an event, place, time, or scientific concept. What you can do is adhere to good research practices and paint as honest and accurate a picture as you can.

Personal Style

Another characteristic that impacts perceived credibility is the confidence with which you speak. Judgments of confidence are based on elements such as eye contact, voice, body language, and physical appearance.

Eye contact is probably one of the most important factors in visitors' perceptions of confidence. You shouldn't stare at visitors but, instead, maintain two or three seconds of eye contact with individuals. Try to look at everyone at least once. For large audiences, don't focus your attention and eye contact on one side of the group; try to sweep the entire audience.

Voice quality also reflects your confidence. Meek, mild, and high-pitched voices are not perceived as confident and certainly do not command as much attention as low-pitched,

> *Studies have found that, whatever the status, age, gender or physical size of individuals, those who maintain effective eye contact are perceived as more honest, warmer, and more knowledgeable than those who look away from their listeners.*
>
> —Brownell, 1982

authoritative voices. In the midst of various distracting stimuli in a resource setting, voice quality is essential to command attention. In addition, talking too fast or too slowly impacts perceptions of credibility. Filling in pauses with *ums* and *ahs* also has a negative impact on visitor perceptions. There is great power in a dramatic pause. Know when to stop talking. Your voice should be loud enough in tone and pitch to hear, fluid in pattern, and slow enough to understand. Refer to Chapter 6 for (more) discussion of voice and vocabulary.

Body language is the third element that impacts visitor perceptions of the interpreter's confidence and thus impacts the overall judgments of credibility. "The cues your body sends are often more accurate indicators of the way you feel and what you think than the words you choose" (Brownell 1982, 33). In fact, it is estimated that approximately "60–95 percent of the meaning transfer in a communication system is accomplished through non-verbals" (Jurin, Danter, and Roush 2000, 143). We use body language, often subconsciously, about two-thirds of the time when communicating. The trick for an interpreter is to consciously channel that use of body language in appropriate ways. Standing up straight, holding your head up, and using your body for emphasis are all ways of improving your body language. The number-two fear in America (dying is number one) is speaking in front of others (Wallenechinsky, Wallace, and Wallace 1977). Although this book cannot remove that fear, using simple techniques that prevent the visitor from knowing how you feel, and thus impacting your perceived credibility, is easy. Some tips for overcoming stage fright can be found in Chapter 6.

The physical appearance of the speaker also impacts credibility judgments. The old saying "beauty is in the eye of the beholder" is certainly applicable in this situation; however, there are generalities that can be identified regarding how appearance impacts

Table 3.1
Tilden's Principles of Interpretation

Any interpretation that does not somehow relate what is being displayed or described to something within the personality or experience of the visitor will be sterile.

Information, as such, is not interpretation. Interpretation is revelation based on information, but they are entirely different things; however, all interpretation includes information.

Interpretation is an art, which combines many arts, whether the materials presented are scientific, historical, or architectural. Any art is, to some degree, teachable.

The chief aim of interpretation is not instruction but provocation.

Interpretation should aim to present a whole, rather than a part, and must address itself to the whole man, rather than any phase.

Interpretation addressed to children (say up to the age of twelve) should not be a dilution of the presentation to adults, but should follow a fundamentally different approach. To be at its best it will require a separate program.

—Freeman Tilden, 1957

credibility. One element that will increase credibility is a uniform. Wearing a uniform typically signifies having authority and being of an expert status. Always be sure your uniform is neat, pressed, and clean. If you do not wear a uniform, be sure to dress in professional, appropriate attire.

Delivery
Finally, the manner in which the message is delivered impacts credibility judgments. The

Interpreter Characteristics Impacting Communication

➤ Voice quality
➤ Body language
➤ Accuracy
➤ Appearance
➤ Eye contact
➤ Passion
➤ Sincerity
➤ Uniform
➤ Title

passion, enthusiasm, and sincerity with which you deliver the message impacts the communication process (Ham and Weiler 2002). Tilden (1957) called this the "priceless ingredient." Visitors respond to and can sense the innate interest of the speaker. In a study conducted by Ham and Weiler (2002), visitors cited "passion" the most frequently when evaluating the quality of a guide. Varying voice inflection through changing the pace, rhythm, and tone of speech all help to convey interest in the subject matter. Active, animated body language and facial expressions help convey passion. Think about listening to monotone speakers. It is hard to think that they are really interested in what they are saying. The best method to improve and convey your sincerity is to have it. Believe in what you are doing, the agency for which you work, and the message you are conveying to the public. The audience forgives many technical mistakes *if* they believe you are sincere in the attempt.

Message
The second step in the communication process is the message itself and is the reason communication takes place: it is the heart of

> *Dry words and dry facts will not*
> *fire hearts.*
>
> —John Muir, 1838–1914

the communication process. There are several techniques and strategies that can be used to create successful messages. Freeman Tilden (1957) outlined six principles that will help build successful messages (table 3.1).

In addition, there are several considerations to message formation. The following section reviews some of the basic characteristics of an effective message and examines more advanced techniques for improving persuasive communication. Keep in mind that the overall goal is minimal distortion of the original message between the sender (interpreter) and the receiver (visitor).

CREATES

The basics of good message delivery are things we instinctively know. Think about telling a good joke. It has a beginning, middle, and end. Each has its place in the story and must be told in the appropriate order and with the right emphasis. Communicating interpretively is not some new form of communication; it is simply being able to tell a good story. And, in our case, that story has a moral or message we are trying to convey. The message *creates* the foundation of all communication. In fact, the acronym CREATES (table 3.2) identifies the basic characteristics of an effective interpretive message and can help guide successful message formation.

Connects

One of the key elements of an effective message is that it connects visitors to the

Table 3.2 CREATES

C **Connects**—Messages must link directly to the inherent meanings and purposes of the resources.

R **Relevant**—The audience can understand the message within the context of something they already know or personally relate to.

E **Enjoyable**—Communication that is pleasurable and fun.

A **Appropriate**—Messages tailored to meet audience, resource, and management needs.

T **Thematic**—One central message that guides program creation and addresses the overall purpose of the communication.

E **Engaging**—Communication that incorporates visitor senses and produces a mindful state.

S **Structured**—Messages must follow a logical sequence of ideas.

Table 3.3
Field Tips to Increase Relevance

Analogies—Drawing similarities between two things. *A shaken soda can is a way to think of a volcanic eruption.*

Examples—Referring to something that is representative of what you are talking about. *A redwood is an example of a living fossil.*

Stories—The telling or accounting of an event that explains or describes what you want to interpret. *Tell the creation story of the Cherokee to convey how they revere the earth.*

Metaphors—A figure of speech using a word or phrase to describe something not usually associated with the word. *You are my sunshine.*

Similes—Comparing two things using like or as. *Tectonic plates can hit together like bumper cars.*

Visual aids—Using a tangible object to demonstrate, represent, or explain something. *Pour water onto a dry sponge to represent how marshes soak up and hold on to water.*

Universal concepts—Anything that is known, felt, or believed regardless of most demographic characteristics. *Most emotions and Maslow's basic needs are known, felt, or believed.*

Practical application—Demonstrating the usefulness or application of something. *Showing visitors the medicinal qualities of plants and indicating potential uses in the future.*

resource. Each resource is set aside, protected, and managed for specific reasons. Program messages must be driven by those inherent messages. There should always be a clear connection between program content and the resource. The National Park Service talks about linking tangibles in the resource to the intangible ideas, attitudes, emotions, or concepts that might relate to the visitor. Interpretation helps form basic visitor connections to the resource, but only if our messages are well connected to the resource itself.

Relevant

An effective message must be relevant to the audience. There are numerous approaches for increasing the relevance of a message (table 3.3). Visitors must be able to under-

People are out for recreation and need restful, intellectual visions, and not dull, dry facts, rules, and manuals.

—Enos Mills, 1870–1922

Your need to talk does not create in me a need to listen.

—Mason Cooley, 1927–present

stand the concept in terms of something they already know or something with which they can associate. For example, to explain an erupting volcano, you could shake a can of soda and ask visitors what will happen if you pull the tab. This analogy makes the concept of eruption clear because most people understand or even have firsthand experience with a shaken carbonated drink. Without contextual understanding, new information is sterile and will quickly be forgotten. In addition, if information is not contextually relevant for an audience, it could cause them to become bored or feel stupid.

Sam H. Ham (1992) suggests making information personal to visitors using *self-referencing*, a technique that helps visitors tap into their own experiences and memories as new information is conveyed. *How many of*

Visual aids are effective tools for helping visitors relate to the information conveyed in programs. Courtesy of Oregon Caves N.M., NPS

you have ever? … or *Remember the first time you made a snowball with your bare hands?* are examples of self-referencing. Self-referencing is a simple technique that can increase visitors' connections to the information by tapping into their own memories.

Another technique, called *labeling* (Ham 1992), involves using more specific terms to relate to the audience besides generic pronouns, such as you, us, and we. *As Americans, we can all relate to the sense of tragedy from the events of September 11, 2001.* The phrase *As Americans* is labeling. Use care when labeling, so you do not exclude people needlessly or

Field Tips for Infusing Enjoyment into Facts

➢ Smile.

➢ Tell stories; don't just give facts.

➢ Encourage participation.

➢ Do hands-on demonstrations.

➢ Ask questions.

➢ Use analogies.

➢ Be enthusiastic.

➢ Use visual aids.

➢ Engage visitors' senses.

➢ Relate it to the visitor.

➢ Mainly, *love* what you do!

include people into negative or derogatory categories.

Another way to relate to the audience is through the use of things that we all share in common regardless of our background, age, ethnicity, and so on. The National Park Service calls these *universal concepts*. Universal concepts are things such as family, love, hate, fear, hunger, and so on. Most of the basic needs on Abraham Maslow's hierarchy of needs (figure 2.1) are universal concepts. Tapping into basic needs and emotions is always a sure way of reaching visitors on a personal level.

Enjoyable

Creating enjoyable or pleasurable presentations is a primary on-site goal for our programs. Ham (1992) talks about the entertaining and pleasurable aspects of interpretation and identifies them as essential characteristics of successful programs, primarily because visitors who attend interpretive programs are a noncaptive audience. Although we hope they don't, they can get up and leave the program anytime they choose. In addition, the experience itself is a recreational experience. We provide programs, in part, to help increase visitor enjoyment of the resource. It is our job to make presentations interesting and enjoyable. There is nothing that is inherently boring; instead, it is our interpretation of it that makes it boring or interesting. In fact, it is our *job* to make science, history, culture, and management come to life for visitors. If we make learning fun and enjoyable, we create lifelong learners.

Appropriate

Another characteristic of an effective message is that it is appropriate in three realms: the visitor, the resource, and the management. The message must be tailored for the target audience. This includes both age-appropriate content and messages that meet expressed visitor needs. Messages must also be appropriate to the resource and clearly

> There are no inherently
> boring topics,
> only boring interpreters.

address the needs of the resource. What stories should be told to best facilitate resource protection and promotion? Messages that encourage visitor appreciation for and connection to the resource are those most appropriate. Messages must also be tailored to the management's needs. Each organization has specific mission, goals, and objectives upon which all programs and message should be based.

Thematic

The theme is the anchor point around which all of the information presented must relate. It is the message of the program. Subthemes are the submessages of each main point within the program. Using themes and subthemes around which the information is organized serves three main purposes. First, as indicated above, it provides an organizational hierarchy for the program. The theme guides the selection of the most appropriate material and the order in which to present the information. Second, the theme is the reason you are presenting the program. The theme directly relates to the resource, the visitor, and the management. Creating a theme facilitates a clear linkage between the resource and the visitor and is an indication of the appropriateness of the program itself. The third function of a theme is to help increase message understanding and retention. In other words, the theme and subthemes guide your research, establish the structure of your presentation, and convey the reason or message of the program.

Having a theme is what makes communication interpretation. The theme is the reason you interpret. It is your message for the visitor to take home. A story with a lot of facts and bits of information, after time, will be forgotten; however, if the story has a message, that message will likely be retained longer than any of the individual details that made up the story. In a study conducted in 2003 (Tarlton and Ward 2006), children exposed to a thematic interpretive program retained more information than those exposed to an identical program in content but with no thematic structure. In addition to remembering more factual information, those students receiving the thematic program were three times more able to identify the main message of the program. The true success of an interpretive program is not that the visitor walks away knowing all the plants you talked about, but that they retained the bigger message or theme. In Chapter 5, we will review techniques and methods of developing good themes.

Engaging

A message must be engaging. Including visitors in the program through participation, incorporating their senses, provoking their minds, and providing them with opportunities to act on or share their knowledge all facilitate keeping visitors actively engaged in the message. Keeping participants engaged encourages the formation of visitors' own connections to and meanings of the resource. Hands-on participation promotes minds-on learning and processing of the content of the message (Moscardo 1999).

Provoking the visitors to be curious, to want to know more, and to seek more information on their own is the primary off-site goal of our programs. Given the nature of science, knowledge, and of interpretation itself, one of the great achievements of an interpretive program happens when the visitor begins to question. As important as a skillfully conveyed message is the result of having visitors wonder, question, and desire to know more!

Methods of accomplishing this wonderment are not easily put into a list. In fact, it is the success of myriad things that results in provocation. There are some things you can do to help facilitate provocation through your programs. Ask good, thought-provoking questions—don't always have "the answer." In addition, always encourage discussion and feedback during your programs.

The aim is to illuminate and reveal the alluring world outdoors by introducing determining influences and the respondent tendencies.

—Enos Mills, 1870–1922

Structured

Giving an organized presentation is a fundamental characteristic of good interpretation. Information that is organized is presented in an easy-to-understand manner that follows a logical progression of ideas. Again, this is like telling a good joke. It has a beginning that sets up the punch line and a middle that makes the punch line funny. If information is not presented in an easily understood manner, then the audience will soon get frustrated and lose interest.

There are many creative ways to help visitors follow the organizational structure of a program. Charts and illustrations are especially useful for visual learners. Courtesy of Carolyn Widner Ward

A Cognitive Map? Here's an Example ...

Today, we will journey together and discover what the forest provides for survival. That way, if you're ever lost in the woods, you'll be able to survive! We will discover the easiest way to find water, what the most nutritious thing is to eat, how to build a fire, seek shelter, and, finally, how to find your way out. We will take an easy, short walk around the visitor center and end up right back here in about one hour.

There are four methods to help organize a presentation: a cognitive map, transition sentences, theme/subthemes, and practice. The use of advanced organizers or cognitive maps are proven ways of increasing organization and thus impacting knowledge acquisition and understanding from communication (Hammit 1981; Knopf 1981). Just as you would use a spatial map to find your way in a foreign place, cognitive maps provide the mental orientation for the interpretive journey. Cognitive map theory suggests that providing an initial structure through which the listener can organize the information helps facilitate understanding and comprehension of that message. Learners are said to construct new information, and cognitive maps serve as the blueprints for that construction. A cognitive map tells the visitor what is going to happen.

A second technique to increase organization is to use transition sentences. These sentences provide listeners with the verbal cues that you have finished one main point and are continuing onto the next. They allow the listener to fade in and out of attention while retaining the ability to follow the program. For example, a listener who has been watching a bird and not listening to your program could hear the transition—*Now that we have discovered how to find water in the forest, let's turn to three primary ways to find food for survival*—and return to the program without feeling lost.

The third method of increasing organization is to structure your presentation with a theme and five or so main points/subthemes. It is important not to have too many main points (subthemes) in an interpretive presentation. Studies have shown that people can only process seven (plus or minus two) new pieces of information at one time. In fact, most literature recommends around five main points (Ham 1992; Knudson, Cable, and Beck 1995; Miller 1956). That is why students (in school) have to take notes, because they could not possibly remember all the new information presented at one time. Remember, your audience will not be taking notes and will certainly not be able to process too much new information. At the same time, too little information could cause them to become bored.

A fourth method for improving organization is practice. How well an interpreter knows the program directly results in the subsequent ability to present that information to the public in an organized fashion. Trying to remember what you are supposed to say results in a choppy, jumbled program. Being prepared directly affects the outward organizational appearance of information.

Persuasive Techniques

As discussed in Chapter 2, there are informational/orientational, educational, and inspirational types of messages; however, we could consider all messages to be persuasive in nature. All of the messages we provide are aimed at influencing visitors in some manner, whether that influence is aimed at what they know (cognitive), think (attitudes), feel (emotions), or do (behaviors). Whether the goal is to alleviate fear or to educate them about the resource, we are trying to influence them in some fashion. Given this relationship, there are several methods that can be used to increase the overall effectiveness of any type of persuasive message.

Attitudes

Message effectiveness matches the message to the target audience. As covered in the CREATES section on "Relevant," understanding the visitors' needs, attitudes, and motives enhances the success of message formation. For example, if you are presenting a message identifying the need to remove horseback riding from an area to a group of horseback riders, your approach should be very different than if presenting the same program to a group of backpackers. Visitor attitudes about any given subject are either for it, against it, or neutral. Let's look at some appropriate strategies for each.

Visitors who hold attitudes in agreement with your position respond to messages that encourage action and that focus on their ability to contribute and share. Spend as little time on facts and evidence as possible, because these visitors already agree with your position.

One of the most difficult groups to address are those who are in opposition to your position. Messages targeted for these audiences should begin by establishing common ground. Starting the message with commonalities keeps those who disagree with you from erecting emotional barriers early on in the communication process. Next, acknowledge their position and primary arguments, as it encourages their attention and increases your credibility. Then, only present items from your position that can be easily demonstrated with clear evidence. Credibility is crucial in this step. Remember, you will not easily change visitors' opinions and attitudes with one appeal or program; however, if the message is fashioned carefully, you can ensure they will at least be open to hearing your position. Ending the program with common actions and messages that both sides can agree upon helps promote overall message success.

For groups that are neutral, or for those in which attitude positions are unknown, the message should focus on providing information. Educating visitors with messages that include both positions, provide opportunities to learn more, and encourage visitors' involvement will be the most successful.

Sometimes visitors just need to be reminded about an existing attitude. Most visitors to our site already care about the resources within them, and our messages simply need to remind or prime beliefs already held. Successful persuasive messages must also convey that the visitors' behavior makes a difference and that they are responsible for that difference (Fishbein and Manfredo 1992; Petty and Cacioppo 1984; Vincent and Fazio 1992). Research supports this theory and indicates that if messages are to affect behavior through attitudes, the appropriate attitude regarding the behavior must be primed. Visitors must be able to predict what will happen after a behavior and must be willing to accept responsibility for those consequences.

Priming—An Example

It is so nice to see everyone out here because you love and care about our natural resources. Remember, the tide-pool animals need your help to survive. If you remove them from the rocks even once, it can kill them. It is up to you to keep your tide pools alive and healthy.

Norms

Effective messages make use of the expected and accepted norms for behavior. Every situation, social group, and setting has a set of expected norms for behavior. For example, laughing during a funeral is not the accepted norm for behavior. Two types of norms are social norms and descriptive norms. Social

norms reflect the most accepted form of behavior in any given situation that people *should* be doing, and descriptive norms tell us what others *are* doing. The most successful messages will incorporate both types of norms in conjunction with each other (Cialdini 1996). In other words, what we tell visitors to do (social norm), e.g., *Do not litter*, should be in line with what we say others are doing (descriptive norm), e.g., *Ninety-nine percent of visitors do not litter*. Using norms to affect behavior works well, because people are influenced by the expectations of others and by the social pressure of what they think others are doing (Eagly and Chaiken 1993). For example, if visitors believe that everyone walks off the trail (descriptive norm), it will be difficult to convince them that they should not (social norm). *After all, everyone's doing it, how much more could I hurt it?*

Specific Requests

When trying to influence behavior, it is important to be specific with behavioral requests. Avoid general statements, such as *Help us protect the resource*. Remember, most depreciative behavior occurs out of ignorance, and asking someone to protect the resource assumes that they know how to do so. *Help us protect the resource by staying on the trail* conveys the specific behavior you want them to perform. Compliance with this request will be much higher than with the general one.

Positive Spin

Frame messages in a positive light. For example, *Help us protect the resource by staying on the trail* is positive. *Do not hike off the trail, as it damages the resource* is the same message framed in a negative way. People respond more readily to positive messages than to negative ones.

Reasons Why

Always explain why you want visitors to do something. Identifying the reason behind the

Reason Why—An Example

The plants here are very fragile and even one step can crush them. Please stay on the trail as we pass through this area. Like you, there are thousands of other visitors who come to this meadow every year to see the wildflowers. Staying on the trail will assure that the next visitors get to have the same experience you are having now.

rule prevents visitors from guessing at the reason and deciding that it isn't that important. In addition, George Wallace (1990) suggests reasons for behavioral requests should be told in reference to the resource first, the visitor second, and the management third. Visitors are more likely to modify their behavior to protect the resource or other people than to satisfy management. In addition, knowing the reasons behind the rules makes *you* more informed and thus a better interpreter. If you cannot identify the reason behind the rule in terms of the resource or the visitor, how can you expect a visitor to do so on his or her own?

Moral Reasoning

Moral reasoning theories suggest that persuasive messages should include both a message addressing lower stages of moral develop-

Moral Reasoning— An Example

Preconventional message—
> There is a $1,000 fine for littering.

Postconventional message—
> Leave the resource as you found it—without litter.

ment (preconventional) and higher levels of moral development (postconventional) (Christensen and Dustin 1989; Kohlberg, Levine, and Hewer 1983). Individuals in lower or preconventional stages of moral development respond to messages that promise a reward or threaten punishment. Children most closely reflect this level of moral development. Individuals in the postconventional moral stages of development respond to what others think and the ethics associated with a behavior. Messages should be tailored to the stage of moral reasoning held by the target individual. For example, individuals in the preconventional stage of moral development will be more likely to change behavior in response to threats of punishment or promises of rewards than to ethical appeals. On the other hand, individuals in the postconventional stages of moral reasoning will tend to be more responsive to ethical appeals.

Multiple Methods (Shotgun) Approach

The final suggestion for improving persuasive message appeal is to use a combination of several of the approaches previously discussed. Many researchers have concluded that no one strategy is likely to effectively control all depreciative behaviors (Knopf and

Shotgun Approach— An Example

Look around our group. We all care deeply about the natural resources here in the park. Protecting the park's resources is up to each one of you. Although 99 percent of park visitors do not steal petrified wood, the small fraction who do cause an enormous amount of damage. Please do not steal even one small piece. The fine for theft of petrified wood is $250, but the cost for future generations is far larger. Thanks for helping us protect your treasures.

The moment one gives close attention to anything, even a blade of grass, it becomes a mysterious, awesome, indescribably magnificent world in itself.

—Henry Miller, 1891–1980

Dustin 1992; Vande Kamp, Johnson, and Swearingen 1994; Widner and Roggenbuck 2000). In other words, incorporating multiple persuasive techniques should increase the overall effectiveness of a single message. For example, if appeals to visitor norms or attitudes reach some people and moral reasoning messages influence others, a message that includes both approaches should be more effective overall than messages based on any single approach.

Characteristics of an effective message

➢ Connects the message to the resource

➢ Makes it relevant to the visitor

➢ Is fun

➢ Uses a thematic approach

➢ Creates an engaging experience

➢ Presents organized information

➢ Relates the consequences for behavior

➢ Leaves them wanting to know more

➢ Ensures program accessibility

➢ Presents accurate information

➢ Helps visitors to retain messages

➢ Primes visitor attitudes

➢ Always tells why

➢ Positively frames messages

➢ Appeals to morals

➢ Gives specific behavioral request

Translation

There are various methods through which a message can be translated to visitors. Verbal, visual, hands-on, and written mediums of communication are the four primary methods used to translate a message to visitors.

Translating is the process of coding a message into a particular channel to be communicated to visitors. Deciding which channel will be the most effective depends on numerous factors, including the target audience, the message itself, the time frame, the interpreter, and the resource being interpreted. Each channel has its own characteristics and benefits. As more of the channels are incorporated, the visitor remembers more. Do you remember more if someone *tells* you something or if you *do* it? The most retention occurs when we see it, hear it, *and* do it.

Visitor

The next step of the communication process is the actual reception of the message by the visitor. Although we can't change or affect the visitors' characteristics, it is important to be aware of their potential impact on the communication process (table 3.4).

There are often hindrances to the communication process inherent to the individual, such as language and physical barriers. Differences in semantics, dialect, language origin, and jargon present language barriers. The inclusion of more sensory exploration, hands-on demonstrations, analogies, and avoidance of too much technical vocabulary overcomes language barriers.

An individual's physical barriers to communication could also be inherent. For example, can the visitor see, hear, or navigate adequately to experience the program? What is the trail surface like? Is there another more accessible trail where you could do the same program? These and other similar questions are important for you to consider when designing communication opportunities.

Table 3.4
Visitor Characteristics

Worldview—The visitor's view of and belief system about the world influences communication. Visitors selectively receive and process information that supports an established belief system. This is known as emotional deafness.

Knowledge/experience level—What a visitor knows about a subject affects communication. Previous knowledge can positively or negatively affect the process, depending upon perceived credibility of the sender.

Personal distractions—Visitors' social, physical, and emotional settings create various degrees of distraction.

Attitude toward the agency—A visitor's belief system and attitudes regarding the organization will impact judgments of credibility and trustworthiness.

Information needs/motives—Visitors' motives and needs for information impact what is retained.

Significant others—The social group that the visitor is with impacts communication. For example, a teenage boy surrounded by his friends will react differently than the same boy in his family group. This could be considered peer pressure.

Filter

Filtering is the process that happens after information is translated from the interpreter to the visitor. Only 10 percent of what is actually communicated is retained by the listener (Grater 1976). There are three primary steps that information goes through once it has been communicated. Each of these steps impacts the ultimate goal of communication, the understanding or exchange of meaning. The first step is reception. Not all information is heard, remembered, or comprehended. The second

The Filtering Process—
An Example

When communication is sent ...

➤ What did you hear

➤ What did you understand?

➤ What do you remember from what you heard and understood?

➤ What do you think about what you remembered?

➤ Do you believe it?

➤ Do you think it is valuable and useful information for you?

➤ If so, how will you integrate it into your worldview?

➤ Will it impact your behavior?

Visitors' inherent characteristics impact the communication process in numerous ways. Courtesy of Oregon Caves N.M., NPS

Field Tips for Increasing Filtering Success

➤ Incorporate all the senses.

➤ Tell stories and paint pictures.

➤ Engage visitors directly with the resource.

➤ Use visual aids and props.

➤ Convey facts and information.

➤ Highlight relationships and ideas.

➤ Demonstrate concepts.

step is acceptance or rejection of the information. Given what a visitor heard and understood, value judgments about the information are then made. Once the information has been judged, then appropriate parts are assimilated (or not) into the existing belief system.

There are many elements that impact how the information is filtered. One of the primary elements is that individuals learn and process information differently. For example, many people need visual cues to understand a new concept, while others may only need to hear it to understand. Even within the individual, there are times when details are needed for comprehension and other times when the big picture will do. Although we cannot control how a visitor filters our messages, understanding the basic approaches to processing information will assist us in creating interpretive opportunities that incorporate all visitors. Tilden's fifth principle reminds us that interpretation must address itself to the many phases of an individual (1957). This means that at any given time or for any one individual, there are numerous ways that information is processed or learned.

One way to distinguish information-processing styles is the brain. Right-brain processing involves visual, intuitive, emotional, and spatial elements. It is the creative

side of the brain. Techniques for involving right-brain thinkers include anything that incorporates the senses or emotions. To reach this group, remember that emotions are often more important than facts. Left-brain processing involves factual, linear, logical thought. To engage these logical processors, include facts, ideas, concepts, and the relationships among them.

Another way to discuss filtering is to consider the three main styles of learning, including visual, auditory, and kinesthetic. Visual learners must see the information in order to understand it. Whether it is seeing the printed word, a picture, or the object itself, a visual learner must engage visually with information. Auditory learners must hear information. The voice of the interpreter and the sounds of the resource serve best to reach auditory learners. Kinesthetic learners must interact with information. Demonstrations, hands-on activities, and tactile sensory involvement with the resources address these learners.

Although individuals may align more closely with one information-processing style or the other, the manner in which information is processed depends on numerous

Minimize Setting Distractions

➤ Place the sun in your eyes, not the audiences'.

➤ Don't forget Maslow ... Is it too hot? Too cold? Too windy? Too scary?

➤ Be aware of noise distractions, especially unnatural ones.

➤ The interpretation should not be a distraction to the awe-inspiring moment.

➤ Avoid unnatural physical elements (parking lots, houses).

factors. At any given moment, you will not know how an individual is processing information, much less the variety of individuals within your audience, therefore your success results from including myriad information-processing opportunities.

Feedback

An interpreter can determine if communication is effective through feedback. This is essentially evaluating message reception. Feedback is also considered to be communication in reverse, from the receiver back to the sender of the original message. Thus communication is a two-way process of sending and receiving information. The three basic types of feedback are verbal, visual, and written. Each method has its own limitations and benefits in the communication process. For example, written feedback may be some of the most rigorous, but it's often the most time-consuming to review and difficult to acquire. Conversely, visual feedback is quick but often not very informative. For example, as you describe something, you see an audience with furrowed brows. This might tell you they do not understand what you are saying and you should try another method of explanation; however, it will not tell you why they don't understand. For each type of feedback (written, visual, and verbal), there are various methods of modification possible for improving communication. We will discuss evaluation and other methods of ascertaining feedback at length in Chapter 13.

Real World

The final element of the communication model is the context within which communication takes place. The resource and setting impact the communication process. Although you can't change the resource, you can change the place you choose to present the information. For example, standing next to a loud waterfall is probably not the best place to talk about water dynamics. Sometimes distractions are impossible to avoid. Minimize them as much as possible and always be aware of the factors in the setting that pose distracting components for the audience.

Another element to consider is whether or not the environment imposes an unnecessary barrier to communication. In other words, is the trail too difficult or too long? Are there any unnecessary physical barriers in place in the environment that might prevent the participation of anyone with limited physical ability?

In the Next Chapter ...

The basic principles of communication are the foundation of all interpretation. Now that we have a grasp of the generic communication model, let's examine the steps involved with planning specific programs using chosen mediums for target audiences in a particular location. We will examine the basic steps of the planning process and how planning is used to create maximum effectiveness of our messages.

Review

1. Communication is the process of transferring information from one source to another with minimal distortion of the original message.

2. On average, the receiver of the message retains only 10 percent of what is verbally communicated.

3. It does not matter how credible the sender of the message actually is. What matters is the receiver's perception of credibility.

4. The content of the message, the interpreter's communication style, and the method of message delivery all impact perceived credibility.

5. Eye contact is a primary indicator of credibility.

6. More than 60 percent of meaning transfer is accomplished through nonverbal means.

7. CREATES is an acronym for the basic elements of a successful message.

8. A successful message must connect to the resource and its inherent meanings.

9. An effective message must also be relevant, enjoyable, appropriate, thematic, engaging, and structured.

10. Self-referencing, labeling, and universal concepts are all methods of making information relevant to visitors.

11. The theme is the anchor around which an interpretive program is developed.

12. The theme guides the research for the program, establishes the organizational structure, and helps visitors retain and understand the information.

13. Outlines, themes, cognitive maps, and transition sentences all help create the organizational structure for the interpretive program.

14. Matching visitor-held attitudes with an appropriate message increases overall communication success.

15. Making specific behavioral requests, using a positive spin, and always telling why are methods of increasing the persuasiveness of a message.

16. Messages can be translated into verbal, written, visual, or hands-on communication mediums.

17. Visitors filter incoming messages through their attitudes, values, beliefs, and prior knowledge.

18. Feedback is the process of monitoring the listener response to the message.

19. Message reception is impacted by the distracting conditions inherent in the resource.

Questions and Exercises

1. The primary goal of all communication is

2. Are descriptive or social norms more indicative of behavioral choices? Why?

3. Which step of the communication process is the most crucial for overall success? Why?

4. You have been asked to give a presentation to a group of horseback riders to tell them that they can no longer ride on a particular trail. What things can you do to both maximize the effectiveness of the message and reduce negative reactions?

5. You witness a visitor picking up a fragile fossil on display. There is a large crowd around the area. How should you handle the situation?

References

Articles

Brownell, J. 1982. "Increasing Your Credibility." *Journal of Supervisory Management* 27 (12): 31–36.

Christensen, Harriet H. and Daniel L. Dustin. 1989. "Reaching Recreationists at Different Levels of Moral Development." *Journal of Park and Recreation Administration* 7 (4): 72–80.

Cialdini, Robert B. 1996. "Activating and Aligning Two Kinds of Norms in Persuasive Communications." *Journal of Interpretation Research* 1 (1): 3–10.

Ham, Sam H. and Betty Weiler. 2002. "Toward a Theory of Quality in Cruise-Based Interpretive Guiding." *Journal of Interpretation Research* 7 (2): 29–49.

Hammit, William. 1981. "A Theoretical Foundation for Tilden's Interpretive Principles." *Journal of Environmental Education* 12 (3): 13–16.

Knopf, Richard C. 1981. "Cognitive Map Formation as a Tool for Facilitating Information Transfer in Interpretive Programming." *Journal of Leisure Research* 13 (3): 232–242.

Miller, George. 1956. "The Magical Number Seven, Plus or Minus Two: Some Limits on Our Capacity for Processing Information." *Psychological Review* 63 (2): 81–97.

Petty, Richard E. and John T. Cacioppo. 1984. "The Effects of Involvement on Responses to Argument Quantity and Quality: Central and Peripheral Routes to Persuasion." *Journal of Personality and Social Psychology* 46: 69–81.

Tarlton, Jennifer and Carolyn Ward. 2006. "The Effect of Thematic Interpretation on a Child's Knowledge of an Interpretive Program." *Journal of Interpretation Research* 11 (1).

Wallace, George. 1990. "The Authority of the Resource." *Legacy* 1 (2): 4–9.

Widner, Carolyn and Joseph Roggenbuck. 2000. "Reducing Theft of Petrified Wood at Petrified Forest National Park." *Journal of Interpretation Research* 5 (1): 1–18.

Books

Cialdini, Robert B. 1993. *Influence: Science and Practice, Third Edition.* New York: HarperCollins.

Eagly, Alice H. and Shelly Chaiken. 1993. *The Psychology of Attitudes.* Fort Worth, Texas: Harcourt Brace Jovanovich College Publishers.

Fazio, James R. and Douglas L. Gilbert. 2000. *Public Relations and Communications for Natural Resource Managers, Third Edition.* Dubuque, Iowa: Kendall/Hunt Publishing Company.

Fishbein, Martin and Michael Manfredo. 1992. "A Theory of Behavior Change." In M. Manfredo, ed., *Influencing Human Behavior: Theory and Applications in Recreation, Tourism, and Natural Resources Management.* Champaign, Ill.: Sagamore Publishing.

Grater, Russell K. 1976. *The Interpreter's Handbook: Methods, Skills, and Techniques.* Globe, Ariz.: Southwest Parks and Monuments Association.

Ham, Sam H. 1992. *Environmental Interpretation: A Practical Guide for People with Big Ideas and Small Budgets.* Golden, Colo.: Fulcrum Publishing.

Jacobson, Susan K. 1999. *Communication Skills for Conservation Professionals.* Washington, D.C.: Island Press.

Jurin, Richard, K. Danter, and Donald Roush. 2000. *Environmental Communication: Skills and Principles for Natural Resource Managers, Scientists, and Engineers.* Boston, Mass.: Pearson Publishing.

Knopf, Richard C. and Daniel L. Dustin. 1992. "A Multidisciplinary Model for Managing Vandalism and Depreciative Behavior in Recreation Settings." In M.

Manfredo, ed., *Influencing Human Behavior: Theory and Applications in Recreation, Tourism, and Natural Resources Management*. Champaign, Ill.: Sagamore Publishing.

Knudson, Douglas, Ted T. Cable, and Larry Beck. 1995. *Interpretation of Cultural and Natural Resources*. State College, Pa.: Venture Publishing.

Kohlberg, Lawrence, Charles Levine, and Alexandra Hewer. 1983. "Moral Stages: A Current Formulation and Response to Critics." In J. A. Meacham, ed., *Contributions to Human Development*, vol. 10. New York: Karger.

Manfredo, Michael, ed. 1992. *Influencing Human Behavior: Theory and Applications in Recreation, Tourism, and Natural Resources Management*. Champaign, Ill.: Sagamore Publishing.

Maslow, Abraham H. 1954. *Motivation and Personality*. New York: Harper & Row.

Moscardo, Gianna. 1999. *Making Visitors Mindful: Principles for Creating Sustainable Visitor Experiences through Effective Communication*. Champaign, Ill.: Sagamore Publishing.

O'Conner, Patricia T. 2003. *Woe Is I: The Grammarphobe's Guide to Better English in Plain English*. New York: Riverhead Books.

Tilden, Freeman. 1957. *Interpreting Our Heritage*. Chapel Hill: University of North Carolina Press.

Vincent, Mark A. and Russell H. Fazio. 1992. "Attitude Accessibility and Its Consequences of Judgment and Behavior." In Michael Manfredo, ed., *Influencing Human Behavior: Theory and Applications in Recreation, Tourism, and Natural Resources Management*. Champaign, Ill.: Sagamore Publishing.

Wallenechinsky, David, Irving Wallace, and Amy Wallace. 1977. *The People's Almanac Presents the Book of Lists*. New York: William Morrow.

Paper

Vande Kamp, Mark, Darryll Johnson, and Thomas Swearingen. 1994. "Deterring Minor Acts of Noncompliance: A Literature Review." Tech Rep. NPS/PNRUN/NRTR-92/08. Seattle: Cooperative Park Studies Unit College of Forest Resources, University of Washington.

Chapter 4

Planning for Success

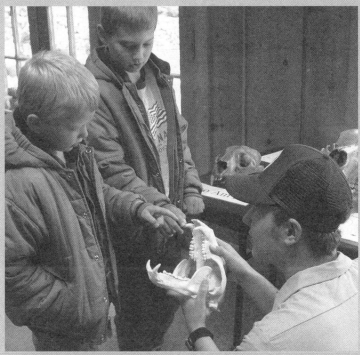

Successful visitor interaction requires careful planning. Courtesy of Oregon Caves N.M., NPS

Planning is a systematic process of researching, designing, and preparing for interpretive programs.

Careful planning is the key to conducting successful interpretation. Even if the interpretation seems spur-of-the-moment, contacts with the public should be carefully planned. Good interpretive planning asks and answers a few basic questions: *What resources do we have? Who is coming and why? What do we need to tell them? What will our facilities, staff, and budget allow us to do? How well did*

Our plans miscarry because they have no aim. When a man does not know what harbor he is making for, no wind is the right wind.

—Marcus Annaeus Seneca,
4 B.C.–A.D. 65

If you fail to plan, plan to fail.

—James Fazio and
Douglas Gilbert, 2000

we do? In this chapter, we'll review each step in the planning process and discuss how to use planning to increase the overall success of our interpretive efforts. While planning occurs at many levels within an organization, this chapter will focus on personal interpretive planning.

The Planning Process

Planning involves researching the site and its importance, the visitors' demographics and motives, and management goals and objectives. After completing this initial research regarding the site, the visitor, and the management goals and objectives, interpretive themes and messages can be identified. Once target messages and themes are identified, interpretive opportunities can be designed that meet the needs of visitors and management while maximizing the inherent characteristics and recreational opportunities presented by the resource. As with any planning effort, the final step in the process is to evaluate and provide for feedback to improve the product or outcome of the program.

Research

Interpreters need to know and understand the site before programs can be prepared successfully. The first step in any planning process is to conduct research. Some planning paradigms call this the *scoping* process. John Veverka (1994) calls it conducting an *inventory*. There are three main elements that should be considered in the research phase of the planning process: the resource itself, the visitors, and the management. Each element must be inventoried before successful interpretive programs can be designed. In this

RIDE—The Planning Process

R Research resources, publics, management

I Identify primary messages

D Design interpretive opportunities

E Evaluate and provide feedback

section, we will review *what* each element is, followed by a discussion of *how* to conduct research on that element.

Resources

The physical resources drive the interpretive-planning process. These resources often constitute the interpretive priorities of the place, the natural and the cultural world. These components form the foundation of much of the interpretive messages you communicate. Interpretation is, after all, a communication process designed to help connect the visitor to the resource. Interpreters can't connect visitors with a resource with which interpreters themselves are unfamiliar. Having the most current and accurate resource information allows for the creation of successful programs, promotes credibility with the audience, and produces personal growth in knowledge of the resource.

Resource inventories may exist somewhere already, but it's more likely that you will develop them over time. Observations about the site should be physically recorded in some fashion (labeled photos, written descriptions, electronic databases, etc.) and kept in a central location for interpreters and other staff to access. Although all staff can contribute input for the resource inventory, the interpreter conducting the interpretive programs should be a major contributor to the physical

resource inventory. The interpreter is in a unique position to continuously observe the resource and note changes when roving and/or providing interpretive walks. The interpreter is also the one who will use the resource-inventory information to create programs.

We will now briefly discuss the resource categories, natural and cultural, and review common methods for conducting research in each area.

Natural Resources

A natural resource inventory involves observing, identifying, and surveying the flora, fauna, and physical characteristics of the resources. This activity should be conducted periodically and as resources change. In addition, there are often seasonal variations in natural resources that should be documented. For example, birds found in the spring may be different from fall migratory species; however, some natural resources, such as those associated with geological formations, don't need to be inventoried as frequently. Storm surges, heavy precipitation, wind, and other weather phenomenon can often uncover fossil beds, rock outcroppings, and other geological features of an area. Geological aspects of a natural resource

There is no substitute for knowing your resource. Familiarity enables you to facilitate visitor connections to those resources. Courtesy of Carolyn Widner Ward

A Natural Resource Inventory Includes:

- ➤ Climate
- ➤ Scenic/vista points
- ➤ Elevations and topography
- ➤ Dominant vegetation
- ➤ Primary animals
- ➤ Rare, threatened, or endangered species
- ➤ Species of special concern
- ➤ Water sources in number and size
- ➤ Habitat types
- ➤ Unique and seasonal features
- ➤ Superlatives or outstanding features of the site
- ➤ Historical changes in flora or fauna numbers, patterns, and distribution
- ➤ Natural hazards or dangers
- ➤ Geologic features
- ➤ Geological development and history of the area
- ➤ Significant geological events
- ➤ Relationships between geological, biological, and cultural elements

inventory should be updated whenever such events take place.

Cultural Resources

A cultural resource inventory is conducted to determine what significant cultural resources are found at the site and on adjacent lands. These resources may be as significant as the reason the site itself was protected or as obscure as overlooked, infrequently visited sites. Cultural resource surveys do not need to be conducted as often as natural resource surveys, because major changes are infrequent in cultural resources. In addition, seasonal changes don't often affect cultural resources; however, there can be seasonal events or celebrations that should be included in a cultural resource inventory.

Methods of Collecting Resource Data

There are two approaches for collecting data: primary and secondary. A combination of both is highly recommended. Primary data tells you *what* is on the site, and secondary data tells you *about* the resources on the site.

Primary data collection involves firsthand data collection on the site where resources are reviewed and inventoried. It is the first step to designing interpretive programs. It promotes familiarity and knowledge of the resource and is invaluable for conducting natural and cultural resource–based interpretation.

Secondary data collection begins once the primary data collection is completed and familiarity with the resource begins to grow. Secondary data collection is information that someone else has collected or conveyed to you based on their firsthand experiences. Secondary research uses libraries, museums, personal testimonials and interviews, Web sites, books, reports, peer-reviewed journals,

A Cultural Resource Inventory Includes:

- ➤ Significant cultural groups
- ➤ Historic events
- ➤ Historic highlights
- ➤ Significance of site resources for cultural groups
- ➤ Existing historic structures, features, and collections
- ➤ Significant cultural places and landscapes
- ➤ Archaeological sites and artifacts
- ➤ Seasonal celebrations and events
- ➤ Historic changes in makeup, distribution, and populations of associated cultural groups

Primary materials are derived from
an actual event.
Secondary materials generally are
about an event.

longtime employees, and so on. This type of
data is essential for conducting interpretation
of any kind.

Public

A careful examination of the public is a
second element that must be considered in
the research phase of the program-planning
process. This is the *market* and, as such,
should be a driving force behind program
creation. As public servants, meeting the
needs of our constituents and visitors should
be of primary importance. There are two
publics that we should consider: the visiting
public and the local public.

In order to meet needs and satisfy expectations, you must know who is coming and why
and who is *not* coming and why (Ham,
Housego, and Weiler 2004; Veverka 1994). We
need to know who is *not* coming to ensure
that lack of participation is not due to a lack

Field Tips for Conducting Primary Data Collection

**Visit the site at different times of the day,
week, and month.**

**Use a camera to document special or unusual
resources.**

**Record and date all observations, site visits,
and photographs.**

**Note conditions under which observations
were made.**

**Take care not to alter any historical or cultural
resources.**

**Use guides to verify identification of species,
architectural details, etc.**

Call in an expert if identification is in question.

**Indicate any resources too fragile to withstand
visitor use or traffic.**

of services, facilities, programs, or outreach to
that segment of the public (Knudson, Cable,
and Beck 1995). After we know who is
coming and the motives for the visit, we can
examine what they do when there. This
information will allow us to create and deliver
programs that are more successful in meeting
visitor needs. Now let's review aspects of the
public that should be examined and recommended methods of conducting research.

Sources of Secondary Data

➢ Historians, biologists, archaeologists, etc.

➢ Historic structures reports

➢ Interpretive prospectus, general plans, etc.

➢ Scope of collection statement

➢ Artifact collection reports

➢ Agency resource inventories

➢ Libraries, museums, and historical
  societies

➢ Books, research journals, newspapers,
  Internet, etc.

➢ Current and former residents, employees,
  and community members

Take the time to get to know your visitors. Courtesy of
Carolyn Widner Ward

Examples of Helpful Demographic Data

➤ Gender

➤ Age

➤ Group structure (family, adult groups with no children, single, etc.)

➤ Place of residence (local versus nonlocal, in- versus out-of-state, foreign, etc.)

➤ Education level

➤ Cultural or ethnicity identification

➤ Previous site experience

➤ Knowledge regarding the site

The Visiting Public

Analysis of our visiting public includes an examination of demographics, motives, and use and activity patterns. Each of these will be discussed, followed by a section on methods and sources for collecting visitor data.

Planning is everything;
the plan is nothing.
—Dwight D. Eisenhower,
1890–1969

DEMOGRAPHICS

Demographic data is some of the easiest data to collect and is very useful in program design. Think about how your program offerings would vary if your visiting public were primarily families with young children versus adult groups with no children. What if the majority of your users are elderly? The education level of your audience can impact the information included in programs. Place of residence and previous site experience inform about the visitors' prior knowledge regarding the site and the history and culture of the area. Cultural associations or ethnic-background information can be helpful in deciding what facilities, programs, topics, and recreational opportunities should be provided.

Field Tips for Conducting Secondary Data Collection

Apply the rule of three—Make every effort to present only correct and accurate information. One method is to use only information that you can find repeated in three different sources. This helps protect from using inaccurate or incomplete information.

Use current sources—Use the most up-to-date information sources. Science is changing and theories develop as scientists test and learn new ideas. In addition, current information and perspectives on historical events are always evolving. Be aware of the date and perspectives of your sources.

Know the source—Part of evaluating the credibility of information is to know the source of the information. Is it from a reputable source? What makes a source reputable? Perspectives

on issues, facts, science, and history can vary vastly. The source of the information might impact the *slant* on the story. No source is free of bias.

Use caution when utilizing the Internet—Anyone can create a Web site. There are some great sources on the computer, such as peer-reviewed journal articles, university search engines, etc. The key is the credibility of the information source.

Keep good notes—Record notes from your research in a consistent and systematic manner. Include the source of the information and the date it was collected. Organize collected information in an easy-to-use manner so future interpreters can build on the data.

MOTIVATIONS

Information on visitors' motives for visiting can be very useful in preparing programs that meet their needs and satisfy their expectations. "Understanding what motivates visitors to come to parks and seek out interpretation will enable you to use the best strategies and methodologies for reading your audience" (Helmich 1997, 13). Research conducted on why visitors come to parks and heritage areas reveals some basic categories of motivation within which most visitors probably fit (Knopf 1988) (table 4.1). Think about how

each of these motivations would impact your program design.

USE AND ACTIVITY PATTERNS

It is fairly easy and useful to collect visitor activity–based data. Use levels of trails, programs, parking lots, visitor centers, boat ramps, contact/entrance stations, and so on, should *all* be included when trying to gather data. This information is very beneficial in showing time, location, density, and frequency of visits. *Site use level* information is often collected and supplemented with

Table 4.1
Motivations for Visiting Natural and Cultural Sites

Curiosity—Many visitors are simply curious about something in the park they have heard, seen, or read about. Their expectations are usually not specific and their needs are typically not well formed. They don't know what to expect and will take what comes more openly than visitors with specific expectations.

Meaning—Visitors often come to parks seeking meaning, which includes social meaning and personal/individual meaning. Social meaning includes things such as: 1.) coming to pay homage to natural wonders; 2.) visiting a cultural heritage site; 3.) gaining a sense of nationalism; and 4.) exploring family history and roots. Other meanings are highly individualized and arise from experiences, memories, special events, spiritual associations, and eras in one's lifetime.

Socialize—Almost all visitors (an average of 80 to 90 percent) come in groups. They seek social experiences that are rewarding, gratifying, and nonjudgmental. Visitors can assume that others there probably share similar values, beliefs, and attitudes. This makes the social experience a rewarding one.

Escape—Some visitors come to escape everyday work, stress, stimuli, etc. They seek sensory input that is different from their *normal* day. They desire natural or cultural stimuli that

are slower and more predictable than their usual surroundings.

Enjoyment—Virtually all visitors come to recreation areas to have a good time. Interpretive programs should always strive to increase visitor enjoyment of the recreational experience.

See the real thing/pilgrimage—Many sites have attractions that serve as a draw for visitors to "come see it for themselves." Some consider it a very special, almost spiritual, experience. For example, many visitors go to Grand Canyon National Park to "see it for themselves." Similarly, historical and cultural sites, such as Gettysburg National Military Park or Mount Rushmore National Memorial, often draw visitors paying homage to a significant thing, place, person, or event.

Esteem/confidence—Some visitors are motivated to "prove themselves" through a recreational experience. In a recreational setting, visitors can match competency levels with challenges and create situations most likely to provide a rewarding experience. Proper advertisement of programs, including describing how difficult or easy an activity will be, is an essential component for visitors motivated to build esteem or confidence.

Field Tips for Conducting Visitor Observations

Record the state or county of origin from license plates on cars. This can give some indication of how far visitors traveled.

Collect information on the basic group structure. This is most easily done in a parking lot before the group splits up to participate in different activities. Make categories ahead of time to save time and *discreetly* collect the information.

Conduct trailhead or entry counts. This can help determine the number and type of users throughout the resource.

Observe visitor center use patterns. Frequency and flow of use can be used to identify which exhibits/signs are the most popular, how traffic flow can be improved, and how long visitors spend at the site.

program use level information to paint a fairly accurate picture of visitor use in the resource.

By conducting inventories of visitor activities, you can tailor programs to meet specific activity preferences. "Visitation use patterns allow you to see when your site and services are most in demand" (Veverka 1994, 53). For example, if 50 percent of users ride bikes, having an interpretive bike program would likely be popular.

METHODS OF COLLECTING VISITOR DATA

Primary and secondary data collection is also collected on visitors. Primary data collection methods include observation and self-report. Observation data involves observing the visitor in the setting to determine use patterns and demographics. Some data is more easily observed than others. For example, simple observation can identify visitor-use type, but motives are less obvious. Self-report data collection simply means that the visitor is asked questions and then reports informa-

tion in any number of formats. Each primary data-collection method has negative and positive characteristics depending on who is collecting the data, who the target audience is, and how the data will be used. Secondary data collection can also be useful to learn about the visitors.

Observation

Observing visitors can be very useful. The key is to randomly pick days and times to observe the place, activity type, and so on. Focus on one place, activity, or attraction at a time. One of the goals of observation data is to identify use patterns over time. As such, you must observe the phenomenon long enough and at a variety of times to identify these use patterns. You must be discreet. Visitors who think they are being watched may change their behavior.

Program-attendance data is easy to collect and priceless when it comes to understanding program-specific patterns. Over time, you will see variations in attendance depending on time of day, day of the week, program topics, and so on. Analyzing this information assists in making program modifications. Basic demographic data combined with attendance levels paint a very useful picture of the target audience for each program.

Knowing what activities visitors participate in can help you provide the appropriate interpretive opportunities to meet their needs. Courtesy of Bob Wick

Self-Report

The second primary visitor data-collection method is self-report. There are many types of self-report data-collection methods. We will review many methods in detail in Chapter 13. One of the most commonly used self-report data-collection methods is a survey. All survey data is self-report data, because we are asking the visitor to give us the information. The following is a brief overview of survey methods useful for collecting demographic, use level, activity type, and informational-needs data.

Have a specific pattern of randomly asking visitors, e.g., every fourth visitor through the gate. This provides a more unbiased, representative sample of the population of users. Use mostly closed-ended questions that ask the visitor to check a category rather than to write in an answer. This type of data is the easiest to tabulate. Open-ended questions allow visitors to write in individual responses but are very time-consuming and difficult to tabulate; however, these questions are useful for informing us of issues, concerns, and so on that we may not understand enough to create a category for a closed-ended question. Use open-ended questions, but use them sparingly.

Secondary Data

Secondary data collection regarding visitor demographics, use, and motivations involves using information that has been previously collected and compiled. This data can be found through the local chamber of commerce, neighboring parks and recreation areas, census data, planning commissions, and even courthouse records departments.

Secondary data collection, although perhaps not as accurate a reflection of users as primary data, provides good information. Secondary data may be the practical first choice for interpreters because it is easier to acquire. It is quicker, cheaper, and requires less skill and expertise to collect than primary data.

Field Tips for Survey Design

➤ Keep total length of surveys short and simple (between 5 and 10 questions).
➤ Use jargon-free language.
➤ Ask only critical-issue questions.
➤ Provide a drop box at the exit or a central location for those who want to fill out the survey later.
➤ Randomly ask visitors to participate.

The Nonvisiting Public

Who is not coming is an important question to answer when assessing public needs for programs and services. Is nonparticipation due to a lack of appropriate facilities, programs, services, or outreach? Trying to assess who is not coming is a very difficult task. The only practical way for interpreters to answer this question is through the use of secondary data regarding the local general public.

BENEFITS

There are two benefits of collecting data regarding the local public. First, through the use of census information and local (county, city) statistics regarding the population, it can be determined if visitor demographics match similar numbers as represented in the local community. This information is a good indicator of which populations may be missing from the visitor-use population. The second benefit is that you discover the characteristics of your local population and can identify unmet needs. School programs, outreach events, and other special off-site activities can then be created to reach these missed local publics.

METHODS OF COLLECTING LOCAL PUBLIC DATA

The methods of collecting this type of data are similar to those previously mentioned. You can conduct a primary data-collection survey

Goals and Objectives— An Example

Goal: Increase public understanding and support for park protection

Objective 1: By December of 2006, 50 percent of visitors will, when asked in an exit survey, correctly identify two reasons for resource protection.

Objective 2: By December of 2006, 25 percent of visitors to the park will take a membership brochure for the interpretive association.

Objective 3: By December of 2006, when reviewed by agency supervisors, 100 percent of all interpretive programs will address resource-protection issues.

of the local public, including items such as: 1.) current activity-participation levels and types; 2.) demographic data; 3.) needs and skill-level information; 4.) attitudes, beliefs, and values regarding relevant issues; and 5.) management preferences, opinions, and issues. Most of the time, staff resources and skills necessary to conduct such an extensive public survey are lacking. That's why the use of secondary data sources, such as the federal census, almanacs, and social-indicator data, are the most common methods of obtaining data on the local publics.

Management

The third element that must be included in the research phase of the program-planning process is management. In order to develop interpretive programs that accomplish management goals and objectives, an examination of what those goals and objectives are must be conducted. In addition, a review of current methods of communication, topics offered, facilities, and locations used in programming should also be undertaken. Consideration of these elements will ensure

the appropriate use of resources needed to meet the overall mission of the agency.

The Organizational Philosophy

Knowing and understanding the purpose and guiding philosophy of the organization determines the overall direction of the interpretive services provided. "A philosophy is a framework which reflects the values and beliefs of an individual or organization" (DeGraaf, Jordan, and DeGraaf 1999, 58). An organization's philosophy is made up of mission, vision, goals, and objectives statements. The primary guiding component of an organization is often the enabling legislation or mandate that created the organization. The mission and vision provide the overall guiding direction for the organization. They are generally overarching ideals, principles, hopes, and dreams for the organization.

Goals and objectives are another level of the organization's philosophy that must be considered when planning programs. Goals are broad statements that provide direction for the organization but are more focused than mission or vision statements. Within each goal are objectives. Objectives are very specific statements that guide how to meet the goals. Good objectives should be specific, measurable, include a time frame for accomplishment, and indicate the methods of measurement. Each goal may have several subsequent objectives.

Current Program Offerings

Once the guiding framework for interpretation is reviewed, a second aspect of management that should be inventoried is the current status of interpretive services. This includes what is offered, when, where, and for whom. When trying to determine what programs you should create, it is imperative to ask what has or is being done. How many walks are provided versus more sedentary programs? How many evening programs versus day programs? How many children's programs? This inventory should be conducted at least for the past year of programming. This data collection is essentially an overview of all existing interpretive programs. Once this information is collected, categories of data will begin to emerge. These categories will then guide the choices of programs to offer in the future. We will discuss this in more detail later in this chapter.

Some categories to examine include the time of day, day of the week, program length, topic, location, program type (slide show, hike, talk, etc.), target audience, and historical attendance levels. A final component is to identify what goals and objectives are addressed by each program; this will enable you to see which goals and objectives are not currently addressed and which ones may be overemphasized.

Facilities, Equipment, Resources, and Supplies

When determining what interpretive programs to conduct, an important area to examine is the facilities, equipment, resources, and supplies that currently exist that can be of use in interpretive programming. All of these things together can be considered to be the infrastructure supporting interpretation. For example, designing an interpretive slide program is not a very effective approach if you don't have a facility that allows for showing slides or the equipment necessary to show them. Is there a visitor center? What about an amphitheater? How many people does it seat? Is there a facility to show slides? What type of interpretive equipment and supplies do you have? Do you have a facility to conduct programs out of inclement weather? These and other questions are critical for determining what types of programs you can offer and where.

Another aspect of the infrastructure is the financial resources available. Know what the available interpretation budget is and plan ahead for needs. If end-of-the-fiscal-year

> ## Inventorying the Tools of the Trade
>
> **Facilities**—Physical structures in the park (amphitheater, visitor center, meeting rooms, historic buildings, etc.)
>
> **Equipment**—Typically considered things that can be used over and over again (slide projector, camera, computer, etc.)
>
> **Resources**—Not as durable as equipment, but not as quickly used up as supplies (field guides, props, slides, costumes, etc.)
>
> **Supplies**—Things that can be used up (glue, tape, film, etc.)

money becomes available, do you have a list of your needs ready? Do you have an interpretive cooperating association working with your site? These nonprofit associations can be a great help for interpreters to acquire needed equipment and supplies.

Methods of Collecting Management Data

The easiest approach to collecting management data is by using secondary data-collection methods. Existing program reports, enabling legislation, and year-end program summaries are secondary data-collection sources that should be helpful in determining management issues relevant to programming. Primary data collection can also be used to review management issues, existing facilities, and equipment. For example, personally performing equipment and supply inventories is one method of conducting primary data collection of park-management resources.

> *It's easy to come up with new ideas; the hard part is letting go of what worked for you two years ago, but will soon be out-of-date.*
>
> —John Veverka, 1994

Sources of Organizational Information

➤ Strategic plan
➤ Scope of collections
➤ Interpretive prospectus/plans
➤ Legislation
➤ General plan and amendments
➤ Mission statement
➤ Organizational philosophy
➤ Program goals and objectives

Because individual organizations have different levels of guiding management documents, specific recommendations cannot be made regarding information sources. For example, some organizations have an interpretive prospectus outlining goals, objectives, and themes, while others have little. Some documents provide very specific detailed information regarding interpretive programming. Many organizations may have developed an interpretive-planning team, while other locations may not even mention interpretation in their overall management plan. It is imperative to assess what, if any, documents guide the interpretive services provided at your site.

Identifying Primary Messages

After resource, public, and management research is conducted, the next step of the planning process is to determine what messages need to be delivered to the public. By now, we should know what is special about the resource, what it has to offer, why it was protected, what the management objectives are, and who is and isn't coming. This information provides the structure for creating the targeted messages to deliver to our publics. Identifying program messages will then determine how interpretive opportunities should be developed to meet agency goals and objectives. Remember, specific targeted messages may already be identified in management-planning documents or general goals for the messages may be specified. (See example below.) However, many times, site messages are not readily identified in any agency literature. In these cases, it is up to the interpreter to create themes and messages that clearly meet management goals and objectives, provide for visitor enjoyment of the resource(s), and promote visitor and resource protection.

Strategic Goal	To ensure that the reasons for the national significance of the Victoria-Esquimalt fortifications, and of Fort Rodd Hill and Fisgard Lighthouse, will be effectively communicated to the public.
Objectives	To communicate to Canadians and visitors to Canada the key components of the sites' national significance and their commemorative integrity;
	To provide for the public an understanding of the reasons for the construction of the Victoria-Esquimalt fortifications;
	To communicate the history of the sites in such a way that visitors have an understanding of why these places are nationally significant to Canada.

—Fort Rodd Hill and Fisgard Lighthouse
National Historic Sites of Canada,
Management Plan, 2003

We will review in detail how to write effective messages or themes in the next chapter; however, in the planning phase, the specific wording and formatting of the messages is not important. For now, it is critical only to identify the overall messages.

Designing Interpretive Opportunities

Once the basic research is conducted and primary messages (themes) are identified, the next task is to determine how to deliver to the target audiences the messages that will best meet the overall goals and objectives. The easiest way to discuss this step of the planning process is to offer an example of how an interpretive opportunity would be created to meet a management goal using the planning steps discussed thus far.

Program Goals and Objectives

This example illustrates how the steps of the process fit together to assist in program planning. Once individual program goals are outlined, program objectives and target audiences can be identified. In the example below, the program goal is to protect the nonrenewable resource—petrified wood—from theft. Once goals are identified, program objectives should be outlined. Just as with park site objectives, program objectives specifically outline how goals will be accomplished. (See example on page 64.)

Objectives for interpretive programs fall into three categories: behavioral, cognitive, and affective. In other words, interpretive programs could influence behavior (behavioral objectives), increase knowledge levels (cognitive objectives), or reach emotions (affective objectives). Site needs and goals often determine what types of objectives programs target. An interpretive program can target all three objectives simultaneously.

Creating an Interpretive Opportunity— An Example

Step One: Research

Natural Data—Research revealed that petrified wood was disappearing from Petrified Forest National Park in visitors' pockets at a rate of approximately 12 tons per year.

Visitor Data—Visitor surveys and interviews revealed that most visitors to the park come to see the petrified wood. Observations of visitor behavior suggest that only 2 percent take wood from the park.

Management Data—The main reason the park was established was to protect the petrified wood. A primary concern of managers is the theft of this nonrenewable resource.

Step Two: Identify messages

One primary message outlined in the management plan is that visitors need to understand why it is important to protect the petrified wood. The message that petrified wood is a nonrenewable resource and needs to be protected is identified as a park priority message.

Step Three: Interpretive opportunity

Given the low percentage of visitors who steal wood from the park, a formal interpretive program may not reach the targeted population with the appropriate message. To reach the targeted population, a roving presence providing interpretive messages to encountered visitors would be the appropriate interpretive approach.

Program Goals and Objectives—An Example

Goal	Protect petrified wood from visitor removal
Behavioral Objective	In June of 2006, resource inventories of random plots conducted during a week with roving interpretive programs and a week without roving will show an 80 percent reduction in the amount of wood removed during the week with a roving presence.
Cognitive Objectives	In June of 2006, when exiting the site, 80 percent of randomly surveyed visitors exposed to roving programs will be able to correctly identify two reasons to protect petrified wood.
Affective Objective	In June of 2006, 90 percent of randomly interviewed visitors exposed to roving will indicate positive support for petrified-wood protection.

Writing Objectives— A Step-by-Step Approach

Objectives are specific, time limited, measurable, and have clearly stated standards. The most common problem encountered when writing objectives is not making them measurable. Objectives often end up very similar to goals if measurement is not carefully considered. This is one of the most important elements of writing an objective. If it is not quantifiable, evaluation of program success is difficult, if not impossible.

The acronym WAMS will assist in writing good measurable objectives. It stands for When, Audience, Method, and Standard. *When* will the evaluation take place? Who is the target *audience*? What *method* will be used to evaluate success? And what is the *standard* for measuring success or failure? Using the WAMS method prevents writing objectives that are not measurable.

Target Audiences

The target audience is another element to consider when designing interpretive opportunities. This part of the planning process pulls everything together. For example, the information collected during the research phase of the planning process will indicate what audiences have typically attended various programs, what the characteristics of the local population are, and what populations are not currently being addressed through program offerings. This information will be used to help identify target audiences for future programs. Although we do not often limit programs to certain audience types, there are some things that can be done to promote participation by certain groups. For example, the time of day programs are offered would impact whether or not local families would be able to participate.

Identifying the target audience is a critical component of successful interpretive programming. Courtesy of Carolyn Widner Ward

Elements for Influencing the Target Audience

- ➢ Where programs are advertised
- ➢ How programs are advertised
- ➢ When programs are offered
- ➢ Where programs are conducted
- ➢ Program topics
- ➢ Program length
- ➢ Program type (walk, slide talk, etc.)

Using the elements for influencing the audience, think about how you might target local families with children. Although certain groups may be targeted, those who actually show up are often unpredictable. With this in mind, programs should always be created with enough flexibility to be conducted for

the "average" audience. The average audience would be a representation of the general public consisting of families with children, adults with no children, a mixture of males and females, and a fairly even age spread among the adults and children.

There are some *special* audiences to consider when designing programs. These audiences introduce special concerns, needs, and issues. Teenagers, children, elderly, and people with disabilities are among some of the groups of special concern when program planning. Children and teenagers will be reviewed in Chapter 9, and the elderly and people with physical and mental impairments will be discussed in Chapter 11.

Evaluation and Feedback

Evaluation and feedback combine to form the final stage of the program-planning process. This brings the process full circle back to the

Writing Program Objectives—An Example

WAMS Method	**Identified Message:** The remaining coastal redwoods should be protected and preserved.
	Program Goal: Create a program that increases awareness of and support for the preservation of the redwoods.
	Objective One: After an interpretive walk, when quizzed, at least 50 percent of visitors will be able to identify two reasons why redwoods should be protected. When = after the walk Audience = visitors Method = a quiz Standard = 50 percent will identify two reasons why redwoods should be protected
	Objective Two: When offered a Save-the-Redwoods League membership application at the end of the walk, at least 10 percent of visitors will take one. When = end of the walk Audience = visitors Method = offer a membership form Standard = 10 percent will take one

research phase. Although we dedicate Chapter 13 to discussing evaluation, it is important to discuss it here to clarify that evaluation is part of the planning process. It should not happen as a separate function but as an integral part of the program-planning process.

Evaluation is examining whether or not program objectives were met. Evaluation and feedback should inform you of the current status of program offerings based on program objectives and suggest modifications and changes for the future. This data is then used as the research for the next cycle of programming. Evaluation and feedback is a critical stage in the planning process. It is through evaluation that assessments of meeting goals and objectives are made. If the planning process doesn't have an evaluation phase, then there is little indication of the success or failure of the planning efforts.

Evaluation and feedback techniques and strategies should be based on the program content, goals and objectives, budgets, expertise, target audiences, program communication mediums used, and the time frame available for feedback. Veverka (1994)

Basic Steps for Evaluation

➤ Identify the objectives that you need to evaluate. This should have been done when the program was created (WAMS method).

➤ Select the most appropriate evaluation tool or technique. (We will discuss this in detail in Chapter 13.)

➤ Conduct the evaluation. Programs can be evaluated before, during, and after the actual delivery.

➤ Compare results to the desired objectives. Program success must be based on accomplishment of desired objectives.

➤ Analyze results. Assess why or why not objectives were met.

➤ Provide feedback. Make recommendations for improvement.

—Adapted from
John Veverka, 1994

recommends a six-step sequence to the evaluation process.

In the Next Chapter ...

Understanding the planning process is necessary in order to create successful interpretive programs. Now let's turn our attention to a review of the interpretive program itself. In the next chapter, we will review the basic elements of an interpretive program and introduce the steps of creating that program.

Evaluating whether your interpretive efforts met objectives is a critical step in the planning process and provides important feedback for future program design. Courtesy of Carolyn Widner Ward

Review

1. Careful planning is the key to successful interpretive programming.

2. Planning can be a simple RIDE if you remember to research, identify themes and messages, design interpretive opportunities, and evaluate and provide feedback.

3. The three elements that must be researched for successful program planning are the resources, the public, and the management.

4. Both natural and cultural resources must be inventoried before successful programs can be designed.

5. Primary data collection involves firsthand data collection from the site itself. It reveals what is on the site.

6. Secondhand data collection is information *about* the resources identified through primary data collection.

7. Data must be reliable, valid, and defensible.

8. Visiting-public data collection enables program creation to meet visitor wants and needs.

9. Demographics, motivations, and use and activity patterns are helpful data to collect regarding visitors.

10. Visitor data can be collected by either observation of behavior or survey methods (self-report data).

11. Identifying characteristics of the nonvisiting public can provide insight into unmet local community and potential constituent needs.

12. Management data should also be collected during the research phase of planning to identify management needs, critical issues, goals, and objectives for programs.

13. Current program offerings, management plans, facilities, equipment, and past programming data should all be collected.

14. After the research phase of the planning process, appropriate themes and messages should be identified.

15. Identification of themes and messages enables interpretive opportunities to be created to meet the needs of the visitors, the resource, and the management.

16. Program objectives should be specific, time limited, measurable, and have clearly stated standards.

17. Evaluation and feedback are the final steps of the planning process.

Questions and Exercises

1. What are the four basic steps of the program-planning process?

2. What are some practical things you can do the first week on the job to become acquainted with the three primary aspects of the research phase of the planning process: the resource itself, the visitors, and the management?

3. Is primary or secondary data more accurate? Why or why not?

4. Where could you find data regarding the local population surrounding your site?

References

Article

Knopf, Richard. 1988. "Human Experience of Wildlife: A Review of Needs and Policy." *Western Wildlands* 2–7.

Books

Brochu, Lisa. 2002. *Interpretive Planning: The 5-M Model for Success (Republication Draft)*. Fort Collins, Colo.: National Association for Interpretation.

DeGraaf, Donald G., Debra J. Jordan, and Kathy H. DeGraaf. 1999. *Programming for Parks, Recreation, and Leisure Services: A Servant Leadership Approach*. State College, Pa.: Venture Publishing.

Diamond, Judy. 1999. *Practical Evaluation Guide: Tools for Museums & Other Informal Educational Settings*. Walnut Creek, Calif.: Alta Mira Press.

Fazio, James and Douglas L. Gilbert. 2000. *Public Relations and Communications for Natural Resource Managers, Third Edition*. Dubuque, Iowa: Kendall/Hunt Publishing Company.

Fort Rodd Hill and Fisgard Lighthouse National Historic Sites of Canada Management Plan. 2003.

Grinder, Alison L. and E. Sue McCoy. 1985. *The Good Guide: A Sourcebook for Interpreters, Docents and Tour Guides*. Scottsdale, Ariz.: Ironwood Press.

Ham, Sam H., A. Housego, and B. Weiler. 2004. *Tasmanian Thematic Interpretation Planning Manual*. Tourism Tasmanian.

Helmich, Mary. 1997. *Workbook for Planning Interpretive Projects in California State Parks*. Sacramento: California Department of Parks and Recreation.

Knudson, Douglas, Ted T. Cable, and Larry Beck. 1995. *Interpretation of Cultural and Natural Resources*. State College, Pa.: Venture Publishing.

Machlis, Gary E. and Donald R. Field, eds. 1992. *On Interpretation, Revised Edition*. Corvallis, Oreg.: Oregon State University Press.

Tilden, Freeman. 1967. *Interpreting Our Heritage, Revised Edition*. Chapel Hill: University of North Carolina Press.

Veverka, John A. 1994. *Interpretive Master Planning*. Helena, Mont.: Falcon Press.

Chapter 5

A Basic Structure: Program

All successful interpretive programs begin with a basic structure that follows a similar design. Courtesy of Kara Murtey

All interpretive programs begin with a basic structure.

Thematic communication is something most of us do every day, more or less intuitively.

—Sam H. Ham, 1992

This chapter introduces the basic components of an interpretive program. Although there are many forms of personal interpretive programs, including walks, talks, and roving, there are basic building blocks of successful interpretive programs regardless of the delivery form. We will review these elements, including the theme, research, introduction, body, and conclusion, in this chapter. For each of these elements, we will discuss its purpose, the various types, and methods of implementation.

The Message

Defined

The primary element of an interpretive presentation is the message or theme. The theme is the one defining characteristic that separates all other communication forms from that of interpretation. Some presentations are simply laundry lists of facts and information;

True interpretation is distinguished by the conveyance of a discernible message driven by an expressed need.

these are known as show-and-tell presentations. You walk visitors through the resource and *show* them the plants (or buildings, or artifacts) and *tell* them some information about each one. This is not true interpretation. True interpretation is distinguished by the conveyance of a discernible message driven by an expressed need. It is the reason we are giving the program. It is identified through careful examination of the site significances, resources, management needs, and the public. Once targeted messages have been identified through careful planning, a theme can be developed.

Purpose

Themes outline the way that interpreters connect visitors to the resource. We use themes for four key reasons. They help us identify the message, or "big picture." A good theme should answer the question, "So what?" (Ham 1992; Lewis 1981). In other words, why is this program worthy of visitors' time and effort? The NPS approach to interpretation indicates that a great theme will link the tangibles in a park (the object, place, etc.) to the intangibles (the meanings, ideas, and emotions, etc.) (Kohen and Sikoryak 2000). The theme also helps guide our research, saving time and focusing our attention on the relevant pieces of information for the story. For example, if the presentation is on birds, think about how many books and sources of information you would have to wade through. If your theme is "Birds take flight for life," your research is now narrowed and certainly more manageable. The theme also provides the overarching organizational structure for the program. All main points, or subthemes, in the program should fit within and complement the main message, or theme.

Perhaps the main reason to use a theme is the increased knowledge acquisition and understanding associated with its use. In a study conducted comparing the effects of a thematic interpretive program versus a nonthematic program, children retained more main points, processed information at higher levels of understanding, and were more likely to identify the main message of the program in the thematic program (Tarlton 2004).

Creation

Before we discuss how to develop a theme for an individual program, remember from Chapter 4 that overarching themes may already be identified in planning documents. Be sure to thoroughly complete the research phases of the planning process before you create program themes. Once you have identified the topic of the program and the target message based on program planning, themes can be developed using a few easy steps.

The first step for developing a theme is to brainstorm. Brainstorming is essentially freeform thinking to generate ideas regarding a particular topic. Brainstorming is used to promote creativity for finding different approaches for programs. Familiarity with a topic often breeds a lack of ability to see it creatively. Brainstorming works best when done with a group of people. The goal is to generate a large number of new ideas about a topic. Get started by writing the topic or subject in the center of a piece of paper, chalkboard, and so on, and then record all ideas and thoughts that are verbalized by participants (figure 5.1). Hearing what others think often generates new and creative ideas.

After brainstorming, ideas need to be categorized and grouped. This is called mind mapping or clustering (DeGraaf, Jordan, and DeGraaf 1999; Regnier, Gross, and Zimmerman 1994). It is a simple technique that is used to link generated ideas into potential subcategories that can then be used to produce themes. Generated ideas can be placed in more than one category, so be sure to use different-colored pens or different shapes for grouping ideas (figure 5.2). Once ideas are subgrouped, brainstorming can focus on a particular subgrouping of interest, which might develop into your theme. Notice how many potential messages (themes) about birds are starting to emerge from the example in figure 5.2.

As Sam H. Ham, Anna Housego, and Betty Weiler (2004) stated, this method produces the raw material for a great theme. Once you have narrowed your vision down using the above methods, you are ready to refine, edit, and massage the theme so that it is ready to light the spark of interest in a visitor. Given that our themes are created for programs with clear goals and objectives in mind, a great theme could be considered to be one that "expresses the heart and soul of the learning objectives" (Ham 2003, 11).

Writing good themes is easy using the steps outlined. Take your time and be creative. Writing great themes comes with practice and years of experience. The theme

Site-specific cultural resources should guide the formation of appropriate program target messages. Courtesy of Carolyn Widner Ward

Figure 5.1 Brainstorming—An Example

Field Tips for Conducting Brainstorming

Clearly identify the target topic or subject of the brainstorm. Be sure all participants agree with and understand the topic.

Establish group rules in the beginning. Everyone should agree with the process used for brainstorming.

Record all responses so everyone can see. Ideas spur other ideas, so all recorded responses must be readable.

Have a manageable group size. At least three and no more than 10 participants are recommended. In a large group, have two recorders.

Change the recorder so everyone gets a chance to participate in the brainstorm.

Record *all* answers with no discussion. Discussion and clarification come later in the process. For now, the goal is simply the generation of new ideas.

Figure 5.2 Mind Mapping—An Example

After selecting a grouping of ideas to explore for developing a theme, use Sam H. Ham's (1992) three-sentence method to refine the theme. To test your theme, Ham recommends answering the following questions.

1. **The first sentence simply states the topic of the presentation.**

   "Generally, my presentation is about _____(topic)_____."

   For our example: "Generally, my presentation is about birds."

2. **After the brainstorming and mind mapping, you can more narrowly define your topic.**

   "Specifically, I want to tell my audience about _____(more narrowly defined topic)_____."

   For our example: "Specifically, I want to tell my audience about why and how birds fly."

3. **Once the topic is narrowed, the third sentence begins to create the message that you want the audience to carry away with them.**

   "After hearing my presentation, I want my audience to understand that _____(theme)_____."

   For our example: "After hearing my presentation, I want my audience to understand that birds fly to survive."

The third sentence can be modified to fit the particular objective of the program. For example, we can have emotional, cognitive, or behavioral program objectives. If the program objective is to alter behavior, it might be better to use the verbs "do," "support," "participate," and so on, rather than "understand," as in the original version. The verb that works best will depend on the overall objective(s) guiding the program. A good theme emerges using Ham's three-sentence method, but not a great one … yet.

—Adapted from Sam H. Ham, 1992

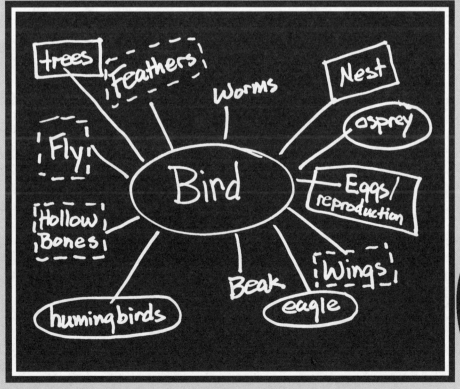

Qualities of a Good Theme

➢ Is specific, simple, and short

➢ Conveys a complete thought or message

➢ Reveals the purpose for the presentation

➢ Contains only one main message

For our example, "Birds fly to survive" is a good theme. It conveys a complete message, reveals the purpose and focus of the talk, and is short and simple.

... A *Great* Theme Also

➢ Paints a picture

➢ Uses active, not passive, language

➢ Answers the question *So what?*

➢ Provokes and promotes attendance

➢ Provides a positive message

Expanding on our previous example, we arrive at "Birds take flight for life" as our theme. This conveys the same meaning but is more interestingly worded, paints a clearer picture, and promotes curiosity. This theme could be improved even more with additional brainstorming.

is the first step of creating successful interpretive programs and should be done with care and patience.

Research

Developing the Theme

After the theme is created, it is time to continue your research. Remember, you conducted research in the planning stages to help set the overall direction for your program. It was through that early research phase of the process that preliminary ideas were generated, helping you to brainstorm and create the target messages. Once you

have created a theme through brainstorming, you are ready to conduct very specific research guided by the theme.

This phase of the research process is used to develop your theme. Your theme will evolve and change as you learn more about your topic. Sometimes the research you uncover may alter the theme altogether; be flexible and allow your theme to accurately reflect what you find.

We conduct research to accurately understand and then convey information to the public. Interpreters are the interface between the resource and the public and, as such, have a responsibility to tell the "truth" of the thing, place, time, or event. There are many perspectives of historical events, and researchers often differ in their interpretations of science. It is the job of the interpreter to communicate as honestly as possible. Conducting good research is the only real method to ensure the reflection of accurate facts.

Conducting Research

As reviewed in detail in Chapter 4, there are two basic approaches used to conduct

Theme Examples

➢ Stars are recyclers of the universe.

➢ The American chestnut tree ruled the ridges of these mountains.

➢ Solar power uses the sun to make your home run.

➢ You can change the world we live in, one solution at a time.

➢ Humboldt Bay starts on your street.

➢ Fire forges every phase of life.

➢ Redwoods: adapting to survive the flames of fire.

➢ The Trail of Tears began with a single step.

research; primary and secondary data collection. Conducting research that is guided by a theme is very similar. The sources for information are the same, but the techniques are a bit more refined. For example, in the planning stages, primary data collection consisted of inventorying the site and assessing all the resources. Conducting primary research after a theme is created involves very specific searches for examples demonstrating main points or ideas in the program.

Remember, one of the goals of interpretation is to link visitors to the resource. In order to accomplish this, primary research of that specific resource must be conducted. Where in the resource are the best places to demonstrate the phenomenon of your program? This information may be used differently depending on how the program will be delivered to the public. For example, you may demonstrate the information in a walk by actually taking visitors there, or in a talk by using the location to direct visitors to go see it for themselves, or show it to them in an audiovisual presentation.

Regardless of the method used, the purpose of the primary research is to identify the places, sites, and objects that are relevant to or appropriate for a particular theme. For our theme example, "Birds take flight for life," we use primary research to find places in the resource that provide the best opportunities to see birds, and especially birds in flight. The research conducted in this stage should be written and kept in a file under the theme idea you are developing. Be sure to date all observations and any special circumstances under which the observations were made. This information is helpful to change the program in the future and provide insight into its successes and failures.

Secondary research is used to provide a more in-depth understanding of the theme. It provides the background, substance, and information needed to develop your presentation. A good starting point for secondary

Field Tips for Conducting Good Research

Review existing information relevant to the theme—it may have been collected during the inventory phase of the planning process.

Visit the sites applicable to theme—primary research.

Examine books, journals, reports, etc., to support theme development—secondary research. Don't forget the rule of three sources.

Keep notes that are organized by subtopic within the theme with citation included—You may want to return to the source.

research is to review the thematically relevant information that was collected during the resource-inventory stage in the planning process. Review both the primary and secondary data that is appropriate for your theme. After the initial review of compiled data, the search continues for other information that supports your theme. Be sure to use information that is the most current, found

Brainstorming and mind mapping are very effective tools for designing creative interpretive programs. Courtesy of California State Parks, Cahill

The work of the specialist, the historian, the naturalist, the archeologist, is fundamental, then. Without their research the interpreter cannot start.

—Freeman Tilden, 1883–1980

repeated in multiple sources (rule of three), from a wide variety of sources (don't just use the Internet), is relevant and interesting. Research prepares you to tell a *great* story.

The Story

The basic interpretive presentation is like telling a story to visitors. It has a beginning, middle, and an ending. A good story has an introduction that sets the stage for the body or main part of the story and a conclusion that brings it full circle, leaving the audience satisfied. Let's take a look at the process of creating the story.

Sam H. Ham (1992) coined the 2-3-1 rule for the order in which the main parts of an interpretive presentation should be developed. According to Ham, if the introduction of the presentation is #1, the body is #2, and the conclusion is #3, the 2-3-1 rule indicates the order in which the presentation should be developed. How can you write an introduction for a presentation that you have

Use the theme to help guide and narrow your research.
Courtesy of Carolyn Widner Ward

not written yet? You can't! Ham's approach, to developing the body (#2) of the talk first, followed by the conclusion (#3), and the lastly the introduction (#1), is a logical approach and one that we highly recommend. Now that you have developed a theme and have completed much of your research, you are ready to begin developing your story.

Developing the Body

The main points are developed and delivered to the audience in the body of the presentation. Remember, there should be about five main points covered in the body of the presentation. The body is the heart of the talk, allowing the interpreter to relate information to visitors, inspiring them to want to learn more, and promoting management goals and objectives.

There are two structures for developing the body of an interpretive presentation: theme/subthemes and narrative. Although both structures should have an overarching message, these labels will allow for ease of discussion. It should be noted that there are many permutations of these forms. This terminology simply allows us to distinguish between two styles of developing the body of a presentation.

Theme/Subthemes

The theme/subthemes structure of a presentation has a theme that is developed and supported by main points, or subthemes. Most interpretive presentations are developed using this format. For theme/subthemes structure, each main point has four elements (Ham 1992). The first thing each main point should do is *focus attention* on the subtopic covered in that main point: *some bird species mate in flight*. In this example, we are introducing mating behavior as the subtheme supporting the main theme, "Birds take flight for life." The next element of each main point is to describe or explain the information: *There are two species of birds found here*

Theme/Subthemes Structure—An Example

Introduction (story)

Body (middle)

> First main point
>
> > A. Focus attention
> >
> > B. Describe or explain the information
> >
> > C. Connect to theme
> >
> > D. Transition
>
> Second main point
>
> > A. Focus attention
> >
> > B. Describe or explain the information
> >
> > C. Connect to theme
> >
> > D. Transition
>
> Third main point, etc.

Conclusion (ending)

> —Adapted from Sam H. Ham, 1992

that mate in flight. ... After presenting the information, each main point should have a thematic connector, bringing the information back to the theme: *Mating behavior is an example of how birds take flight for life and in this case, to create life.* The final element of each main point should be a *transition* to the next main point (or conclusion): *Now that we have discovered how successful mating depends on flight, let's look at the importance of migration for the life of many birds.* Taken together, this approach to designing the body of the presentation follows a theme/subthemes structure. The program contains a central message (theme), which is developed through the creation of several subthemes (main points), which are all linked or connected together with transition sentences.

Narrative

The second type of structure for developing the body of an interpretive presentation is more narrative in form: historical or living-history presentations often follow this approach. The narrative structure also has a central message or theme, but it may not be as obviously stated as in the theme/subthemes structure, and it follows more of a fluid format. There may be dialogue, conversation, or narrator-style presentation of information. For example, the interpreter who comes out in character and relives a moment in history for the audience will probably not follow the outlined theme/subthemes structure. The presentation will flow more fluidly, like a conversation. There may not be discernible main points and transition sentences.

This type of presentation can be very powerful and provoking. Susan Strauss (1996) talks about the "story way" of communicating and how it can be one of the most effective methods of interpreting science and history. "Story telling is considered a literary art (even though it is oral and not written) because it shapes a narrative to create meaning or address a problem, a question, an imbalance, or a desire" (Strauss 1996, 25). This, in essence, is interpretation. We will review storytelling in much more detail in Chapter 6.

Narrative Structure— An Example

I am the last of my kind still found in these hills. There used to be hundreds of us before the roads, the buildings, and all the trails. I looked for others for years before I finally gave up. I used to hear far-off cries of others, but no more ... the woods have been silent for some time now. We used to travel to this place together in great flocks. ...

Field Tips for Conducting a Conclusion

You must:
➤ Repeat the theme
➤ Provide a clear ending
➤ Thank the audience for attending

You can:
➤ Repeat the subthemes
➤ Give a philosophical ending
➤ Leave the audience with a question
➤ Provide opportunities for action
➤ Show resources for more information
➤ Advertise future programs

There is no set formula that can be outlined for presenting interpretation using the narrative form, because there are numerous methods of developing and presenting a story. It could have a moral, present a problem and resolve it after a climax, be an epic, leave the audience wondering what happens, or bring the information full circle. The narrative structure could be used to tell a person's individual story, recall a historical event, follow the life cycle of an individual animal or plant, or trace the life of a drop of water through the resource.

The Ending

The final part of an interpretive presentation, regardless of its type, is the conclusion. Following the 2-3-1 rule, the conclusion should be created after the body of the presentation has been designed (Ham 1992). The conclusion is a summative message. It is the ending.

Purpose

The reason we have a conclusion is to give the audience a sense of completeness for the program. It also provides an opportunity to repeat the program's theme and subthemes. People are more likely to retain information that has been repeated throughout the presentation. Repeating the theme numerous times, and having it as the last thing visitors hear in the conclusion, maximizes retention. Another reason to "formally end" the presentation is to send a clear signal that the presentation is indeed over.

Creation

There are as many ways to end a presentation as there are presentation styles. Every interpreter has his or her own method of concluding a presentation. There are some things that every conclusion should do and many more things that are appropriate for certain programs with specific program goals and particular presenter styles.

Conclusion—An Example

We have reached the end of our journey together today. Remember, birds take flight for life. Migrating, escaping from predators, and mating are just some of the critical roles flight plays in the survival of birds found in this park.

The next time you see a bird take flight, ask yourself if you think it is for life, love, or longing. I brought some books on the subject if anyone is interested. Let your imagination soar with some of these great resources on the birds of this park. Does anyone have any questions? If not, I would like to thank you all for coming and hope you have a great afternoon.

Every program should have a clear ending with *Thank you for coming* as one of the parting statements. Ending presentations with *That's about it* or *I'm done*, although reflecting an ending, are not very powerful in helping to meet program objectives nor very professional. Every ending should somehow repeat the theme, thus increasing the potential impact of the message. If it was important enough for you to design an entire presentation around, it is important enough to remind visitors.

The remaining suggestions for a conclusion are not necessary but can be powerful and effective if used appropriately. Conclusions can repeat the main points or subthemes of the program. This will help to increase retention of those submessages. Asking for questions from the audience during the conclusion is a popular technique. Conclusions can have a philosophical message, leave an audience with a question to think about, or provide them something to do. Bringing information sources (books, etc.) for the audience to review can also be included as part of the conclusion. You can also announce upcoming events or other programs offered in the park.

The Beginning

After you have designed the body and the conclusion of the presentation, you are finally ready to create a powerful introduction to set the stage for the program. The introduction is critical and must grab and hold attention. It conveys to the audience that there is a reason for them to commit and stay for the duration of the presentation. The introduction serves three primary functions: it serves to orient the audience, introduce the theme, and provide a cognitive map for the audience. A cognitive map is much like a spatial map. You can give directions to your home in two ways, spatially or cognitively. You could provide a spatial map showing the way visually, or you could simply tell the

Field Tips for Conducting an Introduction

Introduce yourself—Tell the audience your name, position in the park, and a little about yourself.

Welcome the visitors—Be a good host.

Establish credibility—Describe your background, expertise, and passion for the topic.

Provide the theme—Introduce the theme for the talk.

Give an attention grabber—Provide a startling fact, visual aid, thought-provoking question, etc.

Introduce the main points for the talk—This is part of the cognitive map.

Tell the audience why you are doing the talk—People respond better if they know why you are doing the talk.

Provide any orientation/information necessary—Abraham Maslow safety, security, and physiological needs, route of the walk, bathroom breaks, any difficulties or dangers encountered during the talk, etc. The specifics of this information will vary greatly depending on the type of presentation.

Be enthusiastic and sincere—Visitors respond to genuine passion and sincerity.

By using the basic building blocks of program design, conducting successful interpretive efforts is systematic and easy. Courtesy of Carolyn Widner Ward

Introduction—An Example

Hi, my name is Carolyn. I've been a state park interpreter for the past 10 years and I just love working in this park. I'd like to welcome you all to San Luis Reservoir State Recreation Area, a popular stop for waterfowl along the Pacific Flyway. How many of you think it would be great to fly? Would you be more likely to fly for love, life, or longing? Today, we will travel down one of the park's trails and search for examples of how birds take flight for life. Many visitors wonder why the birds don't just stay here all year long. We will discover the primary reasons birds take flight to survive, including migrating, hunting for food, mating, and escaping from predators. We will uncover a fifth reason for flight together at the end of the talk.

It is an easy walk, covering about a quarter-mile on fairly level ground. The walk will end back here in about one hour. There is poison oak near this trail, and I will point it out to you when we approach it, so please keep together and let me lead. I have binoculars and field guides with me today if anyone would like to use them. Any questions before we start?

directions, a cognitive map. A cognitive map provides a mental picture or organizing structure for the direction of the presentation (Knopf 1981). It should tell an audience why they are there, what they will get out of the presentation, and what they can expect. According to cognitive-map theory, providing this initial organizing structure should facilitate comprehension and retention of the message (Knopf 1981; Hammit 1981).

Putting the Program Together

All good programs start with a theme. People forget facts, but they remember a good theme and the supporting subthemes. Brainstorming, familiarity with the site and visitor, and understanding management needs and objectives all combine to assist in creating appropriate themes. Themes also focus research efforts, allowing programs to connect visitors with the resource in as accurate and honest a manner as possible. After most of the research is completed, the interpretive story is fashioned. There are two primary structures for developing the interpretive story: we can use both the narrative and theme/subthemes structures to creatively weave our facts and information into an informative, enjoyable, and interesting program. The actual development of the story should follow the 2-3-1 rule. The body of the presentation will have around five main points and should be developed first. After the body of the program is designed, a conclusion is created that repeats the theme and provides a clear ending for the story told during the program. The last thing to be designed is the introduction. The introduction sets the direction for the program and can only be created after the presentation itself has been designed. These components form the basic interpretive presentation regardless of delivery method.

Together, the theme, body, conclusion, and introduction form the basic building blocks of almost all personal interpretive programs. Regardless of the type of program conducted, using these essential elements will increase the likelihood of overall success.

In the Next Chapter ...

Now that we have a clear understanding of the basic components of an interpretive program, individual programs can begin to be created. The most basic program type is the interpretive talk. In the next chapter, we will focus on applying the basic elements of the program to creating the interpretive talk.

Review

1. The theme is the main message of the interpretive program, driven by a discernable need.

2. Themes help guide research and the organizational structure for the program.

3. Thematic communication helps increase knowledge retention and understanding of our messages.

4. Brainstorming and mind mapping are two useful techniques for theme creation.

5. A theme should be short, active, positive, convey one complete message, and paint an interesting picture that makes visitors want to listen to programs.

6. The body of the interpretive presentation should be developed before the conclusion or the introduction.

7. There should be approximately five to seven main points in an hour-long interpretive program.

8. There are two main structures for an interpretive program: the narrative and the theme/subtheme.

9. The narrative program is the "story way" of communicating and is a fluid format without discernable main points.

10. The theme/subtheme structure has clear main points that support the overall theme.

11. The conclusion of the program should be developed after the body of the talk.

12. A good conclusion must provide a clear ending, repeat the theme, and thank everyone for participating.

13. An introduction is the last thing to be developed for an interpretive talk.

14. Introductions should set the stage for the conclusion.

15. The introduction should orient the audience, introduce the theme, and provide a cognitive map for the program to come.

Questions and Exercises

1. Name at least three qualities of a great theme.

2. With at least two other people, choose a topic, brainstorm, mind map, and write a theme.

3. Take the following good themes and make them great.

   Tide-pool life struggles to survive.

   Pioneers traveled west.

   There are many nonnative species causing damage in the park.

   The bay is home for many different species.

   The desert comes alive at night with life.

   Dams prevent salmon from traveling upstream.

4. When do you think a narrative structure would be preferable to a theme/sub-themes structure?

5. Choose a topic, write a theme, and create an outline for a program.

References

Articles

Ham, Sam H. 2003. "Rethinking Goals, Objectives, and Themes." *Interpscan* May/June 2003: 9–12.

Hammit, William. 1981. "A Theoretical Foundation for Tilden's Interpretive Principles." *Journal of Environmental Education* 12 (3): 13–16.

Knopf, Richard. 1981. "Cognitive Map Formation as a Tool for Facilitating Information Transfer in Interpretive Programming." *Journal of Leisure Research* 13 (3): 232–242.

Books

Beck, Larry and Ted T. Cable. 2002. *Interpretation for the 21st Century, Second Edition.* Champaign, Ill.: Sagamore Publishing.

DeGraaf, Donald, Debra Jordan, and Kathy DeGraaf. 1999. *Programming for Parks, Recreation, and Leisure Services: A Servant Leadership Approach.* State College, Pa.: Venture Publishing.

Ham, Sam H. 1992. *Environmental Interpretation: A Practical Guide for People with Big Ideas and Small Budgets.* Golden, Colo.: Fulcrum Publishing.

Ham, Sam H., Anna Housego, and Betty Weiler. 2004. *Tasmanian Thematic Interpretation Planning Manual.* Tourism Tasmanian.

Knudson, Douglas, Ted T. Cable, and Larry Beck. 1995. *Interpretation of Cultural and Natural Resources.* State College, Pa.: Venture Publishing.

Lewis, William J. 1981. *Interpreting for Park Visitors.* Philadelphia, Pa.: Eastern Acorn Press.

Regnier, Kathleen, Michael Gross, and Ron Zimmerman. 1994. *The Interpreter's Guidebook: Techniques for Programs and Presentations, Third Edition.* Stevens Point, Wisc.: UW-SP Foundation Press.

Strauss, Susan. 1996. *The Passionate Fact: Storytelling in Natural History and Cultural Interpretation.* Golden, Colo.: Fulcrum Publishing.

Manuscript and Paper

Tarlton, Jennifer. 2004. "The Effect of Thematic Interpretation on a Child's Knowledge of an Interpretive Program." Unpublished master's thesis. Arcata, Calif.: Humboldt State University.

Kohen, Richard and Kim Sikoryak. 2000. "Theme Guide: Case Studies." U.S. Department of the Interior, National Park Service, Intermountain Support Office.

Chapter 6

The Basic Program: Talk

Whether formal or informal, a good talk entices visitors to explore on their own. Courtesy of Carolyn Widner Ward

Talk is personal dialogue
with audiences to increase
their understanding, appreciation,
and enjoyment of resources.

Main Points

Talk is the most basic form of personal services interpretation. Through the power of speech and the nonverbal adjuncts associated with delivery, we attempt to light the spark of curiosity and wonder. Good communication helps visitors become so familiar with a resource that they want to forge their own path of discovery. In the previous chapters, we discussed in more general terms the whats, whys, and hows of personal interpretation. In the next five chapters, we will address the specific knowledge, skills, and abilities for presenting talks; walks; campfires; children's and roving programs. Before embarking into new territory, following the principles of good interpretation, let's recap a little of what we have already learned.

Interpretation is an artful form of communication that stresses ideas and relationships, not simply isolated facts and figures. This is most frequently done through the use of hands-on illustrative media, firsthand experiences, and/or the use of physical objects. Good interpretation communicates the science of the natural and cultural world to an audience in a manner that is provocative, interesting, and leaves them wanting to discover more.

The goal of interpretation is not the same as teaching. The people who attend interpretive programs are there because they want to be there (noncaptive audience). There are no externally motivating factors keeping an audience from leaving. As such, one of the most important things to remember is the "priceless ingredient" Freeman Tilden (1957) talked about: *love*. Love allows you to be enthusiastic, knowledgeable, engaging, and

A good talk entertains and informs.
A great talk starts out by entertaining,
moves on to interpreting, and
ends by inspiring.

communicate effectively with your audience. We've seen that to effectively communicate, you must establish all the elements embraced in CREATES. Now let's focus on the most fundamental program: the talk.

Types of Talks

Talks are formal, focused, site-specific presentations or informal, spontaneous dialogues. Whether formal or informal, your talk should help visitors move from satisfying their basic needs to fulfilling their growth needs, the ultimate being self-actualization. There are many types of talks that are conducted in diverse venues and presented to varied audiences. Programs are either formal or informal encounters.

Formal

A formal talk consists of a structured presentation with a prepared theme, introduction, body, and conclusion presented to a specific target audience. Talks may utilize audiovisual equipment, guest speakers, demonstrations, storytelling, and a host of other media in an interpretive program that is entertaining, educational, and inspirational. Formal presentations include:

Walk/Hike/Tour

We inclusively call walks, hikes, and tours *walks*. Taking your talk "on the road" provides the opportunity to involve the audience directly with the resource. The interpreter guides the audience through a series of thematically planned and well-researched stops. Walks are covered in detail in Chapter 7.

Site

The purpose of the site talk is to interpret what has happened, is happening, or might happen at a specific location. The site talk may include a demonstration, results of research, or it may feature a specific location focusing on natural and/or cultural topics.

A historic setting provides an ideal venue to interpret cultural topics from a specific time period. Courtesy of Jennifer Graves

Programs in the Dark

Reduced-lighting programs are most often thought of as campfire talks, steeped in tradition and offering a multisensory and participatory opportunity to interpret resources to a diverse audience. Programs conducted in the evening or under reduced-light conditions also provide unique walk, site, or activity opportunities. Chapter 8 details the techniques and skills for providing programs in the dark.

Children

Talks for children, while encompassing all the CREATES elements, are designed and delivered to an audience that has specific needs, developmental phases, and desires. A children's talk shouldn't be a watered-down version of an already existing program, but a talk developed especially for children. Children's interpretation is covered in detail in Chapter 9.

Classroom

The classroom provides a venue for integrating our interpretive messages with academic-content standards. Ranging from

While interpretation is not the same as teaching, the classroom provides an opportunity to take our messages to a receptive audience. Courtesy of Oregon Caves N.M., NPS

elementary to college classes, classroom talks provide an opportunity to present resource themes, discuss pre- and post-site visits, and encourage agency advocacy. Tips for conducting classroom curriculum–based programs are discussed in Chapter 9.

Speaking Engagements

Speaking engagements in the community afford excellent opportunities to connect with constituents who may not routinely visit our sites or attend formal programs. These outreach experiences provide opportunities to present resource topics and issues, develop support for our programs, and extend an invitation to the community to visit their natural, cultural, and recreation areas.

Informal

Spontaneous, or informal, interpretation is a spur-of-the-moment type of dialogue with individual visitors or small groups. The encounters may or may not be planned, but, in most instances, the questions and information requested by the visitors can be anticipated. This type of visitor contact has more of a natural conversational progression.

The two most common locations for spontaneous interpretation are discussed below.

Visitor Center or Information Desk

One of the most common places for providing information and orientation services is the visitor information center or information desk. The key here is to provide interpretive answers, not just give facts. Chapter 2 reviews some techniques useful for accomplishing this goal.

Roving

Roving interpretation is personalized, face-to-face communication where the audience has chosen the venue, the resource is the stage, and the interpreter is the catalyst for knowledge. Roving is planned, personalized communication with visitors in an informal setting. Chapter 10 is devoted to the basic techniques of conducting roving interpretation.

Preparation

Whether you are presenting a formal program or making a spontaneous, informal contact, preparation is the key to success. Being prepared is the best way to combat nervousness and promote self-assurance. Research and study your topic thoroughly. When preparing your talk, you must know the resource, the significant features, and

Initial visitor inquiry is most often conducted at the visitor center or information desk. Anticipate the questions and be prepared to provide clear, concise, and accurate information. Courtesy of Oregon Caves N.M., NPS

> When preparing any talk, it is vital to recognize that SAP is the life of your presentation.
>
> **S**ubject
> **A**udience
> **P**urpose

their importance (subject); have an understanding of your visitors' needs and motives (audience); and incorporate management goals and objectives (purpose). As you begin to really *know* your subject, audience, and purpose, you will gain confidence and be eager to deliver your talk.

Getting Started

It is much better to outline your talk than to write it out completely. If you write it out, you are tempted to memorize or read it. A canned speech sounds like a canned speech. It's not conversational, friendly, or wise. Interpreters who memorize their programs are under pressure to remember every line. If they fall out of sequence, they often panic and become completely lost. Forgetting even one word of a memorized speech can be disaster.

The outline should consist of your theme and subthemes, introduction, and conclusion. Practice without extensive notes. Use just the major points (subthemes) as your guides. Develop focusing sentences, thematic connectors, and transitions (Chapter 5). Make it your goal to feel comfortable enough with the main points, transitions, and the flow of the presentation that you talk with the audience as if they were friends. If you *must* memorize something, limit memorization to the outline, transitions, and the opening and closing statements.

Quotes can be extremely powerful, especially when they directly relate to your topic. Be careful when incorporating quotes:

don't paraphrase or misquote the person. Using the voice/dialect of the person you are quoting certainly enhances the reality. A good technique is to let historical characters speak for themselves through their letters, diaries, and other documents.

Note cards may come in handy and be appropriate for the program agenda, long quotes, and/or the basic outline (subthemes) of your presentation, but avoid having too many as crutches. Use note cards sparingly. Once again, they may get out of sequence and cause you to panic. Having them results in an overwhelming desire to use them. Note cards can hamper eye contact, hand gestures, and the general conversational flow.

Practice

Practice is the crucial step in the transitional phase between planning your talk and actually delivering it. There is no substitute for actual practice. Rehearse as if an audience were in front of you; go through the entire program, using visual aids and body and facial gestures. Anticipate where and when you will have questions. Visualize yourself

Rehearsals Take Many Forms

Technical—Complete verbal program without full development of props, anticipated questions and answers, and costume/uniform.

Personal—Intellectually and physically, work through the progression and details of your talk. Work with your notes, talk to yourself in front of a mirror, and refine what words, actions, and props work best. Stop as many times as necessary to make corrections.

Dress—Complete program without stopping, including props, questions and answers, and in costume/uniform. Videotaping this stage of rehearsal is very beneficial.

Field Tips for Reducing Anxiety

Confidence—Remember, you are organized and ready.

Visualize—Envision every element of your program.

Release tension—Relax and breathe.

Divert audience focus—Ask a question or have a prop that draws attention elsewhere, giving you a moment.

Solid introduction—Successful first moments build confidence.

Enjoy—Recognize that the audience is not the enemy.

introducing yourself, delivering your talk, fielding questions, and concluding the presentation.

A minimum of five rehearsals is recommended; however, be careful not to practice *so much* that you memorize it. Have friends and/or coworkers watch and critique your presentation. If possible, videotape and/or record your practice sessions. This combined with critiques from outside observers will allow you to assess and modify your program more easily. Videotaping and/or recording your talk are excellent practice techniques.

Take advantage of every opportunity to practice in front of strangers. Force yourself to speak to groups, even if you're really frightened. Even the greatest orators get nervous. They overcome their fear by conscious effort and practice. *You can do the same.* Practice, practice, practice! Through practice and preparation, you will begin to

> *The knowledge that most of the audience regards you as worth listening to even before you open your mouth should increase your confidence.*
>
> —Paul Risk, 1982

deliver presentations in a more natural manner, as though talking with friends about a subject for which you are passionate.

Overcoming Stage Fright

Stage fright is normal. Almost all of us share a fear of speaking in front of an audience. Even the most seasoned professional actor may have a nervous stomach, sweaty hands, tremors in the knees, and an accelerated heart rate before each performance. The trick is to use this excess adrenaline to your advantage. "This kind of 'arousal,' as psychologists call it, makes us more alert, more focused and less likely to forget—even though we feel just the opposite" (Ham 1992, 69). Recognize that stage fright is normal and make it work *for* you. Let the heightened sensitivity and energy fuel a more enthusiastic and dynamic presentation.

Remind yourself to breathe. When muscles tighten and you're anxious, you may not be breathing deeply enough. Focus on relaxing. Remind yourself that you are prepared. The audience is on your side and they want you to succeed. Give yourself some flexibility. Don't lock your knees or maintain a rigid posture; move around a little and allow your muscles to release tension. Moderation is the key, so don't pace wildly back and forth either. Smile and watch the audience smile back.

Voice and Vocabulary

Your voice and vocabulary convey friendly, approachable, personal warmth. Talk with the audience, not at them; there is a huge difference. Endeavor to use the same conversational style in your talk as you would with a group of your friends. Speak clearly, avoid using jargon and scientific terms, and don't forget to breathe. Avoid repeating words or phrases such as *actually*, *basically*, *uh*, *um*, or *ah*.

Express your talk in a conversational style, using the full range of your voice. The

Add PEACE to Your Voice

Pleasant—Conversational, friendly

Eloquent—Spontaneous and natural

Audible—Articulate with appropriate volume

Compelling—Makes audience want to listen

Engaging—Actively conveys meanings and feelings

manner and skill with which you use your voice influences the audience's perception of your credibility and their comprehension and retention of the theme. There a several methods you can use to enhance the delivery of your talk.

Even if you possess a strong, audible voice, there are times when the audience will not easily hear you. Be constantly aware of your surroundings and any distractions that may make hearing difficult. When you are speaking to a large group, or when the ambient noise level is high, a microphone

Delivering Your Talk

Rate—Most people speak 120 to 180 words a minute. Vary the speed at which you talk, but don't speak too fast or too slow. A constant rate is monotonous and boring.

Pitch—Intonation and volume should also vary. A constant pitch is tedious.

Articulate—Enunciate so that each word is heard correctly.

Breathe—A relaxed voice with controlled breathing is easier to understand. Short sentences with pauses and periods help; don't run on and on.

Quality—Emphasis, force, expression, and clarity make all the difference in the effectiveness of a talk.

can be a useful tool. Chapter 12 has tips on the proper use of microphones and other audiovisual equipment.

It is important that you face your audience. This directs your voice toward the audience and, if any participants need to, it allows them to lip-read or infer what you are saying. Don't have anything in your mouth while you are speaking. Items such as gum, a toothpick, or a cigarette are very annoying and reduce your ability to enunciate clearly. They also sabotage credibility and professionalism. How you express yourself helps your audience to be open and receptive, understand what you are saying, and relate to their personal experiences. The words and phrases you use make a difference.

Most often when conveying facts and numbers, it is best to generalize, but there certainly are exceptions. For example, the Declaration of Independence was signed in 1776 not the late 1700s, and water freezes at precisely 32 degrees not the low 30s. Conversely, in many instances, rounding numbers is less tedious and distracting. For example, 397 species of birds should be rounded up to 400, and 14,010 acres should be rounded down to 14,000. Decisions about whether or not the exact number or an average or rounded number is better will only come through knowing your resource and the importance of the facts you are conveying. Where possible, put numerical information into a context to which the audience can relate. For example, to help them relate to how much food a hawk must eat each day in order to survive, you might say something such as *A hawk eats half its body weight every day. If I were to do that, I'd have to eat 75 pounds of food. Let's see ... that's about 150 hamburgers a day!*

Adding Pizzazz

There are many ways to stimulate interest and add excitement to your program. An easy attention-getter is a sentence that is outrageous,

Field Tips for Spicing Up Your Programs

Choose words carefully, they can make a world of difference. Use active, descriptive words to verbally illustrate an idea, not just tell about it. For example, instead of saying, *She tried not to indicate how much my words hurt her.* Say, *As I finished speaking, she lowered her eyes and turned away. In a whispery voice, she said, "Looks like it might rain later."*

Use descriptive verbs instead of adjectives and adverbs. For example, you might say, *The deer ran away scared.* But by saying, *The deer froze, then leaped the fence and bolted across the meadow,* you paint a much clearer verbal image.

Avoid the verb *to be* (is, was, were) whenever possible. For example, the statement *It was a dark and stormy night* doesn't help the audience visualize as much as *The storm raged all night; only the lightning lit my way through the forest.*

Use an active voice for power and strength; use a passive voice for a soft, vague effect. *The grass was bent low by the wind* is an example of describing a scene in a passive voice. An example of active voice might be *The wind presses the grass close to the ground.*

Use simile or metaphor to enhance your descriptions. *The man hopped around and waved his arms* is not as descriptive as the following simile, *The man hopped into the air and waved his arms like a giant prehistoric bird straining to take off into the wind.* Metaphors work well also: *He was a giant prehistoric bird straining to take off into the wind.*

—Adapted from Sam H. Ham, 1992, and Jane Vander Weyden, 1994

to listen carefully and solve the problem. A riddle, a brainteaser, or a trivial-pursuit challenge helps to heighten interest and interaction. Providing your audience with clues in the body of your talk helps them solve the mystery at, or prior to, your conclusion. You might use a phrase that is repeated and gains power with each repetition, e.g., "I have a dream." You might use a turnabout, start a line of thinking in one direction and then abruptly change; or you might use a long pause or whisper.

Incorporate humor into your talk, as long as it relates to your theme. Humor can add lightheartedness to your presentation and help establish rapport. With that said, use humor very carefully. You are an interpreter, not a stand-up comic. Something funny to one person may offend another. A humorous story about your personal experiences or observations that directly relates to your theme can add insight and humanize your presentation. If the humorous story illustrates a point, the punch line should not be at your audience's expense. Remember, befriend your guests and make them feel at home and important.

Questioning Techniques

The technique of questioning involves and intellectually stimulates the audience. Questions entice visitors to share their knowledge, thoughts, and feelings. Questions

Use Questions That Help the Audience

➤ **Focus** by describing, naming, observing, recalling, etc.

➤ **Process** by analyzing, comparing, explaining, grouping, etc.

➤ **Evaluate** by imagining, predicting, theorizing, extrapolating, etc.

rhymes, or is startling. Say something that really captures the audience's attention and makes them want to listen. Foreshadowing, an early reference to something that you will talk about later, adds mystery, suspense, and enhances curiosity. It provokes the audience are either open- or closed-ended. Open-ended questions ask for opinions, feelings, and generally stimulate creative thinking and discussion. Closed-ended questions ask for direct, short, factual type responses, e.g., yes/no or the answer to who, what, or where.

It may seem obvious, but when you ask a question, give your audience enough time to answer. Unless asking a rhetorical question, you should allow 5 to 15 seconds for the audience to think about, formulate an opinion on, and verbalize a response. Direct questions to, and encourage responses from, different members of the audience. Don't let one or a few individuals dominate the conversation and interaction. Do *not* put anyone on the spot by directly singling them out, unless you are sure they will be able to answer the question easily. If no one answers the question, rephrase or leave it open and answer it later in your talk. Try not to answer your own questions. The unanswered question becomes suspenseful foreshadowing. It's important to accept answers gracefully, even if the response is incorrect. *I never thought about it that way ...* or *That's an interesting perspective ...* are methods of gingerly accepting a *wrong* answer. Use follow-up questioning or rephrasing to gently arrive at the correct answer.

You've heard the question a thousand times! By the end of the tourist season, you will probably know what questions the audience will ask before they ask them. It may be a challenge to respond as if this is the first time you have ever heard that question. Remember, be a good host. It is the first time that particular individual has asked, and he/she deserves a clear, courteous answer.

Presentation Strategies

As we learned in Chapter 5, the body of your presentation can be delivered in either the theme/subtheme or narrative style. Whichever style you incorporate, you should

Field Tips for Answering a Question

Always rephrase and repeat a question received from an audience member. This helps ensure that you understand the question being asked and that everyone in the audience heard the question you are responding to.

If you don't know the answer to a question, don't bluff or fake it. Say you don't know. Ask if anyone in the audience has the answer. If not, make arrangements to provide the answer at a later time.

Sometimes it is prudent to not directly answer the question. Help the audience discover the answer on their own with a little encouragement from you. If the question will be answered later in your talk, let them know you will be answering it shortly.

remember that, just as with all interpretation, the only limit to what you can do is your imagination and creativity. Other presentation strategies may be employed to help convey your interpretive messages, including characterization and costumed interpretation, demonstrations, storytelling, puppets, a guest speaker, and guided imagery. Audiovisual and specific types of programs presented in the dark will be discussed in Chapter 8.

Answering techniques are very important. Act the role of a person who is hearing the question the first time. Interpreters in the cultural setting get into the habit of explaining everything in the room that they know will be of interest to the visitor. Interpreters need to allow the visitors to ask questions. We need to encourage a conversational style, participatory with the audience, not a lecture.

—Michael Green, 2002

Field Tips for Putting "Spark" in Your Presentation

Smile—Sixty to 95 percent of communication is unspoken.

Vary your voice—Monotone induces sleep, not interest.

Talk with your audience, not at them—Be conversational and friendly.

Speak from the heart, not your notes—The priceless ingredient is love.

Face your audience—Let them see and hear what you are saying.

Use appropriate gestures and positive body language—Engage the audience.

Don't memorize your talk—Remember your outline.

Make smooth transitions—Compel the audience to listen.

Employ good questioning techniques—Involve and intellectually stimulate the audience.

Add pizzazz—Incorporate suspense, mystery, foreshadowing, humor, and active words.

Close the program with an ending that punctuates your theme—It's the story they'll remember.

Don't fret, stage fright is normal—Use the energy to your advantage.

Characterization

Costumed interpretation of a real or imaginary creature requires considerable preparation, but the rewards can be great. "Characters engage the imagination and evoke a whole range of emotions—humor, drama, pathos. Characters humanize events and concepts, making them personal and real to visitors" (Regnier, Gross, and Zimmerman 1994, 46).

There are two types of characterizations: first-person characterization, sometimes called costumed/living history, and third-person interpretation. In first-person, the interpreter *becomes* the character in every aspect: dress, dialogue, mannerism, and delivery. The interpreter must know the character and the time period so well that he/she can ad-lib responses. The interpreter stays in character at all times. In third-person, the interpreter may look like a person from a particular era but speaks about the people and events of the portrayed time period from a current perspective.

Consider carefully whether to use first- or third-person characterization. First-person generally requires help from another person to introduce the audience to someone from the past.

> First-person interpretation generally requires another person to prepare the audience, set the stage, and close the program. Without someone to provide a cognitive map to the program, visitors may not understand the depiction and may become confused or feel disoriented.

First-Person—"Living History"

In addition to physical voice, there is another voice we can use in our interpretation. The voice of first-person interpretation is that of an individual from a specific time or period. This type of interpretation is known as *living history*. To work well, you must *become* the person who lived or was at the site. You must not only accurately look like the character, but your speech, dialect, vocabulary, and style must also be an accurate reflection of that era. First-person interpretation may use a "canned presentation," but more commonly relies on spontaneous interaction with the audience. As you interact with the audience,

> *In essence, living interpretation involves on-site re-creation of the lives of a people, wearing their clothing, speaking their dialect, reviewing their decisions.*
>
> —Inger Garrison, 1992

acknowledge only things from the appropriate time period. For example, you are portraying a rancher's wife baking bread in an adobe oven. An audience member says something about storing bread in the freezer. You know nothing about a freezer, but you could say that the rodents tend to burrow into the basement cold-storage area, so bread doesn't store well. First-person interpretation takes considerable research, concentration, theatrical skill, and practice to stay in character. Although it is one of the most difficult voices to master, when performed correctly, first-person interpretation can be a powerful presentation tool.

To portray someone successfully takes lots of practice. Allow plenty of time to develop your specific character. The character should have a name, a history, a personality, and must support your theme. You will have the best results if you choose common characters. For example, become Lincoln's neighbor, not Lincoln himself. Most audience members will relate better to the common person.

Third-Person—Costumed Interpretation

Third-person interpretation uses a costume and associated items as props for the time period being discussed. The interpreter does not need to *become* a certain character, and the dialogue and discussion can be in modern terms. Visitors generally find it easier to interact and ask questions of someone doing third-person, costumed interpretation. Craft and skill demonstrations are greatly enhanced when the interpreter dresses in suitable clothing and uses authentic-looking tools and props. Third-person interpretation allows more-comfortable interaction with the audience and may be more effective at conveying a given message.

Demonstration

A demonstration is a program that incorporates activities with narrative. It shows how

---

Field Tips for Making Your Characters Believable

Clothing—Choose comfortable, authentic wear with appropriate age indications.

Makeup—Use sparingly. Most of the time, the best makeup is the real thing: mud, dirt, grease, flour.

Details—Small items make your character come alive, especially those things that contribute to sensory awareness: smoke, food, music, tools, or any items that are connected to the era. The stage for your character can be enhanced with visual effects: candles, kerosene lantern, a rocking chair, or any prop that helps convey the time period of the character.

---

something works or is used. Demonstrations entice questions and can provoke visitors to think more about what is happening and why. The interpreter may or may not be the one doing the demonstration.

Demonstrations range from the interpreter explaining, demonstrating, and showing

A costume greatly enhances the visual impact of your presentation. Clothing, makeup, and attention to details make your messages more understandable and believable. Courtesy of Jennifer Graves

A demonstration integrates narrative with a specific activity. Performing the task and providing interpretive narrative greatly increases comprehension.

Cultural demonstrations can be powerful and enlightening. The presentation should have an ongoing dialogue that supports the theme. Preplanning where to position the audience is critical for success. Courtesy of Alan E. Wilkinson

examples of one step in a process and/or activity to an audience participating in the activity/process and helping reveal the larger significance. The audience, or at least individuals from the audience who are actively participating, may actually gain a new skill.

Historic and cultural sites are common venues for demonstrations, but demonstrations can also be effective at recreational locations. Often, interpretive objectives can best be attained through demonstration. As with any talk, a demonstration should be a strong thematic presentation. You are still telling a story with a theme and objectives, simply using objects, activities, and props to tell this story.

Be aware of how you position the audience for the demonstration. One of the main drawbacks of the demonstration is lack of visibility. With larger groups, the object you are using or the activity you are demonstrating may not be visible to all. Demonstrations for smaller audiences work best.

Storytelling

Everyone loves to listen to a story ... if it is well told. Storytelling is as old as humanity itself. A good story can be told any time and anywhere. A well-told story is one of the best ways to capture the audience's attention and pique their interest in the subject.

Anyone can learn to tell stories. We tell stories daily when describing an adventure we've had or a movie we've recently seen.

Demonstration Suggestions

Clothes, gear, and tools of an 1800s mountain man, 1840s housewife, or 1850s miner—Help the visitor understand events, issues, and/or hardships of early inhabitants of your area.

Camping skills and equipment—The underlying message might be safety, resource protection, or appreciation of the outdoors.

Trail building—Show the skills and effort it takes to keep the trails open, yet remain sensitive to the resources.

Care and use of firefighting equipment—Aim toward preventing forest fires.

Costumes, facial expressions, and visual aids all enhance the storytelling presentation. Use your voice and gestures to draw in the audience. Courtesy of Carolyn Widner Ward

Field Tips and Techniques for Storytelling

Relaxation exercises—Take a moment before starting a story to relax. Use exercises to release tension.

Humming exercises—Storytelling and any public speaking takes a strong voice. One way to strengthen and not strain your voice is to hum. Try changing the volume, pitch, and expression in your voice as you hum.

Different parts of your voice—It's important to be aware of the different types of sound you can make with the parts of your voice. The nasal long "ē" sound comes from the front of your head or through your nose. The long "ā" sound comes from the front of your mouth. The "ah" sound comes from the back of your throat, the "oh" from your chest, and the deep, short "uh" from way down in your stomach.

Inflection—Use inflection to keep an audience interested and to sustain a feeling or mood. Drop your voice only at the end of a complete thought.

Diction—Your language must be understandable for the audience. Improve your diction by repeating tongue twisters, such as, "Peter Piper picked a peck of pickled peppers."

Facial expression—Practice expressing different emotions, feelings, attitudes, etc., using only your face. Try showing anger, disgust, joy, surprise, excitement, pride, and sadness, for a start.

Character assumption—Learning how to take on a character is critical in becoming an effective storyteller. Your character may be the narrator of the story, or it may be one of the principal figures in the story.

—Adapted from Linda Yemoto and
Simone Dangles, 1980

Good storytellers have the ability to transport listeners to the scene being described and make them feel involved. *Great* storytelling is a special gift and an art that not everyone possesses, but anyone can learn to tell good stories. All it takes is the ability to be creative in describing a scenario and the willingness to practice, practice, and practice.

As a storyteller, your goal is to become, for a brief moment, something other than a man or woman standing in front of the room—to create a whole new world using words, sounds, gestures, and expressions. To hear a story is an ancient longing, to tell a story an ancient skill. A well-told story can move you to laughter or tears, it can explain or cause you to ponder the wonders of the universe.

—Linda Yemoto and
Simone Dangles, 1980

Storytelling is a powerful tool in the interpreter's repertoire, offering a special magic. Stories provoke interest and emotion. They are great for explaining why we celebrate different events and the meanings behind traditions and legends. Throughout the world, stories teach values, attitudes, and philosophies. Through these stories, we learn about the culture and the character of people.

Select stories that are relevant to your interpretive theme. Remember to tell a story, not a memorized speech. Memorize the sequence of images for the story but not the words. This allows you to be spontaneous and creative. Your voice and gestures should make every member of the audience feel as if you are talking directly to them.

Listening to stories is a universal longing, telling a good story an admired skill. The best way to develop this skill is to practice. If you aren't good at storytelling, don't do it in front of an audience until you are!

Sequence of a Good Story

Set the scene—*Once upon a time* or *Long, long ago ...*

Development—Pull the audience in, sustain the interest, and build up the tension

Crisis—The height of the tension

Solution—Relief of that tension

Moral or wrap-up—The hook, needle, or message

Puppets

Humans have long used puppets to entertain and educate. They help engage and focus attention. Puppets serve well to communicate natural and cultural resource information and ethics to audiences of all ages. They help audiences visualize and comprehend abstract, complex, or controversial issues in humorous, lighthearted ways.

Puppets are portable, three-dimensional, inexpensive, and don't require constant attention. They can be lifelike, representational, or fantastic. They are potentially powerful and useful tools in an interpreter's arsenal. "Puppets command attention and are enjoyed by audiences of all ages. They allow for interaction with the audience and convey controversial issues in a fun and nonthreatening manner" (Helmich 1997, 86).

Guided Imagery

Guided imagery is a process of creative visualization or guided fantasy. It allows you

Field Tips for Effective Storytelling

Do

➢ Speak clearly and loudly with plenty of inflection.

➢ Speak at a measured pace, neither too fast nor too slow.

➢ Wear a mask if you are shy about storytelling, but make sure all can hear.

➢ Tell a relevant story that you really like.

➢ Use silence, pause for effect, whisper to catch attention.

➢ Use sound effects to emphasize a point.

➢ Tell the story spontaneously rather than reading from a script.

➢ Practice, practice, and practice.

Do Not

➢ Tell a story you don't really like.

➢ Begin with an apology.

➢ Start with long story introductions.

➢ Use annoying/unwelcoming body language and facial expressions.

➢ Read the story.

➢ Speak in a monotone.

➢ Express personal opinions or bias.

➢ Get sidetracked.

➢ Leave your listeners without a resolution to the story's conflict.

➢ Begin to talk immediately after finishing your story.

➢ Use a fake or affected voice.

➢ Use weak or distracting gestures.

➢ Be someone who you don't like.

➢ Be too detailed.

—Adapted from Vicky Crosson and Jay Stailey, 1988

Guided imagery is best accomplished
with small groups
in a controlled environment.

to mentally take the audience to places, times, or events they cannot or should not experience physically. It is important that the audience is willing to take this journey, and they must trust the interpreter in order to fully enjoy the experience.

Begin the journey by getting the audience as comfortable as possible. Help them relax by listening to the wind, the babble of the nearby creek, or other white, natural noise. Use your voice to help them discard distracting thoughts. Take your time—pauses allow the audience to get in the mood.

Ask the audience to close their eyes and encourage them to create mental images triggered by your verbal, virtual trip. Then describe, with as lively a narration as possible, the scene, situation, or process you desire to show them. Their active involvement, rather than mere listening, makes for greater understanding and retention. An example of a guided-imagery program is a description of the travels of a water molecule through the water cycle, from vapor to cloud to earth and back again.

Guest Speaker

Guest speakers add variety, substance, and innovation to interpretive programs. A guest speaker may be incorporated into a program to provide specific information and expertise beyond your knowledge, but, remember, the responsibility for the overall program falls to you.

Practically every location has people who are experts in a specific field and would be appropriate for including in a program. Consider local craftspeople, longtime residents

Field Tips for Using Puppets

Move the puppet's mouth "in sync" with what it is saying.

Open and close the mouth with each syllable.

Move the lower jaw. The puppet's head should remain level.

Stay in character.

Puppets should make eye contact with the audience. You should talk to the puppet and be a good listener.

Let the puppet carry the program.

Develop a distinct personality and voice for each puppet.

Keep the program short and active.

—Adapted from Kathleen Regnier, Michael Gross, and Ron Zimmerman, 1994

of the area, Native Americans, and experts on the area's natural and cultural features. Don't overlook the expertise you have on staff and

Field Tips for Successful Virtual Travel

Guided imagery is not effective if there are distractions. Read your audience and let them know ahead of time what to expect. A crying baby or group of unruly teens will spoil the whole mood.

Everyone sees the journey a little differently. A beneficial technique is to ask members of the audience to share their trip. Different and interesting insights and revelations may be discovered.

The audience needs to be comfortable, peaceful, relaxed, and in a receptive mood.

It is the interpreter's job to ensure that the environment is conducive for creative visualization.

Research a guest speaker's qualifications and abilities *before* you make that first invitation.

volunteers. Whomever you select must be articulate, prepared, and the topic must be relevant and appropriate for the site and the audience.

Establish a rapport with the guest speaker long before the program. Thoroughly discuss expectations (both yours and the speaker's), know his/her personal/professional background, and develop a mutually agreeable introduction. Make sure the speaker is aware of the composition of the program. Agree on the time allotment and how you will signal the speaker to end the presentation.

It should be clearly understood what the topic is, how the speaker will present the topic, and what conclusions will be made. Although the guest speaker is in front of the audience, the interpreter is still the one responsible for the program. At a minimum, the welcoming, warm-up/introductions, and closing will be your responsibility.

There are hazards to keep in mind when using a guest speaker. An expert may give a lecture, not an interpretive talk with a theme. Unless you know the speaker's ability in subject matter and manner of presentation, it may be best not to experiment with your audience. Your time with the audience is too valuable. Not only do you need to know your audience's needs and desires, you also need to know your guest speaker's ability.

Techniques

All the planning and preparation efforts will begin to pay dividends when you actually present your talk. Here are several presentation techniques that you should employ that will add to the program's success.

Before the Talk

Plan to arrive early for your talk. Just how early depends on several factors: location, preparation needs, and familiarity with the venue and potential audience. Arriving early allows you time to set up, become comfortable in the environment, gain confidence, and when it is time to start the program, you know you are prepared and ready to go. Arriving early also provides time to socialize and establish a rapport with individuals before they become your audience. As we have previously discussed, this personal linkage is vitally important. Through personal conversations, you directly learn about individual wants, needs, and expectations. Through observation, you indirectly gather information about the composition of the audience, including age, gender, ethnic composition, and so on. Understanding your audience enhances success. Knowing whom you are talking to lets you tailor your presentation. Remember Tilden's first principle, "Any interpretation that does not somehow relate what is being displayed or described to something within the personality or experience of the visitor will be sterile" (Tilden 1957, 9).

If you are presenting your talk at a location you are unfamiliar with, such as an off-site speaking engagement, visit the location prior to the presentation. Room layout, location of switches and plugs,

First Impressions

First impressions are very important. The audience begins assessing you the moment they meet you. Arriving at the talk location early helps establish your dependability. Your posture, appearance, grooming (uniform), and voice reinforce and enhance credibility and confidence. Your eye contact, smile, and warm welcome radiate approachability.

> *An interpreter acts out of authority and humility; confidence and compassion; respect for others and one's own integrity; stability and enthusiasm; and joy. An interpreter treats others with kindness.*
>
> —Larry Beck and Ted Cable, 1998

audiovisual concerns, and so on should all be addressed long before the actual presentation.

Make a Positive Impression

Just as you will be observing the audience and determining their wants, needs, and interests, they will be assessing your competence, approachability, and professionalism. First impressions matter. Appropriate, clean clothes and good grooming standards enhance your credibility. Personal mannerisms, voice, enthusiasm, and presentation style can reinforce or shatter this positive respect the audience has for you.

Credibility, personality, competence, and sincerity manifest themselves in your communication skills, both verbal and nonverbal. In Chapter 3, we discussed credibility and how content, confidence, and appearance impact a visitor's perception of you. Let's briefly revisit how to improve nonverbal messages.

Personal Style

How you come across to the audience is influenced by a combination of your environment, education, and personality. We've all inherited characteristics, been influenced by different experiences, and have personal comfort zones. We are unique. When developing your personal style, borrow techniques that you like from other speakers, but don't try to copy them. Let your own personality shine through.

Personal Characteristics That Impact Communication

- ➤ Voice quality
- ➤ Body language
- ➤ Appearance
- ➤ Eye contact
- ➤ Passion
- ➤ Sincerity
- ➤ Uniform
- ➤ Title

We communicate a lot of information with our body, face, hands, and posture. When interacting with an individual or a group, always stand up straight; don't slouch. Look at your audience and smile. Avoid distracting mannerisms, such as swaying, fidgeting, pacing back and forth, putting your hands in your pockets and fumbling with keys and coins, and so on. You communicate positive signals with good posture. Use tasteful, appropriate, and slightly understated hand gestures to punctuate and illustrate points in your program. Don't hesitate to walk toward your audience to focus attention and make personal connections, but be careful not to intimidate or pace wildly. Once again, be aware of and practice good nonverbal skills. In addition, your attitude is extremely important. Assume a friendly, confident, and enthusiastic demeanor. When you have a positive attitude, all the planning and mechanical details of a talk will come more easily and naturally.

Be a Good Host

Think of yourself as the host and the audience as your guests. Have everything ready when guests arrive. Greet them and exude a warm welcome; a smile is a great charmer. Acknowledge everyone, whether personally or visually. Make a connection and offer a welcoming gesture.

Begin your talk on time. Part of being a good host is introducing yourself, formally welcoming the audience, having an attention grabber, providing information about the theme and subthemes, telling them why you are doing the talk, and presenting a cognitive map.

Constantly gauge your audience's reaction to determine their level of enjoyment and understanding. The language, complexity of issues, and examples that you use to clarify points must be at a comprehension level that is appropriate for your audience. For example, if a large percentage appear to

Field Tips for Grabbing Audience Attention

Change your voice and pace of delivery— Change their focus.

Stop and tell a story—Excite them.

Ask a question—Put them on alert status.

Select someone for role-playing—Change the game.

Use a quote—Bring in the past.

Pull out hand-held objects—Electrify with visual props.

Make a spontaneous discovery—*Oh, look over there.*

Change your facial expression—Get dramatic!

Direct the action—Stay in charge, you're the leader.

Be enthusiastic—Share your excitement at every opportunity.

Recognize and praise someone—*Oh, what a great idea …*

Follow their energy and interests—What appears to be a distraction can be a great discovery, if you make it one. Carpé diem!

Use pauses and silence—Emphasize a point or attract attention.

—Adapted from Ron Russo, 1999

How Is a SMILE Like a Talk? Both Should Be:

➤ **S**incere

➤ **M**eaningful and memorable

➤ **I**nviting and interesting

➤ **L**asting, loving, and linking

➤ **E**ndearing, easy, educational, and engaging

understand only limited English, it would not be effective to present a talk full of terms that they can't understand. As a general guide, plan your presentation for the eighth-grade level, and then adjust as needed. Using standard English and avoiding slang is especially important. (Also refer to special groups in Chapter 11.)

Because we speak at a slower rate than minds think, the attention of all audiences wander. People's thoughts drift to new, unrelated areas or different things to do. The physical signs are obvious to the alert interpreter. For example, fidgeting, looking around, talking, and walking away are all symptoms of mental distractions. Here are some suggested ways to regain attention and keep it.

Props

A good interpreter employs a number of well-chosen tools in an effective talk. Your voice, body language, questioning skills, and enthusiasm are just four of the tools you constantly have available when presenting a talk. There are a host of other aids or props that can help illustrate and accentuate the theme of the talk. Remember, props are *aids* to the presentation. Props help *tell* the story; they are not "the story."

Select props, aids, and specimens that are large enough to see and relevant to the talk. Have props laid out in their order of appearance, but, generally, it is best to keep them hidden until you are ready to exhibit them. This provides suspense and lessens distractions. When using props, don't get into the *This is a …* and *This is a …* mode of explaining the objects. Remember good presentation techniques, including transitions, foreshadowing, questioning, and relevance to theme. The prop should be an integrated part of the program, not just a throw-in gadget.

Continue to talk to the audience when using props. Keep eye contact with the visitors, not your props. Only occasionally glance at the prop to identify points of interest and to add emphasis. Use slow, deliberate hand movements when identifying the feature you are exhibiting. Be careful to position yourself so that you don't block anyone's view.

Whenever possible, let visitors feel, smell, and handle the objects that you are discussing; however, use caution when passing objects through the audience. If it is a small group, you might consider waiting until everyone has had a chance to observe the object. If possible, have an object for each member of the group to explore and discover.

Because you are often trying to show items to a large number of people in a limited amount of time, specific display and distribution techniques should be used. Good lighting is critical. What might be easy to see for the few visitors in the front can be completely lost for those in the back. Be aware of glare, hold the object up high, walk into the group so everyone can get a better look, and let the audience know they are welcome to take a closer look at the end of the program.

If the object that you are planning to pass around is expendable, have several to pass, not just one. Starting an object in the front and expecting it to flow through the audience in a timely fashion doesn't work. If the object is large, fragile, precious, or dangerous, make sure you explain the finer details and don't

Activating all the senses creates a holistic experience for the visitor.

—Larry Beck and Ted Cable, 1998

pass it around. Consider using a graphic, a handout, an image of the item projected on a screen, or a model.

Props can be the real items, reproductions, representational, or graphic. Use props to involve all the senses in your talk; incorporate props that can be smelled, heard, touched, tasted, as well as seen. This will greatly improve theme comprehension and retention. Where possible and prudent, use the real thing. For example, it is much more effective to let the visitors smell for themselves the fragrant bark of the Jeffrey pine rather than telling them it smells like vanilla. Hearing the chimes of the old clock on the mantle helps envision quieter days. Tasting that exquisitely ripe blackberry right off the vine has much more impact than hearing someone's description. Props should be incorporated to effectively engage the senses and heighten understanding.

Visuals

Visuals may be two- or three-dimensional. For example, you could use an illustration, photograph, a projected image of an object (two-dimensional), or you could use the actual object (three-dimensional). Generally, it is far more effective to use the real item rather than a facsimile, but that isn't always possible. Visual aids may increase retention and comprehension by as much as 50 to 200 percent (Ham 1992); however, if your visuals are poorly designed or displayed, they may draw attention away from you and work against the intended goal. Visuals should clarify your theme. They should enhance what you are saying without distracting the audience's attention. Ways to engage the sense of sight include:

ILLUSTRATIONS

Projected images are common visual aids that make graphics large enough for all to easily see. We'll cover how to prepare an audiovisual presentation in more detail in Chapter 8. Here we'll look at how other simple illustrations can support your theme.

Select your illustration prop carefully. First and foremost, make sure that all of the audience can see it clearly. It may seem obvious, but pictures, posters, maps, and other visual aids must be large enough for your audience to view. Limit the amount of information you present with any one visual aid. For example, limit the text to a line or two on any one graphic. Too much reading becomes too much like school and competes with what you say to visitors. If you do use text, the font size and style of the letters should be appropriate for the visual. Use an easy-to-read sans-serif font, such as **Arial**. Avoid using complicated graphs and charts, because they are too difficult to decipher at a glance (no more than six rows or columns should be used on any one graph).

Incorporate extra lighting, projection devices, magnifying glasses, and so on, where appropriate to enhance visual acuity.

OBJECTS

When using handheld objects, be sure the background and lighting are suitable. Hold the object steady, generally at shoulder level, and deliberately point out features and details. Slowly rotating objects allows for visual relationships to be grasped. If the item has a human use, show or pantomime that use. Appeal to the audience's imagination where possible. Ask questions to engage their thoughts. For example, you are showing the audience an antique apple peeler that was a common tool in 19th-century farm life. It is a complicated combination of wheels, cogs, and prongs. Ask if anyone knows what this tool might have been used for. Provide clues to help them guess correctly; a bowl of apples nearby may just do the trick! Then actually peel an apple or use gestures to indicate how the tool was used. If appropriate, invite a volunteer from the audience to try it. Have them comment on how hard or easy it is to use.

REFERENCES

Field guides, local flora and fauna keys, architectural digests, how-to manuals, copies of diaries and letters, and other topic-related references provide visitors opportunities to discover details. Interested individuals can discover additional information beyond that which you are able to present to the general audience.

Let the visitor know where they can purchase or obtain the reference, if they desire. This practice is extremely helpful at increasing the take-home value of a program. It can also be beneficial to everyone if the item is available in your local bookstore. If you think an item is good enough to use as a reference, the visitors may very well benefit by having one of their very own.

Let the audience see, touch, and experience with various senses to aid understanding and comprehension. Courtesy of Oregon Caves N.M., NPS

Audio

Incorporating sound into your talk certainly enhances another dimension of understanding. Stopping to listen to the natural or ambient sounds should be a normal occurrence for the seasoned interpreter. You can enhance the audience's ability to hear sounds with various techniques and tools. Have everyone cup their hands near their ears or put their ear to the ground or tree and listen intently. Ask them to close their eyes and listen to often-unheard sounds. In this all-too-busy world, the art of just listening to the tick of a clock, a birdsong, or rushing water is often forgotten by our visitors and overlooked by the interpreter. Listening can be a vital component of telling the story.

Including mechanical devices, such as tape players, stethoscopes, bat detectors, or parabolic recorders, can help capture sounds not normally heard by visitors. Use all the tools available that effectively improve the experience and illustrate the theme.

Smell

Draw your audience's attention to the aromas of the environment. The stuffiness of the cellar, the pungency of creosote, or the musk of the elk are all smells the visitor will not soon forget. How you employ and deliver these and other smells requires careful planning and forethought. While there is no substitute for the real thing, keeping the door closed to the cellar, rubbing the leaves of the creosote, or bottling the musk oil of an elk are all ways to safely and artificially incorporate smell stimuli into the interpretive experience.

> What's ambrosia to one stinks to another. As with all audience considerations, use good judgment and don't force, shame, or embarrass anyone into smelling, tasting, or touching any of your props.

Field Tips for Handling Handouts

Handout materials help engage and involve the audience, but distribution is an issue. Handouts may be beneficial for providing supplemental information, help with recall at a later date, and offer some take-home value. How and when you distribute the handout materials requires forethought and good techniques. Distributing the material at the start of the talk may relax the audience and make them more receptive to listening, but it might also distract their attention away from your presentation. Passing the materials out during the talk may clarify or help illustrate your theme, but the timing and continuity of the presentation may be thrown off. Waiting until the end of the program may reinforce your presentation and provide additional information, but it might also just be something that distracts from your strong conclusion. Use handouts wisely.

Modeling how the audience should smell the item reduces anxiety. Instead of simply handing people something to smell, show them how to approach it. Any time you ask the audience to do something, always demonstrate first. For example, instead of telling the audience to stick their nose in the Jeffrey pine bark, simply walk up to the tree, hug it, put you face right up to it, take a deep breath, and say, *Ahhhhhh*. Once they know it's safe, they will be far more relaxed and willing to experience the smell.

Taste

Tasting things is a tricky proposition. To the untrained eye, plants that are poisonous may easily be confused with safer ones. In addition, tasting things potentially promotes a dangerous message. Be aware of the hidden messages you send picking the natural resources. Choose carefully what tastes you share with visitors. If done wisely, there are

Field Tips for Tasting in the Wild

Don't encourage tasting unless you are absolutely sure it is edible and safe.

Just because animals eat it doesn't mean you can.

Harvest with respect to the resource and the law.

Explain to visitors why and how you are ethically harvesting. For example, advise your audience to take only every fifth blackberry to ensure enough for others, for animals, for reseeding, etc.

Just because it tastes good doesn't make it safe.

Always give a warning about look-alikes and the dangers of eating in the wild.

Be aware of the lesson visitors, and especially children, may be learning from your example of eating plants from the resource.

life experiences to be had! For example, a city dweller who tastes a ripe wild huckleberry may now be able to understand why a bear is so focused. Someone who has never tasted a cattail corncob may finally understand how innovative the hunter-gatherer cultures were.

Pack your kit bag with appropriate tools to help illustrate the various subthemes of your story. Integrate props throughout the program and use good techniques when exhibiting them.
Courtesy of Kara Murtey

Taste is not routinely incorporated into an interpreter's talk. It's difficult to do effectively, a little scary, and may not always produce the desired effect. But when used correctly and it works, you just may have connected the visitor with the resource in a way they will never forget.

Touch

Incorporating tactile sensation is extremely successful at reinforcing messages. For example, touching the ground to test the temperature with one hand in the sun and the other in the shade clearly illustrates the difference a tree can make. The rough texture of bark or of smooth, polished marble cannot be explained any better than by touch. Touching the hairs on plants shows how they manage to "hitchhike" on your socks and disburse widely. Many visitors become conditioned to "do not touch." Providing tactile opportunities to experience the resource can be a very powerful occurrence.

Kit Bag

Props, aids, gadgets, and all sorts of paraphernalia help the interpreter reveal the true essence of the story. Over time, interpreters develop their own personalized kit bag of tools with items that work for them in any given situation, topic, and location. Mike Freed and David Shafer (1982) list 66 items they suggest could go into your kit bag, and William Krumbein (1983) includes 74 cultural and historic items. Both articles are

What's in Your Bag?

certainly worth reviewing. Other information on interpretive techniques can be found in *The Interpreter's Guidebook* (Regnier, Gross, and Zimmerman, 1994).

Whether you use an all-purpose daypack, a treasure trunk, or an under-the-counter drawer to store your kit bag of tools, you will find that you constantly draw on them to help illustrate your talk.

After the Talk

As discussed in Chapter 5, a conclusion should provide a clear ending to the program by summarizing the theme, thanking the audience members for attending, and giving them a sense of completion. Offering a philosophical idea, or needle, that sends them on their way with food for thought is also a very effective ending technique. Your conclusion could entice visitors to learn more about the subject or announce additional interpretive programs and other resources that are available. Invite them to stay and talk.

Inviting the visitors to linger and chat after the program is just good manners. You can overtly state that you will remain for a while and are open to discussion, or you can simply remain in the area and be receptive to the visitors. A gracious host attempts to satisfy his guests' needs. Simply saying *That's all, folks* and leaving doesn't allow for that informal socialization with the interpreter that many

Tricks of the Trade

Every interpreter will have special issues and concerns to address. Many times, we develop props that work specifically to illustrate a point. For instance, California State Park interpreter Michael Green has included a tool in his kit bag that he finds very useful. Working in historic structures where marble is abundant, Michael realized visitors instinctively want to feel the smooth, cool marble. He carries a piece of marble in his kit bag that he invites everyone to touch. Over the years, the oils from all this touching have discolored the demonstration marble, offering a perfect opportunity for Michael to explain why we ask visitors not to touch the marble walls.

visitors crave … and on which good interpreters thrive. This kind of interaction helps you evaluate the program's content and your delivery skills. Don't forget to include appropriate evaluation measures (Chapter 13).

In the Next Chapter …

Our next chapter will help you develop your skills for conducting a walk, which is nothing more than a moving talk. A walk offers you the chance to directly introduce the visitor to the resource. It can take many forms. Let's take a close look at how to lead an exciting, effective, and engaging walk.

Remember to …

- ➤ Begin and end on time.
- ➤ Tell them what you are going to tell them (introduction).
- ➤ Tell them (body).
- ➤ Tell them again (conclusion).
- ➤ Support your theme with a good story.
- ➤ *Always* be a good host.

It Ain't Over 'Til It's Over

- ➤ Evaluate the program (formal/ informal, audience/self).
- ➤ Record interpretive data.
- ➤ Secure/store/replenish materials and equipment.
- ➤ Follow-up considerations (for visitors, staff, self).

Review

1. Talk is the most basic form of personal services interpretation.

2. Talks are formal, focused, site-specific presentations or informal, spontaneous dialogues.

3. Communicate ideas and relationships, not simply isolated facts.

4. Don't memorize your talk.

5. Preparation eases stress and enhances your delivery. Practice is the crucial step in the transitional phase between planning your talk and actually delivering it. Incorporate personal, technical, and dress rehearsals in your preparation.

6. Stage fright is normal; use that adrenaline rush to your advantage.

7. Know your noncaptive audience. Speak with them in terms, concepts, and ideas to which they can relate.

8. Add interest and excitement to your program by speaking with passion and love. Choose active, descriptive words.

9. Questioning techniques, open- or closed-ended, help the listener to focus, process, and evaluate the material being discussed.

10. Whether you structure your talk in the narrative or thematic style, creative and imaginative presentation strategies can be employed.

11. Smile; more than 60 percent of communication is unspoken.

12. A demonstration integrates narrative with a specific activity, greatly increasing comprehension.

13. Incorporate suspense, mystery, foreshadowing, humor, and active words in your presentations.

14. Be a good host and make a positive impression with your verbal and non-verbal communications.

15. Props enhance and help illustrate the theme of your talk. Props that engage multisensory awareness are most effective.

Questions and Exercises

1. How does first-person "living history" differ from third-person costumed interpretation?

2. Circle all the following that are recommended strategies for developing storytelling techniques.

   Humming exercises

   Memorizing the stories you tell

   Relaxation exercises

   Practicing different facial expressions

3. List four ways you could engage visitors with the resources being interpreted.

4. Much of what we interpret for the public is factual information about resources. Making numbers, dates, and other detailed facts understandable to visitors is a key part of interpreting the information. How could you interpret the following concepts for an audience?

   The tallest redwood is more than 360 feet tall.

   Phalaropes fly 2,000 miles, from Canada to South America, in two days.

   From 1850 to 1880, 75 million buffalo were killed.

References

Articles

Freed, Mike and David Shafer. 1982. "Gimmicks and Gadgets." *The Interpreter* 13 (3).

Krumbein, William. 1983. "A Gimmicks and Gadgets Potpourri." *The Interpreter* 14 (4).

Books

Beck, Larry and Ted T. Cable. 1998. *Interpretation for the 21st Century*. Champaign, Ill.: Sagamore Publishing.

Brown, Vinson. 1980. *The Amateur Naturalist's Handbook*. New York: Prentice Hall.

Crosson, Vicky and Jay C. Stailey. 1988. *Spinning Stories: An Introduction to Storytelling Skills*. Austin: Library Development Division, Texas State Library.

Garrison, Inger. 1982. "Living Interpretation." In Grant Sharpe, ed., *Interpreting the Environment, Second Edition*. New York: John Wiley and Sons, Inc.

Grater, Russell. 1976. *The Interpreter's Handbook: Methods, Skills, and Techniques*. Tucson, Ariz.: Southwest Parks and Monuments Association.

Ham, Sam H. 1992. *Environmental Interpretation: A Practical Guide for People with Big Ideas and Small Budgets*. Golden, Colo.: Fulcrum Publishing.

Helmich, Mary. 1997. *Workbook for Planning Interpretive Projects in California State Parks*. Sacramento: California Department of Parks and Recreation.

Krumbein, William and Linda Leyva. 1977. *The Interpreters' Guide*. Sacramento: California State Parks.

MacDonald, Margaret. 1993. *The Storytellers Start-up Book: Finding, Learning, Performing and Using Folktales*. Little Rock, Ark.: August House Publishers, Inc.

National Storytelling Association. 1994. *Tales as Tools: The Power of a Story in the Classroom*. Jonesboro, Tenn.: Riverbank Press.

Regnier, Kathleen, Michael Gross, and Ron Zimmerman. 1994. *The Interpreter's Guidebook: Techniques for Programs and Presentations, Third Edition*. Stevens Point, Wisc.: UW-SP Foundation Press.

Risk, Paul H. 1982. "The Interpretive Talk." In Grant Sharpe, ed., *Interpreting the Environment, Second Edition*. New York: John Wiley and Sons, Inc.

Roth, Stacy Flora. 1998. *Past into Present: Effective Techniques for First-Person Historical Interpretation*. Chapel Hill: University of North Carolina Press.

Sharpe, Grant. 1982. *Interpreting the Environment, Second Edition*. New York: John Wiley and Sons, Inc.

Stensrud, Carol Jean. 1993. *A Training Manual for Americans with Disabilities Act Compliance in Park and Recreation Settings*. State College, Pa.: Venture Publishing.

Storer, John. 1972. *The Web of Life*. New York: New American Library, Inc.

Strauss, Susan. 1996. *The Passionate Fact: Storytelling in Natural History and Cultural Interpretation*. Golden, Colo.: Fulcrum Publishing.

Summers, Lee. n.d. *A Bag of Tricks: Ideas for Campfire Warm-Ups*. Sacramento: California Department of Parks and Recreation and Monterey Bay Natural Historical Association.

Tilden, Freeman. 1957. *Interpreting Our Heritage*. Chapel Hill: University of North Carolina Press.

Van Matre, Steven. 1983. *The Earth Speaks*. Warrenville, Ill.: Acclimatization Experiences Institute.

Online

National Park Service. Interpretive Competencies, Interpretive Development Program. www.nps.gov/idp/interp/competencies.htm.

Pamphlets

Russo, Ron. 1999. "The Tendency to Wander." Unpublished handout. Oakland, Calif.: East Bay Regional Parks.

Vander Weyden, Jane. 1994. "Writing the Landscape." Unpublished handout. Wyo.: Audubon Camp in the Rockies.

Yemoto, Linda and Simone Dangles. 1980. "Storytelling—Be a Better Bard." Unpublished handout. Berkeley, Calif.: East Bay Regional Park District, Tilden Nature Area.

Personal Communication

Green, Michael. 2002. Personal communication. California State Parks.

Chapter 7

Taking the Talk on the Road: Walk

Be a good host and guide your audience toward better understanding and appreciation of the resource. Courtesy of Alan E. Wilkinson

A walk is a moving talk where the interpreter guides the audience through a series of thematically planned stops, directly involving the audience with the resources.

The moment one gives close attention to anything, even a blade of grass, it becomes a mysterious, awesome, indescribably magnificent world in itself.

—Henry Miller, 1891–1980

Taking your talk "on the road" provides an opportunity to involve the audience directly with the resource being interpreted. For purposes of this chapter, we will call a moving talk a walk. According to Sam H. Ham (1992), the qualities of any good presentation (entertaining, relevant, organized, and thematic) are enhanced by the dynamics of the walk, because something always seems to be happening. Whether the activity is strolling through the historic gardens, canoeing on a lake, exploring a cave system, or hiking in a forest, the visitors are actively involved in the resource. You are the guide on this journey. How you move the group, hold their attention, enhance their understanding of the resource, and keep them safe require techniques beyond simply talking. In this chapter, we will discuss and examine the planning and mechanics of a successful walk.

Types of Walks

We have learned from previous chapters how to develop a theme and put together a talk. Now, let's take a look at how we take our show on the road to deliver it as we move through the resource. Some of the more common types of walks include resource, facility, site, and specialty. Although we will use semantic differentiation to distinguish between types of walks, there are many elements from each that overlap and complement each other. A walk should focus interpretation on specific resources but be flexible enough to encompass the unexpected teachable moment. Walks help immerse the visitors and the interpreter in the resource, providing an opportunity for a multisensory experience and a more comprehensive appreciation of that resource. Suffice it to say, only your imagination, resources, audience, and purpose limit the types of walks you offer. Let's take a brief look at types of walks.

Night Hike

Darkness or reduced lighting provides a different perspective on the environment. While the darkness may lessen our visual acuity, it tends to enhance the use of other senses. We'll discuss various aspects of conducting programs in the dark in Chapter 8.

Wet Walk

Leaving the trail and wading knee-deep in a cool creek may be an adventure some visitors have never experienced. A wet walk can be fun, unusual, revealing, and literally get everyone immersed in the theme.

Moving Mechanically

Visitors who prefer not to walk might wholeheartedly join in an activity that lets them use their car, bicycle, or other mode of transportation. Explore various options for increasing participation.

Resources—Natural and Cultural Settings

A resource walk generally conjures up thoughts of walking along a trail, viewing and discussing the natural history of the flora, fauna, and landscape of the area. This type of walk is equally appropriate for cultural interpretation. Topics that focus on early inhabitants' uses of resources, hardships overcome by settlers to the area, and indications of past habitation all might be discussed as you walk along the path. Historic landscapes provide venues for " … interpreting the life-style, technology, economy, society, and personalities of a particular historic period" (Helmich 1997, 80).

Facility—Visitor Center, Historic Structure, Museum

The focus of this type of walk is in or around a facility. It is generally the facility and the cultural history associated with it that is being interpreted. Exhibits, furnishings, and displays provide interpretive media that assist the interpreter in explaining the cultural and natural history of the site. Historic structures may be original, restored, or reconstructed edifices of a particular period. Facility walks allow the interpreter to make connections between the specific location, the broader issues, the historical context, and the visitors' own experiences.

Site—Demonstration, Research, Cultural, and So On

Site visit walks can also focus on natural and cultural topics. These walks generally orient the visitors to the features or values of a specific location. Many times, walking *to* the site is merely a prelude to a more extensive discussion *at* the site. The walk from the visitor center to the beaver ponds is one example. Another is illustrated by a walk through a historic town site, stopping to examine the architecture of a specific building, and ultimately ending at an archaeological dig taking place on the outskirts of town. The primary interpretive moment occurs at the site itself; the walk is just setting the stage. Site visits certainly may incorporate elements of a resource and facility walk in the continuum of experiences and examples offered by the interpreter.

Specialty—Night, Wet, Vehicle

The time of day, the activities associated with an interpretive program, and even the modes of conveyance are all classifications for types of walks. For purposes of this discussion,

Walks encompass a variety of modes of transport. Knowing your audience's desires and the resources available will help you provide an exciting learning environment. Remember, specialty programs require additional planning and effort. Courtesy of Alan Ward

Bike, Paddle, Drive ...

Advantages

Cover more area, allowing for diverse examples supporting topic/theme development

Appeal to a specific audience, such as the bicycle rider, nonwalker, boat enthusiast, surfer, horseback rider, etc.

Happy visitors are more receptive

Drawbacks

Personal communication occurs only at stops

Logistics—interpreter loses and has to reclaim the group leader status

Takes longer to reassemble the group at each stop

Higher potential for accidents

Equipment can distract attention from theme

specialty walks are something different from the normal offerings. While they may be routine in some locations, specialty walks generally provide a different way to view a resource. Because they are out of the routine, they may require additional preparation, time, and logistical effort and present more safety issues.

Planning

As discussed in Chapter 6, planning a walk begins by determining the SAP (subject, audience, and purpose) of your program. Once the SAP is established, conducting

... the movement of a group of visitors led by an interpreter whose goals are to develop sensitivity, awareness, understanding, appreciation, and commitment in the members of the group.

—Paul Risk, 1982

thorough research, developing a theme, and putting it all together into an interpretive program follows easily. A walk encompasses all the elements of a talk, plus the logistics and mechanics of moving visitors through the resource.

Topic and Theme

Planning, research, theme development, and presentation skills are all elements of a good walk. When developing your walk, research both the cultural and natural features of the location. The primary focus should be on the relevance of the route to your theme, your anticipated audience, and management goals.

To know a thing, what we can call knowing, a man must first love the thing, sympathize with it: that is, be virtuously related to it.

—Thomas Carlyle, 1795–1881

The selection of the route may be dictated by the resource(s) being interpreted. For example, if you are doing a facility walk through a historic building, or a site visit to a cultural location, or even a resource walk along the only trail in the area, your route options may be highly limited. In other instances, you may have more latitude as to where you go and the sequence in which you view various features along the way.

The first order of business, as we learned in Chapter 4, is to research and inventory the features and topics of the location. With management's goals and objectives in mind, begin to develop a thematic interpretive program. To be able to select the best theme for any location, you must really get to know the entire setting. Your research should include walking the route in both directions, looking at features from different perspectives, and considering many issues. The more familiar you are with the location, the more personal experiences you will be able to share with your audience.

Route Selection—Choosing Stops

As you become familiar with the resource, start selecting locations for various stops along the route. Kathleen Regnier, Michael Gross, and Ron Zimmerman (1994) liken various stops along the walk to a string of pearls. "Each pearl is a gem of insight. The strand is held together by a thread of unity, a theme along which all of the pearls are strung. You must carefully prepare each pearl and its placement on the string, but the visitor should only perceive the whole necklace" (68). Let's discuss some of the elements that should be considered for specific stops along the route.

Staging Area

The staging area is the departure point of the walk. It is the advertised meeting point for the walk. It should be easy to find, have adequate space for the group to congregate without interfering with other operations, and be located near the planned route. An open area is preferable, because it allows visitors to easily see the starting point and orient to the location. An open location also allows you to see visitors arriving for the walk, draws in visitors who may not be aware of the scheduled interpretive program, and affords a venue to provide an overview for the walk.

The staging area is where you being the walk. It should be easy to find, have adequate space for the group to assemble, and be near the resources you will interpret. Courtesy of Carolyn Widner Ward

Field Tips for Route Selection

Adequate parking and staging areas are available.

Length, time commitment, difficulty, and accessibility are appropriate for target audience.

Avoids hazardous, distracting, and/or unpleasant areas.

Provides representative examples for good theme development.

Logistically, loop walks are generally best.

Many times, the staging area location is the same for all program offerings; it is a logical location to start a variety of walks. The front door of a historic building, the marina of the reservoir, and the major trailhead parking area are examples of easily recognized staging locations. Good staging areas provide a multitude of options for the interpreter.

The First Stop

The first stop should be within sight of the staging area. This allows latecomers to easily and quietly join the group. The first stop is, in essence, the beginning of the walk. While you have "started" the walk at the staging area—by giving the visitors a cognitive map of the program (time commitment, difficulty, topic, etc.)—it is at this first stop that you really introduce the theme of the walk. This is where you plant the seeds of expectation, wonderment, and mystery and set the scene to begin the journey.

Body of Presentation—Elements of a Stop

With your theme firmly in mind and a thorough understanding of the resources, you are now ready to plan the location of the specific stops. Each stop should be selected carefully, so that it clearly and sequentially adds a "pearl" of information to your thematic "necklace."

Field Tips for Stop Selection

Consider your audience. Physical comfort is conducive to maintaining attention. Is it too cool to be in the shade? Too windy to hear? Too confined a room? Is the sun in their eyes or the footing uneven? Little things may distract from your message.

Have more stops in the first half of the walk— people are more attentive in the beginning of the program.

Stops should not only be selected to best illustrate the subject being discussed, but also must accommodate the audience so that *everyone* can experience the setting, objects, and issues being addressed. When planning your stops, begin to think of what issues and impediments might affect your presentation. Avoid distractions or uncomfortable locations that deflect the audience's focus away from your presentation. Locations with noise, visual clutter, and other annoyances definitely should be avoided. Similarly, plan stops that will allow you to be seen and heard easily. Select locations where the audience can gather around you. Choose settings that

The Number of Stops Depends on Several Factors:

➤ Time allotted for the walk

➤ Anticipated group size

➤ Length and difficulty of route

➤ Theme complexity and elements needed to develop it

Remember, you already have three stops— the staging area, first stop, and an ending location. It's best to plan *no more than* seven additional well-thought-out and focused stops—10 stops total.

provide a natural stage or podium or allow you to step away from the group with the particular subject you are discussing in full view of the audience.

Where to End the Walk

It's nice to select a route that will allow you to end the walk near the starting point, but this isn't always possible. Just like all the other stops, the final one certainly should strongly support the theme of the program. Ham (1992) suggests that if the end of the walk culminates at a spectacular feature (waterfall, vista, impressive architectural feature, etc.), consider doing your conclusion in advance of arriving at this location, unless the feature itself relates directly to the theme. This way, you won't compete for the audience's attention.

Thematic Map and Outline

The more familiar you are with the route, the easier the job of selecting the appropriate stops will be. Select stops much like you would a location to take a photograph. Does the location illustrate the subject, allow you to get close, provide correct lighting, and have a nondistracting background? Will you and your audience to be comfortable in the setting? Careful planning should go into each stop selection. Obviously, the first question you should ask yourself is *Does the stop support the theme?*

During the planning stage, you inventoried and researched the resources. You developed the theme with management objectives in mind. You selected a route with stops that illustrate and support your theme and accommodate your audience. Preparing a map and outline of how all these elements fit within the framework of your walk organizes the planning process. Ham (1992) provides an excellent illustration of a thematic map during his discussion of self-guided media.

An individual location might provide several topic elements. For example, at a stop

> *A thematic map will help you see and evaluate the connection of each stop to the theme of the trail. It also helps you make better decisions about sequence and transitions.*
>
> —Sam H. Ham, 1992

you could discuss bird nesting behavior, the cover provided by the trees, or how habitat destruction is affecting bird reproduction. Because you have mapped these various stops, subthemes begin to determine which locations most appropriately fit into the sequence of the story. In short, a thematic map is a spatial picture of all potential stops along the selected route. This picture assists in the final selection and order of stops used to develop the program (figure 7.1).

As discussed in Chapter 5, there are specific thematic elements you must include at each stop. In outline form, you now develop your focusing sentence, a description

Sometimes talking at the final stop only detracts from the setting. In these instances, conclude the walk with a strong ending before arriving at the final attention-getting location. Courtesy of Carolyn Widner Ward

or explanation, a thematic connector, and the transition (Ham 1992). By outlining these elements, you begin to focus on how each stop is a "pearl" for the entire presentation.

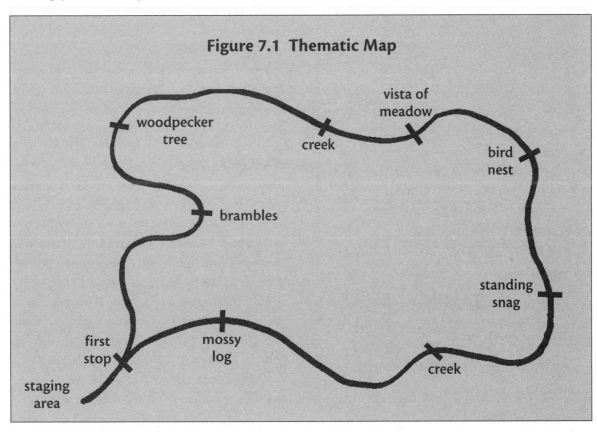

Figure 7.1 Thematic Map

woodpecker tree

creek

vista of meadow

bird nest

brambles

standing snag

first stop

mossy log

creek

staging area

Practice—Transitioning from Planning to Doing

Practice is a crucial step in the transition phase between planning your walk and actually doing it. Practicing on-site is preferable so you become more familiar with each stop. While on-site practice isn't always possible, your thematic map and outline will permit you to focus on the stop and rehearse the presentation. At first, rehearse your presentation by yourself to work out some of the initial logistics and personal internal conflicts. Then it's a good idea to do a dry run with several coworkers and friends. With their help, you'll discover issues and distractions you have overlooked. They can help you refine the narrative, anticipate and prepare for questions, and focus on your timing. This dry run will help physically illustrate the logistics of organizing each stop. It will become clear whether the stop will serve your purposes or present any problems. Practice your presentation at least five times, out loud, all the way through without stopping. Practice thoroughly to boost your confidence.

Practicing your narrative alone or with a small group is one thing, but how do you plan for the unexpected or the extra time a larger group takes to go between stops? With experience, you will gain insight on how to plan your time and how to build in contingency measures. During this practice phase, determine about how much time is needed for each stop. Then add time as the potential group size increases. In a normal one-hour walk, allow an additional five minutes for

> Sometime immediately prior to the walk, check the route to make sure that there are no surprises, such as room lights burned out, areas closed for rehabilitation, litter/graffiti, or a special activity taking place.

> Start on time, but keep in mind that, inevitably, there will be latecomers. Address those who are ready at the starting time while remaining flexible to welcome late arrivals. Use good judgment. You might stretch your opening welcoming remarks and delay just a moment. The selection of your first stop becomes critical when accommodating latecomers.

groups of 12 to 15 people and as much as 10 minutes when the group exceeds 15. Groups larger than 25 may require special attention and planning. Now that we understand the basic elements of planning a walk, we are ready to review the actual mechanics of conducting a walk.

Mechanics

A good talk has an introduction, body, and conclusion. A good walk incorporates these elements into a continuum of the staging area, first stop (introduction), stops along the walk (body of the presentation), and an ending (conclusion). Each stop should have a purpose, a clear subtheme that supports the overall theme. Now, let's turn our focus to the mechanics of *how* to better employ our talk skills in the walk environment.

Getting Started

As with all interpretive programs, it is important that you arrive early. Fifteen minutes early is probably sufficient for a walk. This means that 15 minutes prior to the start time, you are there, unhurried, and ready to go. Be visible, be approachable, and greet everyone as they arrive. Start your formal program at the scheduled time! We can't emphasize this enough! Don't penalize those who arrived on time by making them wait for latecomers.

This doesn't mean that you have to immediately begin to walk. Use the staging area to gather the group, welcome them on behalf of your agency or employer (a little name recognition), introduce yourself, continue to gain information about the audience via visual and spoken clues, and provide a cognitive map for the audience.

> Walks should be expressed in time requirements and mileage. Variations of pace, terrain, number of stops, complexity of the program, and an array of other issues make advertising the length of a walk only in distance a poor indication of commitment for the visitors. Always provide both.

First Stop

The first stop affords many benefits when used wisely. When you begin on time at the staging area, you establish, however subliminally, your credibility. Then you move the group, which helps reinforce that you are the leader. For the visitor, this stop signifies the start of the journey.

The first stop, within sight of the staging area, allows you to determine the group's actual size and composition. Additionally, this short walk provides clues as to how to adjust the tone or pace of the presentation. These are defined by how rapidly you move, how quickly you speak, how you want the

> *Tell them your theme. But, don't do it by saying, "my theme today is ... " Rather, "today I'd like to take you on a walk into the past. Let your imagination guide you as we step back 700 years to a time when household chores were the same as now, but their solutions were somewhat different. As we tour the ruins I think you'll begin to see many similarities to life today, and one of the goals of this walk is to help you develop a kinship with that not so distant or alien past."*
>
> —Paul Risk, 1982

Field Tips for Topics to Include in Your Cognitive Map

Subject—What you expect to see and experience along the route

Route—Time commitment, difficulty, ending location, accessibility

Availability of facilities—Restrooms, drinking water, etc.

Need for appropriate clothing and footwear—Raingear, hat, boots, etc.

Ground rules—You are the leader, receptive to questions, stay on walkway, need for reverence, no flash photography, etc.

Special health and safety issues—Pollen, heights, hazards, low ceilings, etc.

Recommend items to bring—Binoculars, camera, field guide, water, etc.

Equipment needs—Bicycle, personal flotation device, flashlight, etc.

group to gather around, and how knowledgeable and approachable you appear.

The introduction of the theme could be delivered at either the staging area or this first stop. If the staging area is a busy location with distractions and other traffic, then introduce the topic, but wait until this first stop to divulge the theme. The theme is where you plant the seeds of discovery and anticipation. As we discussed in Chapter 5, the theme is the big-picture message, the "So what?" (Ham 1992).

Leading

When you think of yourself as the host of the walk, you will want to arrive early to ensure that everything is ready for your guests. You greet everyone as they arrive, explain the activities that will take place, and invite them on the journey. What host wouldn't want to make sure that all of their guests are comfortable and know who is in charge of the event? Stay in front of the group and *be* the leader.

Field Tips for Managing Latecomers

Inform staff of your planned route of travel. They can direct latecomers where to catch up with the group. Integrating latecomers into the group depends on many factors: group size, how far along you are in the program, how many newcomers are joining the group, and whether you think formal or just visual recognition is most appropriate and less distracting, etc.

Staying in the lead allows you to control the pace and determine when to move briskly and when to saunter. You know the route, so if something unplanned happens, you will most likely be the first to notice and point it out to the whole group. Being in front also lets you better manage and guide the group to avoid potentially hazardous situations.

As the leader, you know the route and when to stop the audience so that everyone can see and hear. This is especially important with large groups. Watch over the whole audience and keep the group together. Remember, you are the host. It is your obligation to ensure that no one gets lost or

Be the leader. Stay visible and in front of the group. Your knowledge of the route and where you want and need to stop allows you to provide the best interpretive presentation possible. Courtesy of Carolyn Widner Ward

left behind and that everyone has an enjoyable and educational experience.

Timing

As we discussed earlier, there are several factors that contribute to program length. Group size, route layout, complexity of topic, and your presentation style all contribute to the length of a walk. Normally, walks range from 45 to 90 minutes. If you lead a longer walk, consider it an extended walk, potentially requiring special considerations. We will discuss this later in the chapter. Remember, the length of time commitment is generally more important to the audience than mileage, but providing them with both is appropriate.

Keep the group moving, with individual stops averaging around five to seven minutes, although some stops may last just a few moments. If the stop is particularly important, or if you want more time for the group to experience the setting, the stop may last 10-plus minutes; however, remember, individual attention spans wane quickly. Walks with larger audiences take more time. We will discuss special considerations for larger groups shortly. When you have a large audience, realize that you may have to curtail, combine, or even eliminate some stops to stay on schedule.

Group Considerations—Field Tips and Techniques

We've already discussed your role as the leader. Remember the concept of being a good host. What are some of the things you need to do to make the journey more inviting and enjoyable for all involved? From the very beginning, use keen observation and sensitivity to assess the physical and mental abilities of the individuals in the group. Describe the physical demands of the walk to the entire audience at the start of the program. Keep in mind that you want to accommodate as many visitors as possible. Certainly, you shouldn't embarrass or exclude anyone, but make it absolutely clear that the physical route may be difficult. Hopefully, the advertising and announcements about the program have forewarned individuals of impediments, but *don't* assume anything. Do your best to select routes that will accommodate as many individual needs as possible while supporting the theme of your walk. Use vocabulary that is appropriate for a diverse audience. As always, a friendly, conversational tone works best.

The safety of your audience is paramount. If there are potential hazards along the route, be sure to explain them fully to your audience at the beginning of the walk, before arriving at the potentially hazardous location, and then again as you approach the specific area of concern. For example, if you know that poison oak occurs alongside the path, it is appropriate to tell the group before encountering it. Then, when you arrive near the poison oak, specifically point it out. Always demonstrate safe practices.

Be sure to take note of the exact number of people attending your walk, not only to keep track of everyone, but also for recording attendance data. Wait for the entire group to arrive at each stop before you resume your commentary. Field questions and chitchat while you wait for the group to collect.

Establish a pace that is comfortable for your audience. This may sound obvious and easy to accomplish, but, in reality, it can be quite a challenge. You should stick to the schedule you announced at the beginning of the walk; however, there are many things that can disrupt the schedule, such as teachable moments. We'll discuss unexpected teachable moments later in this chapter.

Generally speaking, you should set the pace based on the slowest person in the group. Start the walk out briskly from the staging area. This will give you an opportunity to assess the group's abilities. If you are going too fast, you will create large gaps in the group. It will ultimately take longer to

Be a good host. Position yourself where everyone can see and hear you. Plan your stops carefully. Courtesy of Carolyn Widner Ward

reassemble the group at the next stop than to set a slower overall pace. Be careful not to set too slow a pace, because some participants may become bored and distracted, causing you to fall even further behind schedule. Keep track of the entire group's abilities and adjust accordingly. Check behind you periodically to make sure that everything is okay.

Be open to questions and discussion, especially when in transit between stops, but don't let one person monopolize your attention. Include others in the conversation, especially if it relates to the theme. If a particular point is relevant to the group, you should brief everyone at the next stop. Remember, clearly repeat the question asked by a visitor. Not only does this let everyone else know what question you are answering, it also clarifies that you understand the question and keeps the whole group involved in the dialogue.

Much of the time is spent moving between stops. Don't forget to use this time to help accomplish program goals. For example, asking visitors to observe, smell, or count phenomena along the way keeps them involved.

Being Heard

Let's discuss some techniques to help everyone hear. It's okay to chat while you walk, but don't try to make important points; the group is generally too spread out for everyone to hear what you have to say. When you stop, make every attempt to position yourself in the center of the group. Most importantly, face your audience. This directs your voice at them and, if any participants need to, allows them to lip-read or infer what you are saying.

Be constantly aware of the surroundings and any distractions that may make it difficult for you to be heard. Use a conversational tone. Be observant and take note of nonverbal feedback. Are audience members tilting their heads, moving closer, or asking others what you said? Be aware of the cues and don't hesitate to ask the group if they can hear. Adjust your volume accordingly. Speak clearly, avoid using jargon and scientific terms, and don't forget to breathe.

Sometimes you should be quiet. Don't constantly talk. Use pauses and silence to emphasize a point, set the stage, or enjoy the moment. Sunlight streaming through the tiny window of an adobe house may emphasize the hardships endured in that era. The sound of the crashing surf may imply the dangers of being a seaman, and the sunset may require only silence to punctuate its beauty.

> *We should not attempt to describe that which is only—or better—to be comprehended by feeling.*
>
> —Freeman Tilden, 1957

Large Groups

When group size increases above 25, the time needed to organize the group at each stop, the transit time between stops, and the time spent clarifying issues and answering questions also increases. Since you told your audience that the walk will last a certain

Whenever possible, limit the group size to a number that you can adequately address. Large groups require special planning and assistance. Enlist the help of others. Courtesy of Oregon Caves N.M., NPS

length of time, and the pace is generally dependent on the slowest person, your options for keeping on schedule are limited. Reducing the time spent at each stop, eliminating a stop (or more) entirely, or a combination of both are the most obvious remedies. In any case, you will have to make a value judgment on what information can be eliminated without weakening your theme. Don't be tempted to try to make up time by walking and talking at the same time. Some resource locations may not support large groups. For example, 35 people spread along a trail may make it impossible for you to be heard. In those instances, you should limit group size accordingly.

Extended Walk

An extended walk (over one-and-a-half hours) is generally viewed by the visitor as more of an "outing" with the interpreter than a typical program. It requires a little more stamina and a little less structure. This doesn't mean an extended walk is without a purpose, planned stops, or a theme. It does mean you must modify your presentation. Often visitors attend extended walks because they want to spend time with a resource person who knows the area well and can provide in-depth insight into the resources. Other times, they just want to take a walk with "the ranger" who will keep them safe and return them to the starting point in one piece.

It is incumbent on the interpreter to ensure that all participants are aware of the length and difficulty of an extended walk. *Prior* to setting off on the walk, you must directly address personal needs, such as the appropriate clothing and footwear, whether they need to bring food and water, what sanitary facilities to expect, etc.

Since you will most likely be walking longer stretches between formal stops, there will be more opportunities to talk informally with individuals. Be cautious not to let one person dominate your attention; others might feel ignored and become bored or feel left out. Do your best to enhance group dynamics and engage everyone in the experience. Move through the group between stops.

Teachable Moments

When that special something happens during the walk, don't ignore it—let the audience savor the experience. Be watchful for that teachable moment and be flexible. Don't be afraid to diverge from your outline. Build on the unexpected and weave it in to your story,

Field Tips for Working with Large Groups

Limiting the size of the group may be necessary in some instances (facility, night, fragile resources, quality of experience, etc.). Once again, preplanning is the key. For especially large groups (35-plus), have an extra staff person available to assist or take half the group.

When approaching a stop, walk past the targeted spot a little way to place half the group on either side of the topic of focus. Place yourself at the focal point of the stop (in the middle of the group) before beginning to speak. When you start walking again, ask the group to let you resume the lead.

Where possible, request that the group form a semicircle a few feet away from you at each stop. Encourage children and shorter people to stand in the front. Be sure everyone sees the focal point before moving on.

Use elevated or separated positions that increase your visibility. Keep your head lifted and project your voice slightly over the group.

Unexpected Teachable Moment—An Example

On today's walk, you are discussing how cacti have developed adaptations to survive extremely long periods without water. Just then, a snake is spotted nearby, eating a mouse. The snake is the unexpected event, but moving the talk to snake adaptations for survival without water provides linkage for your theme. On the other hand, if you are talking about the architectural style of a historic structure and you spot the snake eating a mouse, it might be too great a stretch to link the two. Just acknowledge and witness the event, interpret the moment, and return to your theme.

if at all possible. Challenge yourself to make that connection from the unexpected teachable moment to the theme, but don't get carried away. Stay on theme. Stay on schedule.

When that unexpected special observation occurs during the walk, embrace it and allow the audience to enjoy it. Incorporate the event into the theme where possible, but don't force the issue. Courtesy of Alan E. Wilkinson

Rules and Reasons—The "Educational Exception"

Set a good example, not only with the rules and regulations, but also with the nuances of stewardship. Don't pass by the gum wrapper or other litter without picking it up. Don't pick flowers, pull the starfish off the rock, or handle the historic document without proper care. People watch your actions and inactions; set a good example and a professional standard.

There are times when you really want to share some experience or examine something more closely with your audience. The vast majority of the time you can do so without infringing on rules and ethics. Instead of picking the bay laurel leaf off of the tree, find some on the ground for the group to smell. Pass around reproductions instead of actual artifacts for the group to examine. In addition, if you walk off trail or go beyond the barrier to better address the group, do so carefully. Explain to the audience that you are doing so as an "educational exception." If it's critical to your program that you must

"disrupt" an object, do so with consideration and respect. Opening the historic book with care when showing different pages or gently turning the salamander over and returning it to where you found it are just two examples of this principle. Don't forget to always tell your audience why you are doing it and that it is not the "norm" for behavior.

Build your kit bag of tools that we discussed in Chapter 6. Use the mirror you carry in your kit bag to show the audience the underside of a mushroom; individuals can view the gills without disturbing the plant. Handheld items and props really help illustrate your point in an ethical manner. Visual aids brought into the field, such as photos, books, or graphics, can greatly increase the visitors' experience and understanding. Don't fail to use them.

Ending

Remember what we said about beginning on time at the staging area? Well, the same is true for ending the program—*on time!* It's *okay* to leave them wanting more.

Have a clear and definite ending to your walk. The conclusion incorporates all the elements we discussed in Chapter 5. Have a strong concluding statement that reinforces the theme, summarizes the walk experiences, and brings the audience full circle with a clear ending. Thank the group for joining you. If you have announcements, need to tell the group about returning to the staging area, or wish to let the group know you will be available at the end of the walk, do so *before* beginning the conclusion. Don't detract from your strong ending with minor, ancillary issues.

If you end the walk at a location other than the staging area, make sure you clearly inform the audience how best to return. Give them the option to stay and enjoy the setting or to join you as you return to the staging area. Notify the whole group of the precise time you will return, should they wish to join you. If you end the presentation at the staging area, you have just made a loop. In both cases, it is a good idea to conclude your program *before* the audience sees the destination. Otherwise, you may lose the attention of the group before you complete your conclusion.

In the Next Chapter ...

Next, we will discuss how to plan and execute the most traditional and well-attended programs offered in parks: campfire and other evening programs. All of the principles we have learned regarding how to present a good talk and walk apply to planning and conducting successful programs in the dark. So … where are the marshmallows?

Review

1. Walks help immerse the visitors and the interpreter in the resource.

2. Walks provide an opportunity for a multisensory experience and a more comprehensive appreciation of that resource.

3. A walk encompasses all the elements of a talk, plus the logistics and mechanics of moving visitors through the resource.

4. The first stop should be within sight of the staging area.

5. Generally, a walk should include no more than ten stops, including staging area (cognitive map), first stop (theme), and the ending (conclusion). Have more stops in the first half of the walk.

6. Individual stops average around five to seven minutes, although some stops may last just a few moments. Longer stops must have critical information or overwhelming interest. Remember, individual attention spans wane quickly.

7. Set the pace of your walk based on the slowest person in the group.

8. Whenever possible, incorporate the unexpected teachable moment into the theme.

9. Before the last stop and prior to your conclusion, make any necessary minor, secondary announcements. Don't dilute your strong ending with ancillary issues.

Questions and Exercises

1. List four considerations for selecting the route of an interpretive walk.

2. What is a teachable moment? What are the pitfalls?

3. Which of the following determine the number of stops for a walk? (Circle all that apply.)

    Time allotted for the walk

    Size of group

    The route

    Topic and theme

4. When planning your stops, what factors should you consider? List at least five elements.

5. What techniques should you employ at each stop to ensure that every participant receives your message?

6. If the walk is taking longer than expected, which of the following are acceptable methods of shortening the planned walk? (Circle all that apply.) Briefly explain your answers.

    Walk and talk at the same time

    Shorten the stops

    Skip stop(s) entirely

    Walk faster

References

Books

Grinder, Alison and E. Sue McCoy. 1985. *The Good Guide: A Sourcebook for Interpreters, Docents, and Tour Guides*. Scottsdale, Ariz.: Ironwood Press.

Ham, Sam H. 1992. *Environmental Interpretation: A Practical Guide for People with Big Ideas and Small Budgets*. Golden, Colo.: Fulcrum Publishing.

Helmich, Mary. 1997. *Workbook for Planning Interpretive Projects in California State Parks*. Sacramento: California Department of Parks and Recreation.

Knudson, Douglas, Ted T. Cable, and Larry Beck. 1995. *Interpretation of Cultural and Natural Resources*. State College, Pa.: Venture Publishing.

Lux, Linda. 1991. *Change, Diversity, and Leadership: Windows on California's Past and Its Future through the Interpretation of Cultural Resources*. San Francisco, Calif.: USDA Forest Service.

Regnier, Kathleen, Michael Gross, and Ron Zimmerman. 1994. *The Interpreter's Guidebook: Techniques for Programs and Presentations, Third Edition*. Stevens Point, Wisc.: UW-SP Foundation Press.

Risk, Paul H. 1982. "The Interpretive Talk." In Grant Sharpe, ed., *Interpreting the Environment, Second Edition*. New York: John Wiley and Sons, Inc.

Sharpe, Grant. 1982. *Interpreting the Environment, Second Edition*. New York: John Wiley and Sons, Inc.

Tilden, Freeman. 1957. *Interpreting Our Heritage*. Chapel Hill: University of North Carolina Press.

Trapp, Suzanne, Michael Gross, and Ron Zimmerman. 1994. *Signs, Trails, and Wayside Exhibits: Connecting People and Places, Second Edition*. Stevens Point, Wisc.: UW-SP Foundation Press.

Online

Britt, Robert Roy. 2003. *Our Tiny Universe: What's Really Visible at Night*. Available online at www.space.com/scienceastronomy/visible_from_earth_031229.html.

Chapter 8

Working in the Dark: Campfires and More!

Whether inside or out, there are ample opportunities to interpret the secrets hidden in the dark.
Courtesy of Oregon Caves N.M., NPS

When the light grows dim,
there are many opportunities
to sparkle.

Program Types

There are several types of programs that are presented in a darkened environment. Generally, we think of programs presented in the dark as evening programs. We'll begin with a discussion of night hikes and stargazing, include a segment emphasizing the traditional campfire program, and end with audiovisual presentations that can take place in any darkened environment. Remember, just as with all interpretation, the only limit to what you can do is your imagination and creativity.

> *To go in the dark with a light is to know the light. To know the dark, go dark, and know that the dark, too, blooms and sings, and is traveled by dark feet and dark wings.*
>
> —Wendell Berry, 1934–present

Nocturnal = nighttime
Diurnal = daytime
Crepuscule = dusk and dawn, twilight

Night Hike

A night hike includes all of the elements we learned about in Chapter 7, with several other important considerations. Many visitors are uncomfortable or afraid of the dark. They are accustomed to turning on the light or being in well-lighted places at night. We'll discuss special strategies to help alleviate their nervousness and allow them an opportunity to use all their senses.

Night Sky

Many visitors come from metropolitan areas where the ambient light is so bright, they rarely have an opportunity to appreciate the stars. Others may have clear views of the evening sky but little understanding of what they are seeing. We'll discuss night-sky interpretation techniques that help make connections for visitors with these distant sights.

Campfire

The mystique of the campfire is universal and probably originated from humans' deepest needs for light, heat, and social interaction. The traditions, camaraderie, and enjoyment the public derives have long made campfire programs a mainstay of interpretive programming. Combine entertainment, information, and education with a high degree of audience interaction, and you'll have a successful program.

Audiovisual

Audiovisual (A/V) programs include slides, computer-generated presentations, film, video, DVD, and audio messages. A/V programs are well suited for telling sequential

Night is a dead monotonous period under a roof; but in the open world it passes lightly, with its stars and dews and perfumes, and the hours are marked by changes in the face of Nature.

—Robert Louis Stevenson, 1850–1894

stories and providing overviews of site resources. A/V media can transport visitors through time and space to experience significant historic events or dramatic natural processes, and they can interpret fragile or inaccessible resources (Helmich 1997, 77). Because A/V programs engage multiple senses, they can be very effective at influencing the audience and offering today's high-tech audience a format that is both engaging and exciting.

Mechanics

The beauty and vastness of the night sky and the secrets of the darkness have created wonder since the beginning of time. The challenge for the interpreter is to unravel the mysteries of the dark and help the audience make connections to their earthly environment.

Exploring in a darkened environment offers a dramatic change from the usual programming and is an exciting activity for participants. Courtesy of Carolyn Widner Ward

Exploration of the nocturnal world can provide insight and appreciation of the natural and cultural resources; however, it can be a challenging task if both the interpreter and the audience are uncomfortable. Working in the dark or reduced lighting requires all the preparation and planning discussed in Chapter 6 and 7, plus addressing some special concerns.

Alleviating Fears

Spending time outside at night or in a darkened environment can make many people uncomfortable or even afraid. Humans are not physically adapted to dark environments. We rely tremendously on vision to the exclusion of other senses. Plan to begin your program by carefully explaining what's going to happen, making sure everyone has a comprehensive cognitive understanding of the activities planned. Speak in reassuring tones.

Darkness Exposes New Perspectives

Instill confidence that this will be a safe experience.

Challenge visitors to use other senses as effectively as they do their sight.

Provide information about "night vision" and how the eyes can adjust to the light when given an opportunity. Objects that you stare at tend to disappear in the dark; coach the group to keep their eyes moving. Tell them to look for shapes, shadows, contrast, and movement.

Provide/use equipment adjuncts to highlight features and to "link" everyone together (laser pointer, rope/string, etc.). Covering a flashlight's beam with red cellophane film provides plenty of light but does not destroy night vision.

Your cognitive map at the beginning of the program must secure the audience's confidence that this will be a safe and fun experience. Speak in reassuring tones, with a smile in your voice. Courtesy of Oregon Caves N.M., NPS

If you're venturing beyond the lighted, safe environment visitors are accustomed to, you've got to let them know you've thoroughly explored the area and it's safe. Assure them that you won't lead them into harmful or dangerous situations. If there are potential hazards that may be encountered (poison oak, low ceilings, etc.), explain this to the group before starting and assure them that you'll notify them when arriving at that location. Set behavior guidelines, such as

Starting an evening program at dusk provides better lighting for the audience to assemble and allow their eyes to naturally adjust. Courtesy of Alan E. Wilkinson

requesting that everyone avoid making loud, abrasive noises and sudden movements. Stress the importance of staying together and helping each other along the journey. Instruct that if anyone gets separated from the group, they should stay put. Assure them you will return directly along the route and find them.

Time Considerations—Dark, Full Moon, or Dusk

If the program is outside, consider starting at dusk, which affords better lighting conditions to assemble the group and provide a cognitive map of the program. This also lets everyone's eyes adjust more gradually to the changing light. Be aware of the moon phases. A full moon will make walking easier, but a new moon makes stargazing spectacular. Use the lunar cycles to your advantage. Starting too late may restrict participation of children who generally go to bed at an early hour. Consider an earlier night walk for families with kids.

Presentations

Exploring in the Dark— Night Hike

Exploring in a darkened environment offers a dramatic change from the usual programming and an exciting activity for participants. Consider how perceptions of the surroundings change with the alteration of ambient lighting. The normal daytime walk through the mission may take on an entirely different character when the rooms are illuminated by candlelight. The nature trail may feel longer and narrower when it is dark.

Placing a red lens (cellophane) on a flashlight is a useful tool that allows humans to see more clearly in the dark without destroying night vision or scaring nocturnal animals away.

Appropriate themes should be developed, different equipment and props may be necessary, and special issues need to be addressed. The biggest issue is that the audience will not be able to see everything as easily with the reduced lighting. There are certainly exceptions to this statement. The historic home with electric lighting may provide just as many visual cues as during the daytime, but, generally speaking, it is more difficult to see at night. This reduction in sight is a benefit to the night walk. Reducing the ability to see in the ordinary way heightens the use of other senses and provides a whole new way to experience the resource. Helping to sharpen this awareness of other senses is a very important element of a night hike. Plan activities that assist visitors to awaken or gain confidence in their sense of touch, smell, hearing, and even taste. Consider selecting a route with good interpretive potential that incorporates various sensory experiences, such as babbling water, fragrant flowers, and rough tree bark. Refer to Chapter 6 for other tips to incorporate props to heighten sensory awareness.

To be effective, night walks must be designed differently from daytime walks.

Field Tips for Night Hike Safety

Select a trail that is wide and level, with no barriers.

Recheck the route the day of the hike for safety and interpretive issues.

Count participants before and after the hike.

Designate someone to be the last of the group.

Advise everyone on the use/nonuse of flashlights during the walk.

Walk slowly and gather the group together at each stop.

Encourage the buddy system, where everyone helps and keeps track of each other.

Because you generally don't have the visual cues to read and keep track of your audience, you must plan accordingly. Consider starting your hike at dusk. This affords enough light for people to find the staging or meeting location. Choose a very safe route; avoid uneven terrain, protruding objects, and areas with hazards. Select a route away from distracting light and noises. Where possible, plan stops in larger, open areas. Trail intersections are good places to plan stops, as they allow you to gather the group and ensure everyone follows you on the correct route. Plan to count and keep the group together more than you normally would. Since safety is always paramount, you may need to restrict group size.

Before beginning the walk, ask the group to help keep track of each other; have each person watch out for a buddy. Explain that it takes time for human eyes to adjust to darkness. Consider providing each person carrying a flashlight with a red covering to avoid those "blinding accidents" (red light allows our eyes to see quite well in the dark, but doesn't scare animals). Request that white lights not be used. Appoint a person to be

Stars, Milky Way, Night Sky ...

The nighttime sky has been a constant in the human experience. It has inspired countless myth, religion, art, literature, and science from every culture around the globe. It is the ultimate common ground for humanity that has been tragically taken for granted. Some who recreate on public lands specifically seek out the night sky with telescopes or simply a warm blanket and their own eyes; but perhaps for everyone the night sky is an integral component of a natural experience.

—Chad Moore, 2003

Light and Color Activities

The human eye, while not as good as most nocturnal animals', is still able to adjust amazingly well to changes in light level. Here are a couple of fun activities to demonstrate how our vision works in light and dark conditions.

Night Vision

This demonstration will help to illustrate how well our eyes adapt to the dark. After you've been in a dark environment for a while, have each person cover one eye (it doesn't matter which one). Explain that you are going to light a match/candle and you want them to stare at the flame for 10 to 15 seconds. After you blow out the flame, have them open and close each eye, switching from eye to eye. There will be a remarkable difference in what they can see, or not see, depending on which eye they are using.

Explanation: Our eyes produce a chemical, rhodopsin, in low-light situations that improves night vision. When eyes are exposed to light, all the rhodopsin is instantly destroyed; however, allowing our eyes to adjust to the dark and produce rhodopsin for even five minutes can improve night vision by as much as 1,000 times!

Colors

When in a darkened environment, give each person a crayon and a piece of paper. Have them write the color they think the crayon is on the piece of paper. At the end of program, when back in a lighted environment, have them examine the color on the paper. How many were correct? Generally, less than 30 percent will be correct. (Note: Use basic colors, such as blue, red, green, brown, etc., and remove the wrappers from the crayons.)

Explanation: Humans have two types of cells in our eyes, called rods and cones. Cones allow for seeing color, rods are light sensitive. We have more cone (color) cells than rods. Our color vision is great when there is plenty of light but poor in the dark. These rods and cones are also why red light does not scare away nocturnal animals.

the last person in the group. This person's job is to make sure no one is left behind or gets lost.

When beginning the hike, allow everyone's eyes time to adjust. Don't walk directly from the lighted room or amphitheater into the darkened environment and expect everyone to "see" where you are going. Walk slowly. You may want to provide your group with some tips for walking in the out-of-doors. Suggestions such as, *Watch the sky, trails have slot openings in the treetops that can help you follow the trail*, or *Feel the trail beneath your feet. Grass, gravel, dirt, leaves all have their own feel*, can help visitors more easily find their way.

Night-Sky Interpretation—Stargazing

Perhaps what first comes to mind when thinking about night-sky interpretation is a beautiful, dark, warm summer evening with millions and millions of stars, a powerful telescope for viewing the planets, and shooting stars everywhere. Although this may be the case, more often, we don't have the expensive telescope or the expertise to

On a clear dark night away from city lights, the star-spangled heavens can create an overwhelming sense of infinity. Seemingly countless points of light, so far away, urge one to contemplate the insignificance of a lone planet amid the incomprehensible breadth of the universe.

—Robert Roy Britt, 2003

Sky Interpretation is the art and process of coupling direct observation with skilled communication for the purpose of informing people about the sky, its objects, and phenomena, with special emphasis on relationships of these to Earth and its occupants.

—Von Del Chamberlain, 1982

adequately use it, nor will the meteorites appear or the clouds stay away. As a result, flexibility, adaptability, and a variety of program presentations may be necessary. Depending on your topic, it might be easier to discuss black holes or pulsars indoors with illustrations, while the emotional impact of the Milky Way Galaxy or stories of navigation and orientation by the North or South Star would be better outside. Whichever venue you select, or a combination of each, the talk and walk presentation strategies, techniques, and mechanics discussed in previous chapters apply.

If you're outside, the best views of the sky are afforded from large, open areas, preferably with as little artificial light as possible. One technique is to have the audience lie down on their backs, let them really enjoy the sky, then slowly tell the story. In the Northern Hemisphere, perhaps begin by orienting them to the Big Dipper. With this landmark, move them to Polaris, the Pole Star, better know as the North Star. Whether your program is about astronomy, legends, navigation, or something else, allowing the audience to relax, gain their night vision, and become accustomed to your

No sight that the human eyes can look upon is more provocative of awe than is the night sky scattered with stars.

—Llewelyn Powys, 1884–1939

voice and style of presentation will pay dividends with receptiveness.

Trying to explain direction and distance is difficult. Orienting your audience to one location, such as the North Star, is useful. Then you can move their focus right, left, up, and down from that location. Using their hand as the reference, you can explain degrees of distance. With their hand at arm's length, their thumb equals one-half degree, three knuckles equals five degrees, and their fist equals 10 degrees. Vast distances in space are measured in light-years. Light travels at 186,000 miles per second. That's seven times around the Earth in one second! Light from the Sun (93 million miles) takes eight minutes to reach us, and light from the next brightest star (Sirius) takes eight years.

Understanding scale or size is another mystery. On a clear night, with good eyesight, you will see approximately 3,000 stars. The Milky Way Galaxy has approximately 100 billion stars! Using the Earth for comparison, you could explain that Mars is one-half the size of the Earth, and Jupiter is 11 times larger. Or, if the Sun were a soccer

The science and myths of the moon and stars provide a wealth of topics to interpret. Courtesy of Alan E. Wilkinson

Whether It's a Night Hike or a Night Sky, the Topics are Endless

➤ Moon and tides
➤ Sun and seasons
➤ Nocturnal animals
➤ Distances—How far? How big?
➤ Astronomy and astrology
➤ Cultures beliefs
➤ Comets and meteorites

From old-fashioned marshmallow roasting to a high-tech audiovisual presentation, campfire programs are universally desired by the public. Courtesy of Jim Absher

ball, Jupiter would be about the size of a baseball, and Earth less than a pea.

Equipment to enhance viewing the sky can also be helpful. If you are employing optical devices, make sure everyone has an opportunity to use them. Looking at the Moon with the naked eye, you can see light and dark "seas" (plains) and craters. With standard binoculars, mountain ranges become visible. With a telescope, details and variations in the color of the surface can be seen. However, as we'll discuss in Chapter 12, the more equipment and technology used, the more time and expertise is needed to use that equipment effectively and properly.

Campfires recall our deepest roots as social beings. They inspire the same feelings of warmth, security, and conviviality that our primitive forebears shared around the fire, safe from the dark, cold, lonely, and dangerous world outside its circle of light. Similarly, campfire centers evoke the archetypical park experience. We can relax and enjoy each other's company in the evening at a campfire center. A colleague calls them the park "family room."

—Joann Weiler, 1990

Make sure the media clarifies, reinforces, and enhances the theme.

Traditional Campfire

The mystique of the campfire is universal. Most visitors who come to parks, recreation areas, and other outdoor sites are on vacation and seeking a slower pace. Many have fond memories of campfire experiences and now wish to share similar occasions with family and friends. They come to the campfire program for entertainment as well as to learn more about the resource. Take advantage of this prime opportunity to reward them with a well-thought-out program that is fun, educational, and relevant.

A campfire program has all the elements in developing a talk as we discussed in Chapter 6, with an added amount of entertainment, site-specific embellishments, and tradition. In this next section, we'll cover the basics of preparing and conducting a good campfire program. The most important things to remember when planning a campfire are to have a strong, site-relevant theme that your media-of-choice supports, know your audience, and practice, practice, practice.

Getting Started

No one enjoys bad surprises; preparation and pretesting ensure success. Become thoroughly familiar with the equipment, location and

Develop an Appropriate Preprogram Checklist for Your Presentation. Here Are Several Ideas to Get You Started:

Agenda—Written list of all the items you want to cover. This is your personal cheat sheet of program reminders.

Operational equipment—Is backup available (spare bulb/projector)? Check connections and switches, microphone, facility lighting.

Materials—Props, slides/movie, audiotape, hand-held objects, samples

Handouts—Song sheets, skit text, prizes/giveaways

Agency awards ready—Pins and signed certificates

Schedule—Upcoming activities and other announcements

Check your appearance—Take care of personal comforts

Supplies—Matches, kindling, and dry firewood, water to put out the fire

Safety items—Small first-aid kit, flashlight, radio

function of switches, and the layout of the campfire facility. Before the program, recheck the facility, confirm the equipment is in place, and make sure that all the supplies needed are there. Is the facility clean, safe, and free of unwanted distractions, such as litter, graffiti, and/or vandalism? If not, give yourself plenty of time to make the necessary corrections.

Busy days seem to get busier just before your program. There are many things you can do to assure success. Nothing can rattle

Appropriate Preprogram Music May Be Beneficial in a Number of Ways:

➤ Music announces that something is happening and provides directional clues.

➤ Music encourages people to chat, since it cuts the silence. This is especially true for the early arrivers.

➤ Music provides foreshadowing for the main program. Use cultural, historic, and/or natural sounds.

➤ Music establishes a mood. Instrumental music is generally preferable. Don't overdo the volume.

your confidence more than being late. Arrive at least 30 minutes before the program is scheduled to begin. Spend this time rechecking that the equipment and facility are ready. Prepare your materials, arrange your props, and construct the fire. If you are hosting a guest speaker, giving a demonstration, or employing any one of several other creative techniques, make sure all is ready. This early arrival time will build your confidence because you know that everything is ready to go as planned.

This is also a good time to start establishing a rapport. Allow yourself enough time to mingle and greet people. Chatting with visitors as they arrive will calm your nerves and make your audience feel welcome. Take this opportunity to evaluate the audience and tailor the program to get the message across more effectively.

Additionally, preprogram arrival of the audience is a good time to identify possible troublemakers and program distractions. Defuse any problems early by simply assigning jobs, such as counting the audience or distributing handouts.

BEGINNING

Start on time; don't penalize those who arrive on time. Remember, everyone is on vacation,

Field Tips for Getting the Word Out—Attention Getters

Have those who arrived on-time yell *Campfire!*

Divide the on-time audience into two groups (right side against left, or adults against kids) and challenge them to outyell each other. Something such as *You're late!* might hurry the latecomers along.

Making group noise is a great energy releaser, establishes a playful mood, and builds a sense of camaraderie.

so don't be too rigid about scheduling. If there is something very important at the beginning of the program, then it bears repeating. Your program should last for 45 minutes to an hour, so don't delay your introduction too long. Stay on track, but be a little flexible, especially at the beginning.

Welcome your guests, introduce yourself, other staff who might be assisting, and your agency. People like to know a little about you personally, so don't be afraid to tell them about yourself. The positive image of the "ranger" and "interpreter" gives you an edge—use it!

Just as they want to know you, it is imperative for you to get to know your audience. One effective technique is to "quiz the audience." Develop questions and mentally note trends, deficiencies, and other

My fire squirmed and struggled as if ill at ease ... the flames, now rushing up in long lances, now flattened and twisted on the rocky ground, roared as if trying to tell the storm stories of the trees they belonged to, as the light given out was telling the story of the sunshine they had gathered in centuries of summers.

—John Muir, 1838–1914

anecdotal data that might be helpful. Some suggested questions:

- First-time visitors to the area? The campfire? Or your program?
- How long have people been coming to this area? For example, who has visited the most times? Years? From the farthest away?
- How many are staying in hotels? Camping in tents? In RVs?
- How did they learn about tonight's program?
- What does the audience know about tonight's topic?

Reward "winners" of quizzing the audience with a map, postcard, or some little relevant prize that will remind them of their visit. The small prize may enhance participation, establish a positive rapport, and it's fun!

➤ Always repeat the question, so everyone can hear what was asked.

➤ By restating the question, you gain a moment to decide what you want to say and to confirm that you are answering the question asked.

➤ Be sure to answer the question to everyone, not just the person who asked it.

OPENING

Remember to provide a clear cognitive map. Give your audience a brief idea of what to expect, such as the length of program and topic. Also use this time to make announcements of upcoming activities scheduled in and around the site. Present awards, if appropriate. Don't forget to promote agency programs and other interpretive activities.

While quizzing the audience, you have a chance to ask the audience questions; immediately after is a good time for them to get some answers from you. Try to direct their questions so they relate to your program's theme and/or the site resources. See "stump the interpreter" later in this chapter (page 141).

FIRE LIGHTING

Lighting the campfire can be accomplished in a number of ways. It can be a ceremony or a task. You may prefer to have the fire already going when the audience arrives, or to light it at the very beginning of the program. Some interpreters use dramatic ways of lighting the fire, such as flint and steel, using only one match, "magic," and so on, while other interpreters prefer to select someone from the audience to have the honor. Be careful, and always be aware of safety issues around the fire; use the opportunity to model the appropriate desired behavior.

Warm-Up—Traditional Elements of a Campfire

The warm-up is steeped in the traditions of activities normally associated with the old-fashioned campfire program. Its intent is to be fun, entertaining, and participation-based. The underlying purpose of the warm-up is to establish a rapport with the audience, put them in a receptive mood, and help move the program on to the topic of the evening. Design your warm-up activities so that they contribute to the overall success of the program objectives.

There is a whole menu of activities to offer the audience during the warm-up.

Warm-Up Activities

➢ Songs
➢ Skits
➢ Games and quizzes
➢ Storytelling
➢ "Stump the interpreter"

Field Tips for Lighting the Fire

Use good tinder. Use good kindling, paper, and dry wood.

Know what you're burning. Don't use chemically treated wood. Know how easily or quickly the wood burns and/or if it smokes excessively.

Remember matches and/or a lighter. If you forget, ask if someone in the audience has one.

Start the fire at the right time. The timing of when to light the fire depends on a number of factors. If showing slides, light the fire early to give it time to die down. If doing a demonstration, storytelling, puppets, or other activities, use the fire to illuminate and enhance the setting.

Select those activities that best suit your style and personality and that are compatible with the main program. Not every interpreter is comfortable singing songs, telling stories, or quizzing the audience, but, surely, some of the activities will work for you. Whatever you do, keep the warm-up lighthearted and enthusiastic.

Throughout the warm-up activities, don't be shy about walking into the audience and directly communicating with individuals. Smile, relax, and have fun.

SONGS

Singing songs at a campfire program is a tradition. It's fun for the group and almost everyone likes to do it. To conduct singing successfully, you need lots of self-confidence, an enthusiastic manner, and strong organization. Leadership is much more important than the quality of your singing voice. If you are uncomfortable with singing, it will show, so invite a volunteer or another employee who can carry a tune and who likes to sing to lead the group. Keep the songs simple and easy for the audience to learn.

Field Tips for Sing-Alongs

Use familiar songs. Song sheets and/or slides are very useful, but make sure lighting is adequate to read them.

Briefly go over the words and tune.

Enlist someone to help you.

Start the song so that everyone starts together.

Use gestures to keep time and rhythm—don't let the song drag.

Maintain contact with all the audience.

Use a variety of songs (rounds, humorous, slow, fast). Usually, songs with a faster tempo are better at the beginning, while slower songs are better at the end.

Incorporate audience actions with the words—clap hands, stand up on a phrase or word, sway like a tree, etc.

SKITS

If you are really uncomfortable with singing, then skits may provide the traditional light-heartedness to the warm-up. Audience participation is the key to success for skits. They are intended to be fun, develop cama-raderie, and, at their very finest, to lead into the theme of the main program. Most people enjoy being involved in these stories and skits, especially children, and it's fun to see parents' responses as they watch their children perform. Don't limit it to just children, and don't force anyone to participate.

Generally, numerous individuals have parts to play, but, if possible, the skit should include the rest of the audience as a group. If you have more volunteers than parts, have several people play a part together; the more people who are actively involved, the better. It's important to allow everyone, including the audience, to practice their parts. The narration or script should be easy to read, and the story should be straightforward to follow. The sayings, words, sounds, and/or actions each player makes should be easy to learn, perform, and remember.

There are numerous tried-and-true scripts to choose from, but they run the risk of being overused and tiresome. Strive to write your own skit that incorporates features of the site and ties to the theme of the main program. Personalizing your skit makes it easier to narrate, shows the audience your interest in the subject, strengthens the message, and adds originality and spontane-ity to the program.

GAMES AND QUIZZES

It is often more effective to present informa-tion in the form of a game, riddle, or quiz than to simply tell the audience. Design them so they lead up to, develop, and support the program's theme.

Friendly competition can be fun, lively, participatory, and educational. It adds a measure of excitement to the program. Divide the audience in half or thirds, and have them compete with each other. The interpreter poses questions, most of which should be related to the theme of the pro-gram, and then judges which group has the correct answer. The reward for the winners might be a round of applause by the losers, but everyone will be a winner because you have actively engaged the audience and have provided additional theme information. Games and quizzes can also help evaluate program effectiveness.

Caution!

Don't overspend your allotted time on the warm-up, generally no more than 10 to 15 minutes. The audience may be having a good time, which is important, but allow yourself sufficient time for the main part of the program.

About those Flashlights

Before the main program begins, invite everyone to shine their light on the screen, on your face, the stars, and so on. Let them get it out of their system. Then ask them to turn their flashlights off until the program is over.

"STUMP THE INTERPRETER"

A warm-up technique that provides great interaction between the interpreter and audience, benefiting both, is "stump the interpreter." This activity offers an opportunity for the audience to ask that question they are just itching to know. It's an opportunity for the interpreter to establish a rapport, be human, and impart information.

The main tenet for all interactions is honesty; if you don't know the answer to a question, admit you don't. As the great American humorist, writer, and storyteller Mark Twain (1835–1910) said, "I was gratified to be able to answer promptly. I said, 'I don't know.'" Perhaps someone in the audience will have the answer. If not, and the question is answerable, have a plan to get the answer to the questioner at a later time. Have interested audience members check at the visitor center, entrance station, or campground host site for the answer the next day. But don't forget to warn the staff to expect inquiries. If you can't find an answer, offer to continue looking and suggest some places visitors themselves might research. Be prepared to make a real effort and to follow through. Another great technique is to have postcards to hand out to visitors who had questions you could not answer. Have them write their name, address, and question on the postcard. Mail it to them when you find the answer. This is wonderful public relations for you and the agency.

Transition

Use final warm-up activities to focus the audience on the program's theme. Plan the warm-up with care. Everyone wants to enjoy the evening activities, and generally you can take this time to develop rapport and focus the audience. It is important to make a smooth transition from the playful warm-up to the more educational segment of the program.

You shouldn't expect the audience to transition from an excited, interactive warm-up to a totally receptive "listen to my story" mind-set without some time and assistance. Choose your transitional activities wisely. Calm the activities at the end of the warm-up and begin the introduction into the program. If singing at the end of the warm-up, conclude with a slower song. A story or "stump the interpreter" question that directly relates to your evening's topic may be an ideal opportunity to transition to the program. Be creative; seize the opportunity.

After the warm-up, the educational and interpretive portion of the campfire program may incorporate a host of options, such as a guest speaker, a demonstration, or audiovisual props. Whichever options you incorporate, after the program, there are several ending chores that should be undertaken before your evening is done.

Closure

The ending of your program helps reinforce the overall message. If appropriate, end the program with a thought-provoking "needle" that will stay with the audience. Close on time. Don't drag the program out. People have other things to do and so do you. Invite the audience to come up and talk with you or the guest speaker, if appropriate. Be a gracious host. After the program is a time to answer questions, clarify issues, and gain valuable feedback on your program. As nice as compliments are, you may discover the questions they ask are ones you didn't adequately

A Suggested Campfire Program Time Allotment

Set-up, preparation, pretesting, and casual conversation—15 to 30 minutes

Opening, introduction, welcome, and announcements—10 minutes

Warm-up activities—10 to 15 minutes

Transition—5 minutes

Program—15 to 20 minutes

Closure—5 minutes

After the program informal social interaction—10 to 15 minutes

Follow-up, pack-up, storage, resupply—10 to 15 minutes

answer in your presentation and are actually most helpful in improving your program. Don't be in a hurry to leave; plan to stay.

Consider offering informal after-campfire activities, such as visiting with the interpreter while roasting marshmallows, popping popcorn, stargazing, or taking a stroll in the dark. You can also use this time to conduct appropriate, planned evaluation measures. Occasionally, there are people who want to visit with others from the audience. Be sure you make them feel welcome; encourage them to linger by the fire for a while. If they wish to remain after you have stored the equipment, extinguished the fire, closed up, and are ready to leave, be sure to warn them you are turning out the lights in a moment.

Follow-Up

Your program is completed, everything went well, you're tired, and want to get on to all the other stuff you have yet to do, but now is not the time to just lock up and leave. Make sure you get everything ready for those following you. Attention to detail makes all the difference for successful interpretive programs.

Audiovisual Presentations

Today, with the high-technology influences of television and computers, audiences are increasingly visually oriented. Enhanced by sight and sound, A/V programs help the audience better experience natural, cultural, remote, or fragile resources. Incorporating projected images into our talk helps capture and hold the audience's attention, allowing you to more effectively deliver your message.

Steps in Creating a Slide or Computer-Generated Projected Program

Whether you use one projector, a multi-projector lapse dissolve, or a computer-projected software presentation, the mechanics for developing and presenting audiovisual program are much the same. When using images to supplement the talk, remember, they are simply visual aids that support the program. The images should illustrate the talk, rather than the talk being a series of verbal captions for the pictures.

Think of visual images as props. Develop your talk then select the images to illustrate the story and reinforce the theme. When developing your story, visualize how to illustrated it. Before you select images,

Last, But Not Least

➤ Have you stored the equipment properly?

➤ Does any equipment or the facility need attention?

➤ Are all materials and supplies replenished?

➤ Do any issues need discussing before the next program?

➤ Do you have unanswered questions to address?

➤ Did you record attendance and other statistical data?

Field Tips for Choosing Images

Images should:

Illustrate the point being discussed

Have good color

Be properly exposed

Be in focus and clean

Have variety and sequencing for effect

In larger venues, an audiovisual-augmented presentation may be the most appropriate method to deliver your interpretive messages. Courtesy of Alan E. Wilkinson.

develop a storyboard. "A storyboard is just a visual plan in which you indicate the kinds of slides that would be best to show in each part of the program, and where they should change. As you do this, you'll undoubtedly make small changes in the script to accommodate or capitalize on the visuals you select" (Ham 1992, 358).

The format for the storyboard is a matter of personal preference. One method is to put the script on note cards, and, next to the script, draw or annotate the visual that would best illustrate the point being made. Later, the note cards can be used to practice your talk. Using note cards may be preferable to developing the program on a sheet of paper, as note cards can be moved to accommodate more or less text and illustrations as you refine the program.

Find the best possible illustrations. When selecting, use only good-quality images. Use variety, including alternating between close-up and vista and sequencing from far away to closer, or vice versa. Don't leave images on the screen longer than 15 seconds. Images that require more viewing time to understand are probably too complicated; find a better image to make your point. Maps and graphs that need explaining may be the exception.

Title and text illustrations might be useful for some programs. Make sure to use a bold, easy-to-read font, with good contrast between letters and background. Allow enough time for the audience to comprehend. Don't have too much text—no more than six words per line and six lines per image. Don't overuse text images, as they can disrupt the flow of the talk. Remember, visitors can't read the visual and listen to you at the same time. Text images can cause the program to become very choppy.

Field Tips for Creating an Illustrated Program

Select the topic.

Develop a theme and objectives.

Research.

Organize the information

Utilize the 2-3-1 process and develop the script.

Integrate the story with visualized illustration on a storyboard.

Select images.

Construct the program.

Know your equipment.

Practice your delivery.

Field Tips for Building a Slide Program

Use a light table and lay out slides in sequence. Allow space between each slide for additional insertions and ease of moving around.

Once you are satisfied with the sequence, number the slides in order.

If you're doing a two-projector program, alternately insert slides between the two trays.

Correct slide placement is upside down, emulsion-side toward screen.

Be sure both vertical and horizontal slides fit on the screen.

Use a blackout image to begin and end your program (newer slide projectors do this already); never have a bright-white screen. Better still, have your first visual ready when you turn on the projector and end with an inspirational, impressive image. Remember, don't talk while the last image is still showing. Give your audience a moment to think about what you have presented. Silence is sometimes the most effective way to make a point.

Field Tips for Building a Computer-Generated Projected Program

The process of image and sequence selection is similar to building a slide program.

Make sure your design template is a visual aid, not a visual distraction. Keep it simple.

Use consistent positions, colors, styles, effects, transitions, and animation.

Don't get carried away with clip art, sounds, and special effects.

Minimize text. No more than six words per line and six lines per image.

If you can't find a good image to illustrate your program, what do you do? Modify your talk, temporarily, at least, to eliminate the point, or adjust your talk to make a point you can illustrate. Let staff know what images you need and continue searching. Don't use a weak fill-in image.

Special effects can be accomplished with ordinary photographs. Incorporate "masks" to progressively reveal more or less information. For example, by sequencing copies of the same image, you'll reveal more/less information on each copy. Each advance thereby gives a zoom in/out effect.

Anticipate the upcoming image. Avoid advancing to a new image before you are ready for it. If you change too soon, the listener will examine the new image and lose the train of thought while being confused as to the meaning of the new image. Don't panic if the equipment (e.g., a bulb) fails. Rely on your preplanning efforts and remember you know the story; the images are there just to help illustrate it.

The question often arises, should you mix horizontal and vertical images in your presentation? Using only horizontals permits you to completely fill the screen without worrying about the verticals being cut-off at the top and bottom; however, good photographic composition dictates you may need to vary the orientation. "Many vertically oriented subjects simply don't look visually pleasing when shot in horizontal format; they must be shot in vertical format for maximum impact. For example, a close-up of the Statue of Liberty looks better if shot vertically" (Hooper 1997, 148).

Showing a Movie

Films, videos, and DVDs should be used sparingly and not as a crutch. They must be properly introduced and relate to and support the theme of the main program. Use them to supplement your personal presentation on the topic. Simply turning the projector on and showing a movie is not an interpretive presentation. Plan a thorough introduction and follow-up discussion.

Many movies are taken in other locales. Help visitors to understand how these movies relate to the area they are visiting or you are discussing. Point out specific episodes or relationships that illustrate points you want to emphasize. After the movie, a relevant conclusion should be given.

In the Next Chapter ...

We'll turn our attention to address an important and specific audience: children. Children's interpretation has long been recognized as being unique in theory, approach, and techniques involved. Chapter 9 will explore the purpose and values of successfully providing programs for the young at heart.

Showing a Movie

The film, video, or DVD should be queued up and ready to go. Be sure to give credit to the producers, etc.

Place the audio speaker(s) as close to the screen as possible.

Field Tips for Showing Images Effectively

Do

➤ Go through your program until you are confident that you know it and the equipment very well.

➤ Know the order of the images without having to look at the screen.

➤ Memorize your outline, not the talk.

➤ Face your audience. Even in the dark, they can see you.

➤ Use your voice rather than gestures. The audience is looking at the screen more than at you.

➤ Let the illustration speak for itself, avoid *This is a photograph of ...* and *Here is a ...* It's okay to call attention to details in the image—*Look closely at ...*—to pull the audience into the scene.

➤ Use voice inflections to keep the narration interesting.

➤ Practice, practice, practice!

Do Not

➤ Stand between the projected image and your audience.

➤ Keep turning around to see what image comes next; you should already know.

➤ Stab or flit pointer around the screen; use it only minimally if you must use a pointer (stick or laser) at all.

➤ Use distracting habits, as the audience can still see everything you do, even with the lights out.

➤ Read from a script. The narration should slightly precede the next image.

➤ Use poor images that are difficult to see or out of focus.

Review

1. Instilling confidence that the visitor will have a safe, fun experience in the darkened environment is a necessary component of a successful reduced-lighting program.

2. Human eyes produce a chemical (rhodopsin) when in low-light environments. Within minutes, this chemical will vastly improve night vision.

3. Putting a red lens (cellophane) on a flashlight permits you to see in the dark; white light destroys night vision.

4. Route selection for a night hike is critical. The trail should be wide, level, with no barriers, and absent of distracting light and noise.

5. Night-sky interpretation can be presented indoors, outdoors, and/or a combination of both. The stunning impact of viewing the night sky in a dark, rural environment can be awe-inspiring.

6. The traditional campfire program is an audience-participation-based talk that combines entertainment and education around the flames of discovery.

7. Preprogram music announces that something is happening at the site, establishes a mood, and, at its best, foreshadows the topic.

8. Songs, skits, games, and stories are a great way to establish a connection with the audience and provide warm-up activities for the main program.

9. The transitional phase from the entertainment portion of the campfire program to the educational message is very important.

10. An audiovisual presentation should illustrate and support the talk and strongly reinforce the theme.

Questions and Exercises

1. Which of the following are recommended practices for conducting a slide presentation? (Circle all that apply.)

   Face the screen to keep organized.

   Do not use animated body language.

   Reference each slide as it appears.

   Use only high-quality slides.

2. You should always light the campfire before visitors arrive to your campfire program.

   True or false?

   Why?

3. List three benefits of using music at a campfire program.

4. When preparing a slide presentation, find your slides first and then build your program around those slides.

   True or false?

   Why?

5. What is a storyboard?

6. Once the human eye has adjusted to the dark, it is easy to see colors.

   True or false?

   Why?

References

Article

Moore, Chad. 2003. "Taking Stock of Night-Sky Visibility." *The Improve Newsletter* 12 (3). Fort Collins, Colo.: Air Resource Specialists, Inc.

Books

Brown, Vinson. 1972. *Reading the Outdoors and Night: A Complete Guide to the Sounds, Sights, and Smells of the Wilderness after Dark.* Harrisburg, Pa.: Stackpole Books.

Caduto, Michael J. and Joseph Bruchac. 1994. *Keepers of the Night: Native American Stories and Nocturnal Activities for Children.* Golden, Colo.: Fulcrum Publishing.

Chamberlain, Von Del. 1982. "Interpreting the Sky." In Grant Sharpe, ed., *Interpreting the Environment, Second Edition.* New York: John Wiley and Sons, Inc.

Ham, Sam H. 1992. *Environmental Interpretation: A Practical Guide for People with Big Ideas and Small Budgets.* Golden, Colo.: Fulcrum Publishing.

Helmich, Mary. 1997. *Workbook for Planning Interpretive Projects in California State Parks.* Sacramento: California Department of Parks and Recreation.

Hooper, Jon K. 1997. *Effective Slide Presentations: A Practical Guide to More Powerful Presentations.* Golden, Colo.: Fulcrum Publishing.

Indiana Department of Natural Resources. 2001. *Interpreter's Guidebook 2001.* Division of State Parks and Reservoirs, Division of Forestry.

Regnier, Kathleen, Michael Gross, and Ron Zimmerman. 1994. *The Interpreter's Guidebook: Techniques for Programs and Presentations, Third Edition.* Stevens Point, Wisc.: UW-SP Foundation Press.

Rinard, Judith. 1977. *Creatures of the Night.* Washington, D.C.: National Geographic Society.

Sharpe, Grant. 1982. *Interpreting the Environment, Second Edition.* New York: John Wiley and Sons, Inc.

Stecker, Elinor. 1987. *Slide Showmanship: How to Put On a Terrific Slide Show.* New York: Watson-Guptill Publications.

Strauss, Susan. 1996. *The Passionate Fact: Storytelling in Natural History and Cultural Interpretation.* Golden, Colo.: Fulcrum Publishing.

Summers, Lee. n.d. *A Bag of Tricks: Ideas for Campfire Warm-Ups.* Sacramento: California Department of Parks and Recreation and Monterey Bay Natural Historical Association.

Weiler, Joann. 1990. *Guidelines for Designing Campfire Centers.* Sacramento: California Department of Parks and Recreation.

Chapter 9

For the Young at Heart: Children's Interpretation

Conducting programs with children can be one of the most challenging and
rewarding experiences you will have as an interpreter. Courtesy of Humboldt
State University

**Successful interpretation
for the young at heart
must incorporate special skills,
techniques, and strategies.**

Main Points

Youth are one of the most important populations to target. Not only may you make a significant difference in the future of our planet, but through children, adults can be influenced as well. It is through the eyes of children that adults often see the clearest vision of their own world. In this age of video games, computers, and virtual reality, it is especially important to help connect kids to the natural and cultural world. Interpretation can definitely do that!

Interpretation addressed to children (say, up to the age of twelve) should not be a dilution of the presentation to adults, but should follow a fundamentally different approach. To be at its best it will require a separate program.

—Freeman Tilden, 1883–1980

Children are the future, and without children rooted in the earth, there can be no future.

—Tom Brown Jr., 1989

Conducting interpretation for children is one of the most rewarding aspects of interpretation. There are numerous types of children's programs, and they occur in many venues. Interpreters take their programs into the classroom, bring classroom groups into the park, work with children as members of a general audience, or create programs specifically for them. Regardless of where or when, there are certain techniques, skills, and opportunities that increase the effectiveness of conducting interpretation with and for children.

In this chapter, we'll discuss why you should develop special interpretation programs and opportunities, review the various types of these programs, and examine how to focus messages for children. We'll also discover ways to involve and address children in a mixed-age audience, techniques and strategies for working with various age groups, and the benefits of conducting specific programs for children.

A Special Need

Conducting interpretation for children must take into account several special needs and issues not often faced in adult programming. Children often lack a connection with nature, and, as Larry Beck and Ted T. Cable (2002) suggest, many children only experience nature on television. Although it may be good that they watch the Discovery Channel as opposed to sitcoms or cartoons, the manner in which children are learning about nature and history may indeed be the very thing that keeps them from experiencing it. For example, if a child learns about nature in a neatly packaged one-hour show filled with the action and excitement of a lion killing a pronghorn, how can the slow, deliberate, often hidden real time of nature capture and hold their attention? Much the same can be said about history. For example, gun-shooting Westerns don't accurately reflect pioneer times. Is TV better than no exposure … or does it prevent real exposure? This, as Beck and Cable point out, is the irony of educational nature TV. One of the values of children's interpretation is that it makes the learning and discovery of natural and cultural resources enjoyable and interesting. Interpretation helps children make the connection.

When children don't connect with nature, it becomes a fearful place (Beck and Cable 2002; Brown 1989). Spiders, snakes, and bees frighten not only kids, but adults as well. Children, however, because their exposure to nature has come through television, also fear animals that aren't even found in their local area, such as elephants and tigers. Remembering Maslow's hierarchy of needs, if a child is afraid, learning, discovering, or enjoying is difficult, at best. Interpretation, appropriately conducted, should always address the basic

Hands-on activities, such as creating a marsh system, are effective methods of helping children explore difficult concepts. Courtesy of Carolyn Widner Ward

needs first, thus alleviating fears. This step is critical for children, as fears can quickly become larger than life.

Introducing nature and history to children through our interpretive efforts may be their first authentic exposure and, as such, can have a life-altering effect. Many of us as children were so moved by natural and/or cultural experiences that we chose interpretation as our careers. Our childhood experiences affect us forever. That is why, as an interpreter, you should always proceed as if each program you create and deliver may change lives. You may never know the impact you and your program have on a child. It is with respect and honor that we provide programs for children.

Types of Programs

There are many types of programs that can be conducted with children. As with all interpretation, you can conduct talks, walks, evening programs, slide talks, and other types of programs with any audience, children included. In addition, there are specific programs that are particularly effective with children. The classifications primarily relate to where and how the programs are conducted and the age structure of the audience. The two most common children's programs are presented either in the resource (informal setting) or in the classroom (formal setting). Programs conducted in the resource can include children as members of a mixed-age audience or programs specifically designed for them. School programs provide another venue for reaching children in a more formal setting. This type of outreach is a great way to increase the overall impact and affect of our resources on local publics.

In the Field (Informal)

One of the most common settings in which children connect with the resources is through the traditional programs conducted on-site.

If we cannot interest with our treasures those carefree young persons whose minds are at the height of receptivity, how can we hope to interest those adults who are inevitably fogged and beset by the personal and social worries of an uneasy world?

—Freeman Tilden, 1883–1980

Families frequently attend interpretive programs, yet a child's special needs in this setting are often overlooked. Because programs for children should follow a "fundamentally different approach" (Tilden 1977) than programs for adults, interpreters often feel that they must address either the adults or the children's need—not both. This is not true. In fact, the best programs engage all ages. As with any interpretive opportunity, the key is to incorporate as many components of learning, experience, senses, and so on, as possible. While children may enjoy stories and pictures, adults may want facts and information. Facts, stories, hands-on opportunities, sensory involvement, analogies, metaphors, pictures, and direct experiences with natural and cultural resources are all components of a successful program designed to meet the needs of individuals at different stages in their lives.

All adults, not just parents or guardians, typically appreciate what you do with children. Children in an audience often create opportunities for adults to be kids again. We should strive to engage the young at heart, not just the young in age. Society usually tempers adult desires with regimented restrictions, but interpretive programs can offer an "approved" setting where adults can play. When conducting programs for a mixed-age audience, provide opportunities to explore, interact, and imagine without minimizing the informational components. The guidelines outlined in this chapter assist in planning appropriate activities for children in a mixed-age audience. Moderation, balance, and awareness of the audience are the keys for successfully including everyone, the young and the young at heart.

In the School (Formal)

Programs conducted with school groups follow a somewhat different approach than those conducted with children who are not part of a school group. For example, in the school-group setting, teachers will often handle behavioral problems that the interpreter may need to address in non-school-group situations. If school-group programs are conducted in the classroom, the lack of distractions from an outdoor setting can be beneficial; however, it is difficult for kids to experience nature and history in the classroom. One of the primary differences between school-group programs and other children's programs is that program content should not only be driven by the resource's significance and messages, but also by mandated curriculum standards.

Programs conducted for school groups should, when possible, be aligned with academic-content standards. These content

Taking interpretive programs into the classroom is an effective method of increasing your resources' impacts beyond their physical boundaries. Courtesy of California State Parks, Cahill

standards direct what each student must learn in each grade on both national and state levels. Schools are held accountable to these content standards for each framework or subject area. Schools are also held accountable through financial rewards or sanctions directly correlated to the academic performance of students on these tests. Since accountability is based on the academic-content standards, creating interpretive opportunities that incorporate these content standards increases the overall benefit for the students, schools, teachers, and the agency. Programs should get students into natural and cultural settings, provide opportunities for them to learn about and experience science and history firsthand, and help meet content standards. By meeting these needs, continued support from our public schools is assured. More importantly, we are reaching our target audience. While standards help us identify and support appropriate concepts, themes should not be based solely on content standards. They should be chosen based on the same reasons all themes are selected: site significance, goals and objectives, and so on. Content standards are not the point of our program, but they should be used to help us make the point.

Remember, conducting a school-group program is no different than conducting any interpretive program. It is based, in part, on the needs and wants of the target audience. Programs should be developed based on our themes, the content standards, teacher input, the site, the target audience, time available for the program, and the number of students and assistants.

School-group interpretive programs, although sometimes challenging, help organizations reach populations that may not otherwise be reached. Interpretive programs conducted with school groups can help address some of the problems we will face in the future if children are disconnected from natural and cultural areas. In addition, reaching children through school-based

Interest makes play of the hardest work.
—Enos Mills, 1870–1922

programs helps integrate the site and resources into school curriculum, benefiting the whole community. Making resource-based education important and an integral part of the formal educational system is a worthy goal. In fact, the basic theories and approaches of interpretation that make learning exciting, interesting, and fun help to create lifelong learners and resource stewards.

Children's Characteristics

Although each child is unique and individual, some characteristics are commonly recognized in all children. It is through understanding these general characteristics that the overall success of interpretive programming for children can be improved.

Energetic

One of the most recognizable characteristics of children is their seemingly boundless energy. Kids are just naturally energetic. They love to play, to run, and to be uninhibited.

Field Tips for Positively Engaging Energy

Allow children frequent opportunities for movement. This helps them focus their energy on channeled, controlled movement. Sitting still for any length of time will likely cause behavioral problems.

Begin programs with physical movement. Allowing children to "get out" their natural energy will help promote quieter, more focused times later.

Provide activities that encourage verbal feedback and sharing. It is important to engage their energy, both physically and mentally.

> *It is a miracle that curiosity survives formal education.*
>
> —Albert Einstein, 1879–1955

Especially when outside the formal, regimented classroom, children are likely to want to express themselves through physical activities. An interpreter who constantly reminds children to sit down, listen, stop talking, and so on is missing learning opportunities. Joseph Cornell's (1998) flow-learning theory is a wonderful approach to working with kids and helping to positively channel their natural energy. Later in the chapter, we'll review this theory and other techniques for focusing a child's natural excitement and energy.

Curiosity

Children are naturally curious. In fact, "the earliest school years find children learning the names of things at a phenomenal rate, never again matched" (Tilden 1977, 49). Adults are curious, too, but are often trained by the conventions of society not to ask too many questions. The very things that can drive parents crazy about their child, such as the constant questions, are the same characteristics that will be of the greatest value when conducting programs. For example, when conducting a program for children, constant questions and interruptions may plague your program. This can be very frustrating … *or* … you can take advantage of this natural curiosity, energy, and excitement and channel it!

> *Another characteristic very pronounced in younger children, partly because of their lack of inhibitions, … is the love of personal examination through (the) senses other than sight and hearing.*
>
> —Freeman Tilden, 1883–1980

Sensory Bound

The natural curiosity of children allows you to get them to do, feel, smell, and otherwise experience nature in ways that adults might not. When a very young child picks up something new, the first reaction is to stick it in his/her mouth. At a young age, the primary method of determining if something is good or bad is based on whether or not it is edible. As a child ages, the tendency to identify objects with the mouth lessens and the desire to touch increases. Adults become accustomed to *not* touching things, especially if they don't know what it is. Children, on the other hand, often do the opposite. In fact, touch helps them determine *what* something is. Senses should be frequently engaged to help maximize the natural tendencies of kids to explore. Care should always be taken to ensure the safety of both the children and the environment when engaging them directly with the resources. Be sure that you are always modeling the appropriate behavior.

Field Tips for Channeling Curiosity

Entertain questions and comments in a controlled, timely fashion. At the start of the program, establish the times and places for stories, comments, and questions. Save comments and stories for the end, but take questions throughout the talk.

Listen! Children respond well if they know you are listening.

Capitalize on their natural desire to learn. Ask questions and engage them in the resource.

Follow their eyes. Find out what interests *them*.

Firsthand experiences make the interpretive program come to life for sensory-bound children. Courtesy of Carolyn Widner Ward

We are all born originals—why is it so many of us die copies?

—Edward Young, 1683–1765

Developmental Level

The word "children" is a broad term describing a wide variety of individuals. It goes without saying that a program for third-graders would not work well for eighth-graders. Distinctions between various ages of children can be associated with their developmental level. Children develop emotionally, physically, intellectually, and socially through several distinct stages at approximately the same age (Piaget 1964; Muuss 1982; Grinder and McCoy 1985; Beck and Cable 2002). These developmental stages can be arrested for physical, emotional, cultural, or social reasons. For example, if a child is malnourished or abused, his age-associated level of development may be below the norm. Because developmental levels so clearly impact appropriate content, overall program success, and correspond to school grade levels, these developmental levels will be discussed based on age categories. Keep in mind that these categories are generalizations. Use them as guidelines for assisting in the development of curriculum, activities, and structure of programs.

Field Tips for Engaging the Senses

Engage at least one sense with every main point. Information that is not clearly connected to the resource through a tangible object is harder for children to understand and relate to.

Promote positive engagements with the resource. Always explain why it's *okay* to touch, taste, smell, etc. Children remember everything, so be sure you are showing and telling the right lesson.

Focus on one sense at a time. All people, but especially children, can experience sensory overload, which can result in an unpleasant experience. Instead, help children hone in on one sense at a time. For example, blindfold kids and hand them something. Ask them to identify it, what produced it, or who uses the object.

Change their perspective on a sense. Help them increase their awareness of their senses. For example, have them lie on their backs and gaze up at a tree. Have them count the shades of green they can find in the forest, in a square foot of ground, etc.

Enjoy yourself. Many times, children just don't know how to experience the environment. They will learn much from simply watching *you.*

Use your senses. Point things out as you notice them, especially the small, often-overlooked things; or, better yet, challenge children to notice what is special or unique.

"Games" versus "Activities"

What's in a name? Does it make a difference whether you call it a "game" or an "activity"? Yes! Games may imply something done solely for entertainment or for competition. With video games, sports games, board games, and so on, children are inundated with the term and all the associated meanings. The term "activities" helps promote the added educational elements of what we do with children. Activities are not just games.

Level I (Ages Two to Six)

Children at this age experience the world through their senses. Everything they discover is "alive" and experiences the world the same way they do. For example, two- to six-year-olds think a tree has feelings and parents, just as they do. Independent play, fantasy, and exploration are the primary ways they discover the world. Language skills

Field Tips for Conducting Level I Programs

Make children feel safe.

Establish behavioral expectations early.

Shift activities, physical location, focuses, etc., frequently.

Keep groups small or allow children to participate in activities as individuals.

Focus on fantasy, play, and guided discovery.

Engage children with stories, puppets, games, and sensory explorations.

Conduct short hikes (one-quarter mile or less). Children this age tire easily. Be sensitive to their needs and abilities.

Anthropomorphize (give human characteristics to things that aren't human) to help illuminate difficult concepts.

begin to emerge (Piaget 1964). Symbols and hands-on discovery guide learning. Children in this stage of development don't typically have the ability to make logical operations in their mind. The world is what they see, feel, smell, taste, hear, and so on.

Socially, two- to six-year-old children are self-centered (egocentric perspective) (Muuss 1982). They see the world through their own eyes and have a difficult time grasping any other perspective (Grinder and McCoy 1985; Knudson, Cable, and Beck 1995; Muuss 1982). They also tend to exhibit the preconventional level of moral reasoning (Kohlberg 1971). This means that they primarily reason the appropriateness of an action based on their perceptions of associated rewards or fears of punishment that directly result from the behavior. This is why stickers, stars, and other methods of rewarding positive behavior work so well in controlling behavior in children at this level of development.

Programs for children at Level I must focus on the tangible aspects of the resource. Programs must be object and experience centered. Children will not be physically able to sit still and listen to you lecture, nor will they be able to readily understand the information that is not grounded by a physical object. The elements in CREATES are especially critical for successful children's programming (see page 36). Activities focusing on fantasy or guided discovery are effective with Level I children. Fantasy can be channeled with puppets, skits, storytelling, and opportunities to draw. Guided discovery involves asking children a series of questions, allowing them to "discover" the world around them.

Level II (Ages Seven to 11)

Children at this level of development can deal with simple logical operations and work well in groups or alone. They can classify objects, understand basic relationships, and grasp specific behavioral requests. Children

Tree identification and classification is a great activity for children in the Level II stage of development. Courtesy of Humboldt State University

ages approximately seven to 11 are in what Piaget (1964) termed the concrete "operational" stage of cognitive development. Although children are very much wedded to the physical world, they can begin to perform simple logical operations in their minds. Santa Claus and the Tooth Fairy are replaced with endless questions and inquiries about the nature, classification, or relationship of things.

Social and moral stages at this level of development result in children beginning to see the world from a perspective other than their own (Kohlberg 1971; Muuss 1982). Social development grows from the subjective perspective (ages five to nine), where children begin to understand that others have different perspectives, to the self-reflective thinking category (ages seven to 12), where they begin to evaluate their own behavior (Grinder and McCoy 1985; Knudson, Cable, and Beck 1995; Muuss 1982). The world begins to open up to the concept of "others." After preconventional morality, the next stage is conventional, which is marked by an ability to reason actions based on reciprocity. Judgments about rightness of an action are now not based solely on the self, but also on significant others and society as a whole.

Programs with Level II children should still involve direct experiences with the

resource; however, you can begin to use metaphors, analogies, and other methods of helping them mentally experience the resource. It is critical to establish behavioral control and management with this often rambunctious, abrasive group early in the process. They can understand the "why" behind the rule. Promoting opportunities for children to understand resources themselves through guided discovery and hands-on experience is a powerful tool. Writing stories to share with others is a successful cognitive outlet for children at this level of development.

Level III (Ages 12 to 14)

By age 12, children typically don't consider themselves children. Children in early adolescence can mentally manipulate hypothetical situations, time relationships, and can conduct inductive and deductive logic.

Field Tips for Conducting Level II Programs

Encourage activities that involve direct experience with the resources.

Allow children to work in small groups or alone.

Use questions and inquiries to help guide discoveries.

Incorporate metaphors, analogies, and other cognitive descriptors to help children understand difficult concepts.

Discuss behavioral requests and rules.

Hikes can be longer (approximately one-quarter to one-half mile).

Help them name and categorize items and relationships.

Manage behavior. Children become louder and more abrasive at this level of development.

Provide opportunities for kids to "help." They often compete for your attention.

They are aware of social norms and expectations and are *painfully* aware of their own physical appearance.

In this stage of cognitive development, children can think systematically about logical relationships that are not necessarily physically present (Piaget 1964). Robert Selman categorizes children ages 10 to 15 in the "mutual-perspective" level of social development (Muuss 1982). Children can now understand something from a neutral third-person perspective or from society as a whole. Discussions of global concepts and ideas now hold meaning.

The main factor influencing success is your consideration of their primary concern: physical development. In this stage, they are acutely aware of themselves and everyone else in terms of physical appearance. Not looking stupid or significantly different and being accepted by their peers are their primary

Field Tips for Conducting Level III Programs

Discuss, debate, and allow them to express their own opinions.

Allow them take on adult roles.

Engage their minds in "what-if" scenarios. Encourage their ability to reason, apply logic, and judge situations.

Provide opportunities for them to guide the discovery, conversation, or direction of the program.

Encourage questions and help them discover the answers. (Demonstrate how to use field guides, research techniques, etc.)

Encourage them and discuss ways they can continue their involvement. (Participation in clubs is high in this level of development.)

Provide opportunities for Level III children to work with Levels I or II. Let them be the guides and leaders.

concerns and should be yours as well. Be sure activities don't single out anyone to stand up in front of others, perform on their own, or otherwise call direct attention to them. There is safety in numbers. Incorporate activities that encourage them to form and share their own opinions. Special programs that encourage them to take on adult roles can be very successful. For example, a research-assistant program where they collect, analyze, and discuss data can have a significant impact on these participants who consider themselves "too old to play."

Level IV (Teenagers)

Teenagers are a special group because of their emotional, cognitive, and social developmental stage (Grinder and McCoy 1985; Knudson, Cable, and Beck 1995). The primary concern for most teenagers is how their peers perceive them. They are very self-conscious and don't like to be singled out for attention. As with Level III participants, most of the time, when they attend programs, they are "too cool to play." Don't address teenagers as children. It is important that they be asked their opinions, feelings, and thoughts about things. Many teenagers are still treated as children by their primary caregivers, so interpretive programs that enable teenagers to express adultlike thoughts in an adult setting will be well received. Try to avoid too much lecturelike material. Instead, provide opportunities for open-ended discussion and problem-solving tasks. Douglas Knudson, Ted T. Cable, and Larry Beck (1995) recommend that programs be designated especially for teenagers. It may be easier to have them feel like adults when not surrounded by their parents or guardians. Provide activities that are meaningful and purposeful. If they feel as if they are making a difference, it can have a great impact. Having teenagers work with kids at the other developmental levels can work, but it can't seem as if they are simply babysitting.

Special Needs

A variety of factors can result in children having visual, mental, mobility, learning, or hearing impairments. These kids, although introducing unique challenges for the interpreter, have the right to be able to attend, with minimal alteration, any programs being offered. Don't assume you know how to accommodate a special-needs child. Ask them what they want to do and how you can help them do it. Let them guide you. As always, include several different kinds of stimuli (visual, auditory, tactile, and so on) to increase success.

Non-English-speaking children also introduce interesting challenges. Many of the techniques listed below will assist in working with this special-needs group as well. In addition, refer to Chapter 11 for more tips on working with special groups. Engaging visitors in the resource, using props, and guiding exploration are all useful techniques.

> We must inspire our children to think and live through their hearts, to be guided by the deeper yearnings of life.
>
> —Tom Brown Jr. 1989

These general characteristics of children are meant to serve as a guide to direct and suggest methods and media to enhance program success. Curiosity, excitement, and the natural desire to experience their surroundings are qualities that help make programming for children so enjoyable for the interpreter. Many adults have forgotten

> If a child is to keep alive his inborn sense of wonder ... he needs the companionship of at least one adult who can share it, rediscovering with him the joy, excitement and mystery of the world we live in.
>
> —Rachel Carson, 1907–1964

> We try to use to the utmost the interest of the child. Interest a child and he thinks. While a child is thinking he is learning.
>
> —Enos Mills, 1920

how to experience wonder, awe, and, especially, how to play. Use children's programming to help *you* remember to be young at heart. With practice, interpreting to children will help *you* increase your overall effectiveness as an interpreter. Techniques and strategies that help *children* discover, grasp, and revel in nature can be very effective when used with *adults*. Let's turn now to a discussion of the theories, techniques, strategies, and specific skills for working with children.

Mechanics

Regardless of the individual developmental level of children, there are some general characteristics that help make all children's programs more successful. Behavior control, sensory engagement, and protecting children's safety affect program success at any developmental level.

Have Fun!

Fun crosses all developmental levels. What *you* love, enjoy, and get excited by, children will, too. Creating a pleasurable experience is much of the battle of interesting a child. "This childish desire to know, to learn, will assure mental development if information be given in a way that appeals. Children can learn but little from cold, unrelated, segregated facts ... " (Mills 1920, 101). Joseph Cornell (1998) discussed enthusiasm and reminds us that "enthusiasm is contagious, and that ... is perhaps your greatest asset as an [interpreter]" (15). Remember what it was like to play, get dirty, and touch the ground? Children will learn more, accept more, and remember more if you play, laugh, and enjoy the experience *with* them.

Having fun is one of the most important criteria for a successful children's program. Enjoy what you do, and they will too! Courtesy of Carolyn Widner Ward

Children may have never interacted with natural and cultural resources before and will look to you for the cues for how to respond to it. Dive in to it!

Manage Behavior

There is a fine line between allowing children to explore and discover something for themselves and letting them run wild and out of control. The trick is to find that line and walk it like a tightrope. Establish parameters for behavior early and allow children to expend some of their energy at the start of a program. Specific techniques for controlling behavior vary, depending on the developmental level, the group's structure, the environment, distractions, and the presence or absence of other adults.

Managing behavior by putting it "on cue" is a great technique and one that helps ensure success. A behavioral cue is when you do or say something and the children have a verbal or physical response that they must give. For example, make your hands into rabbit ears and say "rabbit ears," and the kids

Field Tips for Managing Behavior

Outline behavioral guidelines at the start of the program.* Both the expectations and the consequences should be reviewed.

Put behavior "on cue" early in the program. Don't let behavior stray too far from expectations or it will be hard to regain control.

Use positive reinforcement. Controlling behavior is easiest if you proactively encourage positive behavior. Praise a child who is doing the right thing. This unsolicited positive reinforcement can be so much more powerful than punishing the bad. Don't wait; do this early.

Be consistent, both in behavioral requests and enforcements.*

Disapproving looks. These are powerful tools, but only if you follow through.

Delegate responsibility. Disruptive children make good "helpers." Be sure that you are not rewarding disruptive behavior. It is a fine line.

Enlist others. Parents, teachers, volunteers, etc. make great assistants.

Don't yell. This signifies that you have lost control.

Use proximity. Put a problem child next to you.

If the problem persists, discuss it with the child. As with any visitor, identify the problem behavior, the negative impacts to the resource, to others, and to themselves from the behavior, and address how the situation can be remedied.

Give the child time to comply. Don't expect immediate results.

Judge the nature of your behavioral requests. Is safety of the child or the resource an issue? Is it simply your personal desire for behavior? Is the behavior disrupting others? Make careful distinctions about what you want and why. Some requests may not be practical, reasonable, or possible.

*Keep in mind that managing behavior during programs with children in a school setting may not be an issue.

Field Tips for Conducting Safe Programs

Keep group size small (no more than 15, if possible). This helps you maintain control and protect the children from the actions of themselves or others. If you must work with a larger group, have the teacher, parent, or a fellow employee assist you.

Establish rules and expectations for behavior with the parents and with children.

Know where the parents will be during the program and what the protocol is for dealing with an injury. Be sure you always have a means of contacting other staff to help in the event of an emergency.

Be prepared. Stay current in CPR, first-aid training, etc.

Be sure you ask if there is anything that you should know. Any allergic reactions, conditions, or medicines should be disclosed. Develop a check-in sheet with these and other relevant questions.

Frequently check in with children. Ask them how they are doing. Many children may have never been in a natural or cultural resource before, and basic fears can be strong.

Talk to children about potential dangers. At the beginning of the program, you should discuss any dangerous elements that may be encountered (poison oak, etc.). Be careful not to scare them.

have to put their hands on their head, make rabbit ears, and wiggle their noses. This particular behavioral cue might work well during a program for young children about animals. Be sure that you make *all* the children comply with the behavioral cue before you move on to the next topic, activity, and so on. Noncompliance will spread and multiply over time. In addition, select or develop a behavioral cue that fits the subject matter and is age appropriate. Rabbit ears would not work with Level III kids. You are the leader, but they will exert considerable social pressure on each other to comply.

Focus on the Environment

Keep children focused on the resources. Point out things. Help them become aware of colors, textures, shapes, and differences

We should seek to develop a form of natural education that would heighten the senses. We should take children into nature frequently so the senses are fed, nurtured, and become keen.

—Tom Brown Jr., 1989

between things. Teach them how to observe by being a good observer yourself and sharing what you see. Children want to explore the world through their senses; capitalize on this natural desire. "We must take the initiative to enhance children's sensory awareness, building on their natural gifts" (Brown 1989, 8). Programs will be successful if they help children to see, feel, smell, and so on, the world around them. Even if programs occur in the classroom, help children become aware of the world and their perceptions of it. Highlight the subtle elements of the world around them. Engage their minds and bodies in the environment. Use questions to encourage them to think about what they perceive.

Name Names

Children have an enormous capacity for learning new information. Convey facts, names, dates, and details to children. Stories, analogies, and metaphors are important; however, children also want to know the specifics. Don't stray too far from the planned path, but answer their questions. Better yet, do as Tom Brown Jr. (1989) recommends and

We should set an example, by pointing out subtle sounds, sights, smells, tastes, and feelings. Only through our careful attention and nurturing will children ever hope to reach their full sensory potential. Keen sensory awareness is one of the most important skills children can have in life, and it is sensory awareness that makes life full and rich.

—Tom Brown Jr., 1989

"point [them] in the direction of the answer, or ask a series of questions, all designed to make [them] think" (xi). This is essentially a form of guided discovery (Grinder and McCoy 1985). Children are developing. Use your programs to help them increase their understanding, knowledge, and vocabulary of the natural and cultural world (Lewis 1980).

On Their Level

Children spend much of their lives being talked down to, mentally and physically. Most of the time, you may be seen as a uniformed stranger to these children. Whenever possible, physically get on their level. You can be intimidating, towering over them. Bend down when showing them something or when talking directly to them.

Take advantage of the natural curiosity possessed by children and encourage them to explore the world around them. Courtesy of Humboldt State University

Children are much more receptive to an adult who gets on their level to talk with them. In addition to the appropriate physical level, let the state's academic-content standards guide your selection of appropriate material. The academic standards provide very specific guidelines for the information that children are expected to know at various grades.

Keep It Short

Attention spans are very short for children and "most of them haven't learned to be politely quiet when the span is exceeded" (Lewis 1980, 126). Depending on the developmental level, attention spans range from a few seconds to about 10 minutes. Programs can and should be conducted for longer periods of time than this, but, to be successful, they need to shift focus, location, subject matter, and activity more frequently than programs for adults. One great technique to use when working with children is to move their physical location frequently. For example, having them stand up, sit down, face the other way, and so on is effective in regaining interest and focus.

The most successful programs keep children physically *and* mentally engaged. Keep information in sound bites. Children can't listen for extended periods of time. Weave information with activities to gain a child's interest. Anything done in excess gets tiresome; keep it short.

Use Existing Resources

There are numerous resource books, Web sites, and curriculum guides that can help you develop interpretive programs. Some may have been developed specifically for your resources. Uncover these in the formative planning stages of developing programs. Additionally, there are numerous resources you can use that are not place or resource specific. Skills and strategies for working with children come with time, experience, and practice. Talk to your colleagues, experts, and supervisors about their experiences. Seek out opportunities and training and volunteer at schools and clubs to gain experience working with children. Several of the more popular resources are reviewed below.

Flow Learning

One wonderful system for successfully conducting programs with children is called flow learning. This approach to working with children was developed by Cornell (1989). He has published several books providing activities following flow-learning principles. Flow learning takes advantage of the natural process of learning something new. Cornell created flow learning from four distinct stages that mirror the natural process of learning. Stage 1 is "awaken enthusiasm"; Stage 2 is called "focus attention"; Stage 3 is "direct experience"; and Stage 4 is "share inspiration." Each of the four stages has accompanying activities that help maximize that particular stage of learning.

Stage 1 of flow learning is "awaken enthusiasm." This takes place when children are first exposed to something new. Enthusiasm and limitless energy mark this stage of learning.

Children often come to interpretive programs in a Stage 1 mind-set. They are enthusiastic and have boundless energy. Sitting them down and trying to teach them anything would be difficult, at best. Instead, Cornell recommends beginning the program with activities that "establish a mood of cooperation and fun" (1989, 31). The first activities set the tone for the rest of the program. After an introduction, as outlined in previous modules, select an activity that involves the children physically with the resource. Stage 1 allows kids to expend energy and prepares them to slow down and focus attention.

Stage 2, "focus attention," begins after the initial enthusiasm is channeled. If chil-

dren are too excited and enthusiastic, they can't pay attention, watch, see, or feel anything. Stage 2 activities allow children to begin to focus on one or more of their senses. This careful sensory experience sets the framework for more meaningful, direct interactions.

Stage 3, "direct experience," takes advantage of focused attention and provides opportunities for children to have meaningful, direct experiences. These activities, although closely related to Stage 2 activities, provide a more personal, intimate experience with nature. This stage of flow learning is where inspiration, self-actualization, and peak experiences can occur.

After experiencing the excitement and enjoyment of a new experience, it is natural to want to share that experience with others. Stage 4, "share inspiration," takes advantage of this natural desire to share with others that which excites and inspires us. Children ages seven to 14 are especially receptive to sharing with and teaching others. Communicating the experience can come in the form of stories, pictures, poems, and so on. Cornell's activities in Stage 4, as with the other stages, are numerous and varied. This allows the interpreter to select a specific activity based on the target audience, the time frame, and the subject matter.

Although the activities are used most successfully in sequence, they can also be used to supplement existing children's programs, as icebreaker activities, or as stand-alone activities serving as a means to an end. Cornell's (1989) flow-learning

Every normal child is as avaricious for information as a miser is for gold. This childish desire to know, to learn, will assure mental development if information (is) given in a way that appeals.

—Enos Mills, 1870–1922

There is no formula or guide for working with children that can replace your own natural enthusiasm, creativity, and passion. There is no substitute for you. Your love of the subject and of your audience is the greatest asset you have. Working with children presents wonderful opportunities to share your inspiration, knowledge, and understanding of natural and cultural resources. By engaging them and their families, you are developing stewards who will share your desire to preserve and protect our heritage.

activities can also be adapted nicely to fit with any subject matter and can be modified to work effectively with adults.

Other Resources

There are numerous other resources available for designing programs for children. Project Learning Tree, Project Wild Aquatic, Project Wild, and Project Wet provide guidelines, curriculum, activities, and learning opportunities designed to encourage children to

Adults are obsolete children.
—Dr. Seuss, 1904–1991

think. These activities also serve as supplements to your existing programs. They are not meant to function as stand-alone programs, but instead provide wonderful hands-on opportunities to engage your audiences in the program. Each activity guide is organized to allow ease of activity selection based on numerous variables, such as age, grade level, time allotted, subject matter, theme, and content standards. Courses on how to use these resources are offered throughout all 50 states and are available to everyone. Seek out these opportunities and others to improve your skills and techniques for working with children.

Every child is an artist. The problem is how to remain an artist once he grows up.
—Pablo Picasso, 1881–1973

In the Next Chapter ...

Now that we have reviewed many of the basic types of formal interpretive programs, let's turn to the most common type of informal interpretation in the resources: roving interpretation. It involves taking our techniques, skills, and interpretive messages to the visitors on the trails, in the visitor centers, in the campgrounds, or wherever we may find them.

Review

1. Programs conducted for children are fundamentally different from those for adults.

2. There are several challenges when working with children, including heightened fear, lack of connection to nature, and primary exposure to nature through television.

3. Programs for children can be conducted both in the field (informal) and in the school (formal).

4. Children are naturally energetic, curious, and sensory bound.

5. Children's developmental levels impact their social, mental, and cognitive abilities, and thus directly influences appropriate program content and delivery.

6. Activities for Level I children (ages two to six) need to focus attention on the tangible elements of the resource, be short and simple, and allow for individual participation.

7. Level II children (ages seven to 11) can be guided with questions, helped to understand with analogies and metaphors, and controlled with the use of a behavioral cue.

8. Level III (ages 12 to 14) children do not like to "play" or be put on the spot.

9. Teenagers (Level IV) should be treated like adults and given separate opportunities to discover resources for themselves through careful guided discovery programs.

10. Managing behavior and keeping children safe is a primary concern for conducting children's programming.

11. Getting children involved in the environment through the use of their senses is useful for success.

Questions and Exercises

1. List two benefits of conducting interpretive programs with children.

2. What does it mean to put behavior "on cue"?

3. Describe three ways to manage disruptive behavior during a children's program.

4. Develop an activity for 14-year-olds to educate them about the importance of biodiversity.

5. How would you explain the following to a group of eight-year-old children?

    Volcanic eruptions

    The water cycle

    Endangered species

    Cultural diversity

    Extinct species

    Ceremony

References

Article

Piaget, Jean. 1964. "Development and Learning." *Journal of Research in Science Teaching* 3: 176–186. New York: John Wiley and Sons, Inc.

Books

Beck, Larry and Ted T. Cable. 2002. *Interpretation for the 21st Century, Second Edition.* Champaign, Ill.: Sagamore Publishing.

Brown, Tom, Jr. 1989. *Tom Brown's Field Guide to Nature and Survival for Children.* New York: Berkley Books.

Caduto, Michael and Joseph Bruchac. 1991. *Keepers of the Animals: Native American Stories and Wildlife Activities for Children.* Golden, Colo.: Fulcrum Publishing.

California Department of Education. 1996. *A Child's Place in the Environment Series.* Sacramento, Calif.: California Department of Education, Bureau of Publications.

Cornell, Joseph. 1979. *Sharing Nature with Children: A Parents' and Teachers' Nature Awareness Guidebook.* Nevada City, Calif.: Dawn Publications.

———. 1989. *Sharing the Joy of Nature: Nature Activities for All Ages.* Nevada City, Calif.: Dawn Publications.

———. 1998. *Sharing Nature with Children, 20th Anniversary Edition.* Nevada City, Calif.: Dawn Publications.

Erdoes, Richard and Alfonso Ortiz. 1984. *American Indian Myths and Legends.* New York: Pantheon Books.

Grinder, Alison and E. Sue McCoy. 1985. *The Good Guide: A Sourcebook for Interpreters, Docents and Tour Guides.* Scottsdale, Ariz.: Ironwood Press.

Kesselheim, Alan and Britt Eckhardt Slattery. 1995. *WOW: The Wonders of Wetlands.* St. Michael's, Md.: Environmental Concern, and Bozeman, Mont.: The Watercourse.

Knudson, Douglas, Ted T. Cable, and Larry Beck. 1995. *Interpretation of Cultural and Natural Resources.* State College, Pa.: Venture Publishing.

Kohlberg, Lawrence. 1971. "Stages of Moral Development as a Basis for Moral Education." In C. M. Beck, *Moral Education: Interdisciplinary Approaches, Ninth Edition.* Toronto, ON: University of Toronto Press.

Lewis, William J. 1980. *Interpreting for Park Visitors.* Philadelphia, Pa.: Eastern Acorn Press.

Mills, Enos. 1920. *The Adventures of a Nature Guide.* Garden City, N.Y.: Doubleday, Page, & Co.

Muuss, Rolf E. 1982. *Theories of Adolescence.* New York: Random House.

National Research Council. 2001. *National Science Education Standards: Observe, Interact, Change, Learn, Eighth Printing.* Washington, D.C.: National Academy Press.

North American Association for Environmental Education. 1998. *The Environmental Education Collection: A Review of Educators,* vol. 2. Troy, Ohio.

———. 1999. *Excellence in Environmental Education—Guidelines for Learning (K–12).* Rock Springs, Ga.

Porter, Erika. 1994. *All Visitors Welcome: Accessibility in State Park Interpretive Programs and Facilities.* Sacramento, Calif.: California Department of Parks and Recreation.

Regnier, Kathleen, Michael Gross, and Ron Zimmerman. 1994. *The Interpreter's Guidebook: Techniques for Programs and Presentations, Third Edition.* Stevens Point, Wisc.: UW-SP Foundation Press.

Tilden, Freeman. 1977. *Interpreting Our Heritage, Third Edition.* Chapel Hill: University of North Carolina Press.

Online

Project Learning Tree. www.plt.org.

Chapter 10

Taking the Message to the Visitor: Roving Interpretation

Roving contacts fulfill visitor and management needs while permitting you to research and explore the resource. Courtesy of Carolyn Widner Ward

Roving is planned communication with the visitor in an informal setting.

Roving interpretation is personalized, face-to-face communication where the audience has chosen the venue, the resource is the stage, and the interpreter is a catalyst for knowledge. Roving provides the means to protect the resource and the visitor and to ensure a quality recreational experience. This chance to chat with visitors may be one of the finest opportunities for you to positively represent your agency.

Roving interpretation may *seem* spontaneous, extemporaneous, impromptu, unstructured, ad lib, or unprepared, but this should *not* be the case. When done properly, it is well organized and thoroughly planned. Getting to talk to a real live "ranger," the perceived authority of the resource, is an invaluable bonus for the visitor.

> Eighty percent of park visitors
> don't attend formal interpretive programs.

For the interpreter, roving interpretation, including incidental visitor contacts, will far outnumber opportunities to reach people through more-formal presentations. These informal contacts are often the only chance you have to interpret to visitors, influence behavior, and gain support for agency resources. With only about 20 percent of visitors attending formal interpretive programs, roving presents a great opportunity to reach the majority of our visiting public (Knudson, Cable, and Beck 1995). Roving is the quintessential role for an interpreter and is pure joy!

In this chapter, we will explore the reasons and techniques of roving, how to do it; when and when not to do it, and why.

Reasons for Roving

Some of the more obvious benefits of roving include public relations, providing timely and site-specific information and education, gaining a better understanding of the visitor and the resource, and protecting that resource. Other, less obvious benefits include collecting anecdotal information about use patterns, gaining feedback for better site management, developing your communication skills in a nonformal, nonenforcement, nonbureaucratic setting, and allowing you to refresh your sanity, reconnect with reality, and create lifetime memories.

Selecting the location to rove comes with much forethought and consideration. While it may seem opportunistic to the visitor, in reality you should plan this chance meeting very carefully. There are unique reasons and benefits for roving.

Carpe Diem—Seize the Day!

Many times, there are seasonal events, phenomena, or special occurrences that take place at the site. Roving provides a perfect opportunity to capitalize on these events. Sharing a fleeting event with another person can be extremely gratifying. This type of

If you know the resource, the audience, and the needs and desires of management, selecting the location to rove is easy. Courtesy of Alan E. Wilkinson

Field Tips for Handling Difficult Visitors

➤ Listen carefully.

➤ Think before you act.

➤ Maintain control.

➤ Analyze the situation.

➤ Take appropriate action.

➤ Remember that you are a public servant.

➤ Don't get emotionally entangled.

sharing and learning can be illuminating, and even life changing, for you and the visitors. Many visitors who would never attend formal programs are very often receptive to these more spontaneous discovery opportunities.

Some roving will be truly spur-of-the-moment, but the vast majority, while it may seem spontaneous to the visitor, is actually identified and planned well in advance by good interpreters. You may not be able to predict rainbows, but you are aware of the local weather patterns; the advantage is yours. Likewise, you may not be able to predict where the gray whale will breech, or even if one will be sighted, but you are familiar with their migration patterns and when and where to look. Other seasonal or periodic events, such as cacti in bloom,

Take Advantage of the Moment

➤ Flowers blooming

➤ Fall colors

➤ An animal's birth

➤ Rainbows

➤ Cloud patterns

grunion runnings, a red tide at night, and waterfalls in their full glory may be easier to predict.

Visitor Safety

Roving interpretation can be effective in helping to identify safety issues and informing visitors of those issues. By stationing yourself in locations where there are potential hazards (steep cliffs, strong tides, poisonous plants, and so on), not only can the roving be effective as an interpretive tool, but it also addresses safety concerns. In addition, roving will also provide an opportunity to discover visitor safety issues with which you may have been unaware.

Resource Protection

There are many underlying management issues that precipitate the benefit of roving. The reason for violations by visitors is most often due to their unfamiliarity with resource rules and regulations. The roving interpreter, who may be the first to see the problem brewing, can rectify a transgression long before it becomes a problem.

Direct person-to-person communication can explain management issues and educate the visitor to more fully appreciate the need to comply. Think of all the rules with which the visitor must adhere. Rules can become

Roving in the resource affords an opportunity to provide assistance, explain management issues, and protect both the visitor and the resource. Courtesy of Alan E. Wilkinson

the instruments of mistrust and elitism if not explained and personalized by the interpreter. It is easier to gain compliance with understanding rather than with enforcement. That is a role of the interpreter.

In addition to providing information to visitors, interpretation can help with security and protection of the resources. To the visitors, rules prohibiting feeding the squirrels, dogs off-leash, taking a piece of petrified wood, or touching the artifacts may seem like annoying aggravations. When the interpreter has the opportunity to explain the reasons behind the rules, not only will the visitors more readily comply, but also the agency may have gained a constituent for their cause(s).

How you handle a given situation is ultimately up to you, of course, but good judgment, good listening skills, and an

What is required is sight and insight—then you might add one more: excite.
                                —Robert Frost, 1874–1963

interpretive approach may best serve all involved. Review the section in Chapter 2 on handling depreciative behavior through interpretive means (pages 23–27).

Marketing

Try as we might, visitors just don't always see the postings of interpretive activities. Since statistics indicate that only 20 percent of the visiting public attends scheduled interpretive programs, the more welcome we make the visitors feel, the more likely they are to attend (Knudson, Cable, and Beck 1995). Although large audiences aren't always the best, we should still try to reach as large a population as possible through our interpretive efforts. Roving provides a wonderful opportunity to reach visitors in the field and potentially increase participation in more-formal programs.

Generally, visitors are on vacation and don't want to be dictated by the clock. Your friendly reminder of upcoming activities allows them time to plan to attend if they choose. Additionally, you can provide them with a cognitive map of the activity, including the time, place, and topic. You may also provide other useful information, such as the need to bring water, wear appropriate clothing, or carry a flashlight.

Roving provides an excellent opportunity to personally invite the public to formal interpretive programs. Courtesy of Carolyn Widner Ward

Public Relations

A clear benefit of roving is improved public relations. As stated earlier, roving is pure joy for interpreters because they get to meander through the site enjoying the resource and mingling with visitors. Likewise, it's an opportunity for the public, our constituents, to talk with the person they view as the most knowledgeable about the area. Don't disappoint them; be professional in every respect.

You represent your agency. Appearance, knowledge, demeanor, approachability, and so many other factors go into making a positive impression. Be prepared and set a high standard of excellence.

> Roving provides dual field-research benefits: it affords us an opportunity to get to know our visitors and reconnects us with the resource.

Field Research

Visitors are a valuable resource, but do we truly know and understand their wants and needs? How often during the day do we get to chat with a visitor? Certainly not as often as we would like! Roving through an area and talking with visitors helps us personalize information delivery. This interchange of dialogue is beneficial for both the visitor and the interpreter. The stalwart tenet for good program delivery is to "know your audience." What better way to gain this knowledge than to directly observe and talk with the visitors?

Roving affords the interpreter an oppor-

> With research, interpretive opportunities can be created to meet the needs of visitors and management, as well as to maximize the inherent characteristics and recreational opportunities presented by the resource.

> Roving is the quintessential role of an interpreter ... and it's fun!

tunity to gain knowledge of the audience directly from individuals. This knowledge can then be incorporated into more-formal group presentations. The individuals you talk with while roving may not be the same people who attend your more-formal interpretive programs, but they certainly offer insight into the wants and needs of the visitor. Use this valuable knowledge to improve your program delivery and other resource services.

Roving also provides the interpreter with an opportunity to continue researching the resource. It's a time to recharge your batteries and reconnect with the environment. As we discussed in Chapter 4, this continual primary-resource assessment allows you to update your understanding of the natural and cultural features of the location.

Planning

As discussed earlier, roving is a planned communication opportunity with visitors in the resource. There are several planning issues to address prior to roving: location, visitors' needs and interests, and props and attention grabbers.

Location

It's important to know the location you are planning to rove. It is one thing to be *familiar* with the site, and another to really *know* it. Several visits to a location will begin to open your senses to all of its details; just think of all the discoveries you make each time you return. Now, translate that knowledge of the location into helping the visitor make these and similar discoveries.

Look at a location from various perspectives: the visitor, the interpreter, and the

Roving Is Important Because It ...

➤ Builds a sense of ownership through interaction

➤ Gives a personal connection to the place

➤ Serves as a remembrance with take-home value

➤ Seizes the moment (carpe diem!)

➤ Protects the resource

➤ Advertises events and activities

➤ Promotes public relations

➤ Allows us get to know our visitors

➤ Connects management with the visitor

➤ Reconnects staff to resource

management. Ask yourself, *What is it that draws visitors?* If you yourself are new to the location, the first time you walk through the area, take notes on what catches your eye. What questions do you have as you walk through? Your observations are probably very similar to those of the visitor.

Examine the resource through the eyes of a manager. Explore how this specific location is part of the overall picture, down to the smallest details. Not only do you need to know about those features that can be viewed or experienced, you also should know about the culture, history, and unseen background aspects. What are the critical issues?

Finally, look at the resource through the eyes of an interpreter. What's special about this place? Develop a repertoire of mini stories that you can share. Do your homework.

He who asks is a fool for five minutes, but he who does not ask remains a fool forever.

—Chinese proverb

Visit the site often. If you have an off-season, when the location isn't quite as busy, this might be an ideal time for you to make a reconnaissance.

Visitors' Needs

Experience is a good teacher when it comes to anticipating the needs and interests of the visitor. Some aspects of a location will just naturally be of interest to every visitor. For example, the reason the area became a park or a historic site, that big-ticket item, probably is understandable; however, it's those less obvious curiosities that the visitor has that are most important to plan for. Build on each interaction and begin to predict what you'll be asked. Be sure to prepare for and address basic safety and security needs.

There is no such thing as a stupid question. No matter how many times you have heard a visitor's question, answer it as if it is the first time you've ever heard it. Be sincere.

You have selected this location to rove because it attracts visitors. Ask yourself *What it is that brings them to this location?* If it's the *really big* ... or the *beautiful* ... or the *best* ..., then anticipate what it is the visitor needs to better understand and experience the feature.

Props and Attention Grabbers

Once you have identified the location, the target audience, and know what it is you want to accomplish, there are a host of appropriate props, aids, and attention grabbers to facilitate your initial contact and program delivery. We discussed what might be included in your general kit bag of props and aids in Chapter 6 (see pages 102–107). When roving, you might only need a spotting scope at a vista point or a small table covered with historic photographs to draw in your audience and start the conversation. Costumes, music, handheld items—the list is endless; just choose wisely for the setting and the audience.

Visual aids, uniforms or costumes, music, and a host of other items draw the attention of visitors, providing an ideal opportunity for you interpret the resource. Courtesy of Oregon Caves N.M., NPS

Mechanics

Your uniform, costume, or other distinguishing attire is a magnet for most visitors. Add a prop or two, a cheerful smile, and a welcoming comment, and you're well on your way to a successful encounter. Greeting visitors in the manner that you welcome friends into your home will almost always work.

When

Roving should be scheduled. This is not to say that spontaneous face-to-face interaction with visitors shouldn't be a normal activity, but the good interpreter should allocate a specific time to rove. Roving interpretation should have a focused agenda that best serves the goals and objectives of the site and the interests of the visitors. Scheduled roving ensures that you will actually make the contacts and gives added emphasis that you will spend time one-on-one with the visitor. It also lets other staff know where you will be at a certain time. Depending on the work-

An interpreter on horseback, in uniform or period costume, or associated with a large prop is an attention-getter.

Keep track of the number of interpretive contacts you make. Over time, this will help you and other staff decide when and where to rove by discovering those places that have the greatest potential to connect with visitors.

load, management priorities, and predicted availability, scheduling of roving might only be posted on the staff bulletin board and not necessarily advertised to the public.

Where

The American Heritage Dictionary (2000) defines roving as "to wander about … especially over a wide area; roam." In our case as well, roving generally means moving from location to location. Roving is a very effective method to meet large numbers of visitors, especially if you select locations that ordinarily have high concentration of users. Scenic overlooks, wildlife-viewing areas, visitor-use facilities, and popular trails are all locations

Field Tips for Making That Initial Contact

Smile!

Be professional in dress and demeanor.

Use a friendly greeting.

The icebreaker should make you approachable, not pushy.

Avoid yes or no questions and answers.

Personalize your contact.

Props can draw the visitor into discussion and add interest.

Binoculars or a spotting scope are a subtle way to announce that there is something interesting to see.

Be visible and capitalize on visitor curiosity.

Station yourself at high-visibility locations that provide maximum opportunity to contact visitors. A large map not only draws people in, it is also a great tool to orient visitors to the resource. Courtesy of Carolyn Widner Ward

to consider. Don't overlook other special locations your site offers where visitors gather. Use your imagination!

Remember the benefits of roving—protecting the resource, increasing visitor enjoyment, capitalizing on special occurrences, and educating the public—that we discussed at the beginning of the chapter. Now, place yourself where you can best achieve these results.

How
Reading the Audience

Be observant when approaching visitors; some people just want to enjoy the experience

> *The content and nature of each encounter is usually determined less by something the interpreter planned to say than by what the visitors want to know or what they're doing at the time of the encounter.*
>
> —Sam H. Ham, 1992

Not Everyone *Wants* Your Input

Consider not contacting a visitor when:

➤ They are eating or involved in other activities.

➤ They don't make eye contact or they look away as you approach.

➤ They are obviously in a hurry and don't have time to chat.

➤ Their focus is elsewhere.

➤ They are already enjoying an activity.

The bottom line—respect privacy.

without even well-meant distractions. You don't want to disrupt the solitude of the moment or the group camaraderie they are enjoying. Generally, the situation will be obvious. Don't force yourself on anyone; know when to approach and when to leave. Just remember to watch for the warning signals and be courteous.

Making Meaningful Contacts

With every contact, try to personalize your

The National Park Service Subscribes to This "Visitors' Bill of Rights"

Visitors have a right to:

➤ Have their privacy and independence respected;

➤ Retain and express their own values;

➤ Be treated with courtesy and consideration;

➤ Receive accurate and balanced information.

—National Park Service, 2001

When to Leave—Warning Signals

Generally, you shouldn't stay more than five to 10 minutes, but it may be wise to leave sooner. Watch for these warning signals:

➢ Nonverbal body language— indications from the face, hands/feet, and posture

➢ Conversation lags or strays off the subject

Friendly, personalized dialogue is the goal. Be brief, answer questions, impart management messages, and stimulate that sense of wonder. Courtesy of Carolyn Widner Ward

approach. Read the clues of the individual, the group, and the situation. When contacting a group, assess their age and composition. Is this a family unit, friends, random observers of an event? Look for little things. What are the visitors wearing? Does their T-shirt or hat have any slogans? Are they carrying a camera, fishing pole, or skis? Are there any indications of their home state or country, such as vehicle license plates or an accent? Be observant so you can customize the interaction to the individual or group. Once you have established a meaningful contact, constantly watch for signals that indicate the encounter should end. Brief, positive, friendly dialogue is the goal, not a sermon or long, drawn-out discussion.

Disengaging

On the flip side, some visitors think you are their personal interpreter. So, how do you end a contact when a visitor wants to keep you there forever? With skill and tactful persuasion! Remind them that you have many visitors to serve and a short time to meet everyone. Thank them for their interest and attention and direct them to a trail, other features they might enjoy, or invite them to an upcoming program.

In the Next Chapter ...

In the past five chapters, we've discussed the planning, mechanics, and specific implementation techniques of talks, walks, working in the dark, working with children, and roving programs. While these program types are different, they all have elements that are universal to successful program development and delivery. In the next chapter, we'll discuss common factors, strategies, and concerns that should be considered and implemented in all programs.

Review

1. Roving interpretation may *seem* spontaneous, but when done properly, it is well organized and planned.

2. Roving is a good way to contact the 80 percent of visitors who never attend formal interpretive programs.

3. Roving connects the visitor to a specific site or happening. Your selection of the location to rove should consider visitor, management, and resource concerns.

4. Make meaningful contacts and personalize your approach to each individual.

5. Initiate the contacts with a friendly greeting, employing an open-ended question (one that doesn't require simply yes or no answers), interpret briefly, and be prepared to expand your dialogue as appropriate.

6. Know when not to approach, when to leave, and how to move on gracefully. Respect the Visitors' Bill of Rights.

7. Roving is an opportunity to explain the rules and reasons of proper behavior before it becomes a divisive issue. It is also an occasion to gain support for agency programs and issues.

8. Use attention-getters, such as your uniform, costumes, props, and other items from your kit bag of tools to draw in the audience.

9. The roving interpreter doesn't have a planned script or program, but he/she should anticipate and recognize questions commonly asked by visitors.

Questions and Exercises

1. Roving provides what field research benefits? (Circle the two that are most appropriate.)

   Opportunity to get to know our visitors

   Reconnects the interpreter with the resource

   Advertises our programs

   Ensures visitor safety issues are being addressed

2. When approaching visitors, which of the following practices are *not* recommended? (Circle all that apply.)

   Personalize the contact

   Use props

   Ask yes/no type questions

   Smile and provide a welcoming comment

3. What initial observations may help you personalize visitor contacts? (Circle all that apply.)

   Logos, slogans, pins, and other items on the visitor's clothing

   Recreational and other equipment present

   Age and composition of group

   Direction the visitor is traveling

4. Roving times and locations should be scheduled ahead of time.

   True or false? Why?

5. List five reasons to rove.

6. Do you think informal roving interactions or formal programs are the most effective method of accomplishing goals and objectives?

References

Books

Beck, Larry and Ted Cable. 2002. *Interpretation for the 21st Century, Second Edition.* Champaign, Ill.: Sagamore Publishing.

Ham, Sam H. 1992. *Environmental Interpretation: A Practical Guide for People with Big Ideas and Small Budgets.* Golden, Colo.: Fulcrum Publishing.

Knudson, Douglas, Ted T. Cable, and Larry Beck. 1995. *Interpretation of Cultural and Natural Resources.* State College, Pa.: Venture Publishing.

Lewis, William J. 1981. *Interpreting for Park Visitors.* Philadelphia, Pa.: Eastern Acorn Press.

Sharpe, Grant. 1982. *Interpreting the Environment, Second Edition.* New York: John Wiley and Sons, Inc.

The American Heritage Dictionary of the English Language, Fourth Edition. 2000. New York: Houghton Mifflin Co.

Online

National Park Service. Interpretive Competencies, Interpretive Development Program. www.nps.gov/idp/interp/competencies.htm.

Chapter 11

Essentials for All Programs: Critical Concerns

By addressing the critical issues and challenges, we professionally provide our diverse audiences the answers they sorely desire. Courtesy of Oregon Caves N.M., NPS

No matter what type of presentation, there are several issues and concerns.

As we've discovered in the previous chapters, personal interpretive presentations come in many forms. Whether in uniform or costume during a formal presentation or informal spontaneous contact, personal interpretation offers many opportunities to fulfill visitor, resource, and management needs.

Just as personal interpretation runs the gamut, so to do other considerations. Throughout all program types, there are important additional items to address. In this chapter, we will discuss some critical concerns that may pertain to every interpretive presentation.

> Auxiliary aids are devices or services that help provide equal access to programs or activities. Examples include assistive-listening devices, Braille and large-print materials, video captions, audio recordings, readers for the visually impaired, and sign-language interpreters.

Special Groups

Audiences come with a variety of needs and desires. Just as with children's interpretation, some individuals or groups in our audiences may require particular thoughtfulness. Some groups to consider include persons with special needs, the elderly, and visitors who speak foreign languages.

Visitors with Special Needs

As of the 2000 census, almost 50 million Americans of all ages have some sort of physical or mental impairment; the majority of those have a physical disability. These individuals are members of the public we serve, and, as such, they have the right to access our programs and services. Moreover, in 1990, the Americans with Disabilities Act (ADA) passed. This legislation requires leisure-services providers to facilitate and support the full participation of individuals with disabilities in all leisure programs. Accessibility "means being able to get to the door, through the door, to the second floor, and to participate, independently, and with dignity" (Stensrud 1993, 103).

As the interpreter, it is your responsibility to be familiar with and follow the "letter of the law" for program accessibility: to provide programs where all visitors are included in the interpretive talk. Personal integrity and professionalism also dictate that you embrace the "spirit of the law." Incorporate accessibility along with the elements of CREATES for *all* members of the audience.

The Uniform Federal Accessibility Standards, ADA, State Access Codes, and your agency's policies dictate law. Don't fail to ask people about their needs, show respect and sensitivity, use what works, and be creative. Perhaps most importantly, focus on ability, rather than disability.

The major barrier that people with impairments confront, and often the most difficult to overcome, is other people's negative attitudes and flawed perceptions.

The Americans with Disabilities Act (ADA) is a civil rights law that is intended to protect individuals with disabilities from discrimination.

Always think of the person first. It is important to remember that people with disabilities are individuals who do not all act, think, or move alike. Don't group them as such. When addressing or referring to a person with an impairment, put the person in the statement. For example, if the person can't hear, then acknowledge the disability by saying, " … a person with hearing impairments … " People with disabilities are people. They may happen to have more difficulty than others walking, talking, seeing, hearing, and so on, but they are remarkably like everyone else.

One of the central principles of ADA is that "special" programs are not the desired solution. In fact, programs should be as inclusive of those with disabilities as possible. "Separate but equal" is not the intent of the ADA. Ralph W. Smith, David R. Austin, and Dan W. Kennedy (1996) provide several suggestions for conducting programs for those with disabilities, including changing as little as possible from the original program, involving the person with the disability in the modification process, and not making assumptions regarding preferences for modifications. In the end, maintaining the dignity and rights of the individual should always be the primary concern. Be sure to know what facilities, equipment, and services are available to assist those with impairments.

Field Tips for Integrating ADA Principles

When talking with a person with a disability, speak directly to that person rather than through a companion or sign-language interpreter.

If you offer assistance, wait until the offer is accepted. Then ask how you can best help. Listen to and follow their directions. Don't try to take over.

Relax. If you don't know what to do, allow the person who has an impairment to put you at ease.

Don't be embarrassed if you happen to use accepted, common expressions, such as "See you later," or "Got to be running along," that seem to relate to the person's disability.

When meeting a person with a visual impairment, always identify yourself and others who may be with you.

When talking with a person who has difficulty speaking, be patient and listen attentively. Never pretend to understand if you have difficulty doing so. Instead, repeat what you have understood and ask short questions that require brief answers for clarification.

Don't push a person's wheelchair or grab the arm of someone walking with difficulty without first asking if you can be of assistance. Respect personal space and privacy.

When speaking for more than a few minutes to a person using a wheelchair, place yourself at eye level in front of the person to facilitate the conversation.

Be considerate of the extra time it might take for a person with a disability to get things done or said. Let them set the pace.

Recognize that a person with an impairment offers life experiences that may be different. Embrace these exceptional learning opportunities.

Elderly Visitors

The population of recreational participants is aging. Currently, about 25 percent of Americans are over the age of 50, and 12.4 percent are over the age of 65 (U.S. Census Bureau 2002). With the baby-boom population aging and the average life span increasing, it is expected that by 2025, the median age in the United States will be 41. Projected trends in recreation, such as a decrease in backpacking and an increase in bird-watching, reflect this population shift in age (Dwyer 1993). The older adult population is more sophisticated, typically has more free time, and is more physically fit than in years past. This population generally is influential, votes, and is economically able to participate in recreation; however, as this population continues to age, three primary concerns should be addressed when designing programs: mobility, hearing, and vision. Roy Geiger and W. Kay Ellis (1991) indicated that the three most common ailments for seniors are arthritis, hearing loss, and visual impairment.

Generally, interpretive programs targeted for elderly populations should be conducted as short walks on flat or gently sloping trails or as talks with no walking. Programs should take into account the years of experience of the participants and provide

Elderly audiences may not be able to walk great distances or be as active, but their curiosity, enthusiasm to learn, and desire for social interaction are great. Courtesy of California State Parks, Cahill

Be aware of cultural differences. Some gestures do not universally communicate the same meaning, while some may be disrespectful. For example, many Germans consider it rude if you talk with your hands in your pockets. Roger Axtell's *Gestures: The Do's and Taboos of Body Language around the World* (1991) provides other good examples.

opportunities for them to contribute to the program. Socializing opportunities are important for these visitors. Speak loudly (but don't shout) and clearly. Objects, large graphics, and visual aids assist in illustrating your point. Avoid having the audience read small print. Be sure you know what auxiliary aids are available and always announce to visitors the opportunities to use such devices and services.

Visitors Who Speak Foreign Languages

As travel throughout the world increases, our audiences come from many cultures. Embracing this cultural diversity certainly enhances understanding and appreciation, but language barriers can present challenges for communication if you are not prepared.

When addressing visitors who speak a foreign language, if you don't speak their language, use a language interpreter. If you don't have a translator, ask a member of the group who speaks both languages to help. If they don't feel comfortable translating every word, they can still be a valuable ally in conveying key concepts. Some individuals are very shy about being in the spotlight. Don't insist if they should refuse your invitation to translate. Reduce your content by about half to allow for translation time. It's better for the group to understand half of the program well than to hear it all from you and not understand anything.

Do your best to establish a rapport and camaraderie with the group. Don't be afraid to try out your high school language skills! Even scant knowledge of a language is usually appreciated. Ask how to say something in their language, and then repeat it. Even if (and perhaps *especially* if) your attempt is clumsy, the group will appreciate you for trying. Obvious words to start with are "please" and "thank you." Not only will these prove useful, they also demonstrate respect.

Build a library of foreign words and phrases that pertain to your topic and reflect cultures that commonly visit your resource. Keep them on note cards and refer to them when appropriate.

Where appropriate, use pantomime. Facial expressions, hand and body movements, and actions can help convey messages. Draw pictures, use props, make

Use all your interpretive skills and enthusiasm to communicate with audiences who speak foreign languages. Don't hesitate to use nonverbal forms of communication to convey your messages. Courtesy of Oregon Caves N.M., NPS

sounds, and improvise. Not only will the audience appreciate your efforts, you may have fun in doing so. Don't shout; they aren't hearing impaired.

Many Visitors Will Speak Foreign Languages

Por favour
Thank you
Au revoir
Gracias
Please
Grazie
Hello
Hvala
Xie xie
Merci

Bonjour
Good morning
Ohio Molim
Adios
Good-bye
Ciao
Arigato
Ni hao ma

Distractions

Distractions to your program come in many forms. The crying baby, the loud talker in the back of the room, or an overly energetic child will all test your professionalism. The skills you develop as an interpreter will serve you well in handling disruptive situations. By using your pleasant people skills, you can often quickly correct the problem. Good judgment, a calm demeanor, and appropriate action when handling disruptive issues are skills that you will refine as you gain experience. Don't fail to observe or hesitate to discuss with other interpreters how they handle various situations.

Sometimes you can anticipate a problem and defuse it before it becomes disruptive. Ask the overly energetic child to assist with some aspect of the program, such as counting the number of people in attendance or helping lead a song. Invite the rowdy bunch in the back to come closer to the front so that they can "see better." Enlisting audience and peer pressure can be very effective. Discreetly "discussing" the issue with the troublemaker may *sometimes* be necessary.

Planning for the "What-If" Problems

➤ Who decides when to cancel a program, and how do you notify staff and the potential audience of the cancellation? There should be consistency in this cancellation decision.

➤ Is there an alternate location that would accommodate the program in a timely manner?

➤ Is backup equipment available, and what is its location?

Call on the help of volunteers and/or other staff. Teamwork certainly helps.

The bottom line is you've put a lot of effort into your program. The vast majority of the audience is receptive and appreciative of your efforts, so don't let those very few and occasional distracters ruin the experience for all. Deal with them in a professional manner; don't just ignore them.

Emergencies

Accidents and other emergencies happen, and when they do, they will tax your efficiency and professionalism. Hopefully, there are contingency plans in place to help deal with these situations. Preplanning is paramount.

If someone becomes ill or injured while attending your program, you will be required to make some decisions quickly and under pressure. Depending on a host of variables (communications available, proximity to assistance, seriousness of emergency, and so on), you have two major responsibilities: assist the injured/sick individual and direct the rest of the group. Your immediate concern must be for the injured individual's welfare; however, leadership for the group also remains your responsibility. People in the group understand the higher need, they

The old saying about lemons and lemonade should be tempered with well-thought-out alternative plans. Coordinated actions provide consistency and a professional approach for dealing with surprises. Courtesy of Oregon Caves N.M., NPS

just want to be recognized and directed. Generally, it is best to keep the group together and, where appropriate, enlist their assistance (Is anyone a doctor? Does anyone have a cell phone?). If the emergency requires that you leave the group, consider selecting a reliable individual to act as leader to make sure the entire group gets back to the staging area safely, but choose wisely, because you are still responsible for everyone's safety. Know and understand your agency's policies for handling emergencies and the protocol to follow for seeking and conducting any necessary follow-up after an emergency.

Alternative Plans

A good interpreter will have clear alternative plans in case there are such problems as a power outage, equipment failure, weather issues, and so on. As with all emergencies, preplanning is vitally important. Discuss with staff and mutually agree on what to do when things don't go right. There will be times when one or more minor emergencies occur and you'll be glad you worked with your colleagues to develop a plan for dealing with what-if issues.

Good interpreters should be able to "go on with the show" without electricity or the planned equipment. You may need to alter your presentation, consider the safety and comfort of the audience, and/or decrease the length of the program, but simple inconveniences should not automatically cancel a program. Assume your audience members came just to learn from your program … don't disappoint them!

> *Our job is to integrate these various truths into the whole truth, which should be our only loyalty.*
> —Abraham Maslow, 1908–1970

Table 11.1

Verbal

Speaker's point of view—From what perspective does the interpreter speak? What assumptions does she/he make about the topic and audience?

Pronoun usage—Are masculine pronouns used when referring to gender-neutral objects? Are feminine pronouns used diminutively?

Euphemisms—Are euphemisms used to diminish the importance of sensitive or controversial issues, such as slaves/servants?

Terminology—Are terms used with cultural sensitivity?

Nonverbal

Eye contact—With whom does the interpreter make the most eye contact?

Body language—What does body language communicate about accessibility/ inaccessibility or interest/disinterest?

Gestures—Are gestures used to prompt or silence members of the audience, to communicate interest/disinterest?

Positioning—Where does the interpreter spend the most time?

Inclusion—Who gets called upon? With whom does the interpreter spend time? What questions are asked of different students/visitors?

—Adapted from the National Park Service, 1997

Bias and "Truth"

Dealing with bias and the "truth" can be tricky. Bias in its purest form means prejudice, and each individual's truth is in the eye of the beholder. Bias can be overt or unintended; it can be delivered verbally or with body language, and in written or graphic form. Examples of bias or prejudice in

In Chapter 2, we discussed the three basic types of messages that we interpret for the public: cultural, natural, and managerial. In each of these, it is important to present a fair, unbiased, and accurate picture of one whole story. The key for accuracy is to conduct honest, thorough, and unbiased research in an attempt to truly understand the concept, theory, story, or fact.

personal communication are exhibited through such actions as addressing comments exclusively to the men in the audience, not making eye contact with individuals who are physically disabled, or not directly addressing a person of a particular ethnic group. Interpreters must constantly endeavor to identify and then remove bias from their presentations. The National Park Service interpretive training Module 201 (see table 11.1) offers the following forms of bias, prejudice, and stereotyping (1997, 3). Take time to assess if you recognize any of these in your style.

Truth, especially in the cultural sense, is determined by the historical context in which it occurred. Remember in Chapter 2, we discussed that history is not a fact, but rather an interpretation of an event by a person who recorded it, the time in which it occurred, and by those of us who are receiving it today. As more historical information is discovered, the interpretation of that event is adjusted. There are many perspectives from which to tell a story. Be careful that you accurately reflect the culture and the historic "facts" and are not simply playing into stereotypes. Avoid dogmatic certainty when interpreting a historical event. Incorporating qualifiers such as: *Based on what we now know …* or *It appears that …* will provide the caveat for additional truths and biases to be accommodated.

Conversely, there will be current critical or controversial issues to address. When presenting your agency's perspectives, it is the interpreter's job to present the unbiased truths from various viewpoints and inspire the public to learn more. As Larry Beck and Ted T. Cable state, "The difference between alienating people *over* an issue, educating people *about* an issue or inspiring people *by* an issue is in the interpreter's approach" (1998, 162). As with any talk, we must be a good host and provide our guests with well-researched and impartial information. We should influence decisions based on revelation and inspiration, not dogma.

Live Animals

Using live animals in your interpretive programs can be extremely educational, exciting, and fun; however, in some instances, their use incites controversy. Animals are a sensational prop, offering a real hands-on opportunity to interpret the lives, roles, adaptations, individual characteristics of species, ecology of living creatures, and a host of other topics. If you are employed at a zoo, exhibiting animals comes naturally. If you are employed by a resource-conservation agency, the controversy and conflict arises when the public questions the necessity for causing such stress to a live animal. You must

Using living things adds interest to a presentation, but not without risk. Continuously convey respect and concern for the featured specimen. Courtesy of Carolyn Widner Ward

be able to justify your actions and build visitor confidence in your methods. Many visitors will want to know the rationale for keeping wild animals. It is extremely important that you clarify your constant concern for the animal's welfare. Realize, though, that some visitors may never be comfortable with the use of live animals for any purpose.

Keeping captive animals requires a huge commitment, knowledge of the law, and an effective public-relations program. In most cases, it is more practical to know where animals can be found within the resource and to interpret their habits and habitats on-site. A well-informed interpreter will know where the native bird is nesting, the migratory pattern of the butterflies, or the best time to view the tide pool animals. Experiencing animals in their natural habitat is an extremely effective catalyst for discussion and understanding.

How you stage an on-site live-animal presentation is of the utmost importance. Prepare the audience before they encounter the animal. Explain the ground rules in your cognitive map discussion of expectations. Request a peaceful, respectful atmosphere. Introduce the theme and discuss your sub-themes prior to displaying or "discovering" the animal. Once the animal is exhibited or pointed out, most attention will be on it, not on you. When handling the animal, always show the utmost care, respect, and safety. Your behavior is a model for the audience. In addition, exhibit care and respect for your audience. Some people may only want to watch from afar; some people may possess a genuine fear. Certainly don't force the encounter.

Publicizing

You may have prepared the most wonderful interpretive program, but if no one attends because they don't know about it, what good is it? Informing your potential audience about the *when*, *where*, and *why* of the program is extremely important to its success

> ### Field Tips for Live-Animal Programs
>
> **Set expectations for audience behavior and respect for the animal *before* displaying it.**
>
> **Never endanger an animal's health or well-being.** If it shows stress, stop.
>
> **Emphasize the fact that wild animals require special care, that they are not pets.**
>
> **Avoid humanizing animals.**
>
> **Explain natural behaviors and relate the role of the animal in an ecosystem.**
>
> —Adapted from Kathleen Regnier, Michael Gross, and Ron Zimmerman, 1994

or failure. There are numerous options for getting the word out.

Personal invitations, bulletin-board postings, and advertising through the media are the primary avenues for publicizing interpretive programs. As we learned in Chapter 2, timely, attractive, and attention-getting correspondence will make the difference in whether your announcement gets much interest. Selecting your words carefully will also make a difference. See table 11.2 for an example for developing an attention-getting advertisement for a walk.

Advertising—An Example

An amble, a scramble, a saunter, a stroll, or a strident march—how you *advertise* the walk potentially determines the audience. The description helps visitors decide if they are interested in participating in the walk. It is important that you know the audience and match your description, purpose, and the theme to the group. Visitors who understand what they are getting into will be much more receptive to your interpretive message.

Visitors attend walks for numerous reasons. Hopefully, they want to learn about

Table 11.2
Comparing Two Examples of Program Advertisements

Today's discovery walk is very easy. We will only walk one-half mile.

The short mileage might sound perfect to a more sedentary person, but it could send a message that the walk is too easy for active people. The description also says nothing about what the audience will "discover."

Instead, describe the event this way:

Today's walk along a relatively easy one-half-mile trail will last one hour. Join us for an action-packed tour as we discover many facets of the Yurok culture, present and past.

With a description such as this, you are much more likely to attract both sedentary and active participants. Some people will read "easy," others will read "action-packed," and even others will think "history." Advertise carefully to attract the broadest range of participants.

the resource and are willing to do so in an active manner. When you advertise the program, use terminology that makes it appealing to the broadest audience possible. For instance, some people may be disinclined

Use Titles That Entice

- ➤ Walk along the path of the native peoples.
- ➤ Explore the ancient art of recycling—decomposition.
- ➤ Wade the wetlands to discover nature's recyclers.
- ➤ Stroll through the backstreets of history.

to go on a "hike," but call it "stroll" and you may capture a wider audience.

Walks are generally expressed in time requirements instead of mileage, but it is best to provide both. Variations of pace, terrain, number of stops, complexity of the program, and an array of other issues make advertising just the length of a walk in distance a poor indication of commitment for the visitors.

Activity Schedules

Design activity schedules with visitors in mind. Don't forget that staff, volunteers, other agencies, the media, and other audiences will use the schedules as well. The normal *what*, *when*, and *where* issues need to be addressed in an understandable and brief manner. This doesn't mean that the program announcement should look like a timetable. Your program title should make individuals curious and want to attend the program. The title should convey the essence of your theme, if not the theme itself. The write-up should be short, alluring, and informative.

As we see in table 11.3, how you advertise programs potentially determines your audience. All activity schedules should incorporate the four Cs: clear, concise, correct, and compelling. Use active, eloquent, and positive statements to describe program offerings. Select words that are exciting, informative, and hint at the mysteries of the topic. Words such as "discover," "explore," "reveal," "realize," and "unearth" are likely to entice visitors to attend. Terms such as "study," "learn," "investigate," and "research" sound like you are presenting a

In Chapter 2, we learned that nonpersonal interpretation is nonlinear—the visitors read only what they desire. When advertising your program, give the potential audience more than just the topic (title) of the presentation—grab their attention with the theme.

Table 11.3
Activity Announcement Example

Here's an example of an activity announcement for one day.
Other announcements on the page should have similar formatting.

10:30 A.M.

Walk   *Indians, Explorers, and Settlers: 40-Year Conflict*   One hour

Join volunteer Lee Smith on a moderately difficult one-mile amble exploring sensitive locations that have experienced cultural clashes for centuries. Walk begins in front of the visitor center. Bring water and wear comfortable walking shoes.

3:00 P.M.

Junior Rangers   *Peninsular Bighorn Sheep—Myths and Marvels*   One hour

Children ages seven to 12 are invited to join ranger Chris Doe to investigate the life, legends, and amazing mysteries of the largest park mammal. Meet at the campfire center.

7:30 P.M.

Campfire   *Bats of Borrego and Beyond*   One hour

Bats are in the air, everywhere! Join interpreter Pat Jones for a bat patrol at the campfire center. Discover why these mysterious night hunters are disappearing, why that's bad, and how you can help save them.

---

lecture. Remember, the audience is probably on vacation. They may not mind learning something new, but they probably don't want to work *too* hard at it.

Bulletin Boards

Bulletin boards are often the most underused and neglected communication media in parks. Generally, bulletin boards are used to orient visitors and communicate basic rules and information. Organizing attractive, functional bulletin boards for quick scanning and recognition of topics is the ultimate goal. Do whatever it takes to make it easy for visitors to find the information they are looking for and need to know. Don't forget, as we discussed in Chapter 2, most visitors only read about 20 to 30 seconds' worth of material.

Bulletin boards that are divided into distinct sections using color and graphics to attract attention greatly assist the visitor in

locating information. A picture is worth a thousand words. Visitors may give up finding

Eighty percent of our visitors don't attend programs, activities, and events. Lure them with well-organized and attractive bulletin boards. Courtesy of Carolyn Widner Ward

Field Tips for Good Media Relations

Establish liaisons with media outlets prior to requesting free advertising of your news and activities. Keep in touch with media representatives.

Know media requirements, desired formats, and deadlines. Continually update a list of phone, fax, and e-mail addresses.

Treat all media equally. Be honest.

Remember the four Cs (clear, concise, correct, compelling) when developing your PSA. Answer the who, what, where, when, why, and how information in the opening statement (lead).

Use official letterhead with agency identity, contact information, and topic title easily identified.

For print media, double-space text and/or provide an electronic version.

Provide tape/text for radio/TV in broadcast time frames (10-, 20-, 30-, 60-second). Generally, allow for about 20 to 30 words per 10 seconds air time. When written script is prepared for radio/TV broadcast, provide phonetics for difficult words and names.

James Fazio and Douglas Gilbert state that "News stories usually adhere to a highly structured, standardized format. This is shown as the inverted pyramid." (2000, 245) (figure 11.1).

needed information if the bulletin board is a jumble of stapled pages. Clearly identifying program activities using active titles that reflect the theme and vivid, descriptive, concise information will make the bulletin board more approachable.

Media Releases

Advertising interpretive programs off-site to the general public is a great way to attract the local public and a wider audience than might

otherwise attend programs. Refer to the agency or published media guides for comprehensive direction, structure, and format assistance when writing these public service announcements (PSA). Use PSA for all media, including newspapers, magazines, radio, and television. Develop a good, effective relationship with your local media. Know what type of information they desire, what format they prefer (electronic, hard copy, verbal), and what their deadlines are.

Personal Invitations

The finest and most direct method to publicize interpretive programs is through a warm, sincere, and personal invitation. Don't forget to occasionally invite the local media to your programs. Personal invitations to visitors can be extended while the individuals are attending another program, at staffed entrance stations, visitor centers, and offices. They can also be extended in casual, chance meetings and while roving. In Chapter 10, we discussed the benefits of contacting visitors in diverse locations throughout the resource. Realizing that only about 20 percent of visitors attend our formal programs, and that

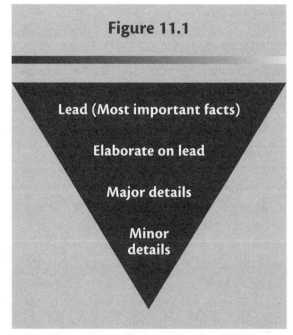

Figure 11.1

Lead (Most important facts)

Elaborate on lead

Major details

Minor details

Adapted from James Fazio and Douglas Gilbert (2000)

Personal invitations are the most effective method for publicizing interpretive programs. Courtesy of Oregon Caves N.M., NPS

bulletin boards are often underused, your personal communication with visitors may be the only way they learn of the interpretive program offerings. Be a good host.

In the Next Chapter ...

Having explored the various personal interpretive program types and essential issues common to all, we'll now focus our attention on multisensory program-delivery devices that can be used to enhance these presentations. Audiovisual equipment options will be highlighted, along with a brief discussion of copyright law and photographic techniques.

Review

1. The Americans with Disabilities Act (ADA) is a civil rights law.

2. ADA legislation legally requires leisure-services providers to facilitate and support the full participation of individuals with disabilities in all leisure programs. As professionals, we should provide interpretive programs where all visitors are included. Special programs are not the desired solution.

3. Auxiliary aids are devices or services that help provide equal access to programs or activities.

4. People with disabilities are individuals. Focus on ability rather than disability. Always think of the person first.

5. The three most common ailments for seniors are arthritis, hearing loss, and visual impairment. Although age is not considered a disability, older adults can benefit from simple modifications or additions to interpretive programs and facilities.

6. Language barriers present an ever-increasing challenge for communication. When using a language translator, reduce your content by about half to allow for translation time.

7. Use your people skills to overcome disruptions to the program. Defuse potential distractions before they become a problem. Don't ignore troublesome issues; your audience deserves your professional approach.

8. Preplanning for potential accidents and other emergencies is paramount. Analyze the situation, maintain control, and take appropriate action. Deal with the immediate emergency, but don't forget you are still responsible for the entire audience.

9. Establish alternative or back-up plans for equipment failures, weather issues, and other program-altering changes well in advance of the problem.

10. Bias is a form of prejudice. It can be overt or unintended.

11. Truth has many versions. Be careful not to take sides.

12. Live animals are sensational props, but their use may be controversial.

13. Market programs so that the maximum number of people know what, when, and where they are available. Entice the potential audience with catchy titles, exciting words, and personal connections.

14. Bulletin-board information must be organized, attractive, and very quickly readable.

15. Establish connections with your local media. Know what they want, how they want it delivered, and when they need it.

16. The most direct method to advertise interpretive programs is through personal invitations.

Questions and Exercises

1. "Special" interpretive programs should be created for the disabled. (Explain your answer.)

   True or false? Why?

2. People with disabilities are individuals. What does "always put the person first" mean?

3. List the three primary concerns that should be addressed when designing programs for elderly adults.

4. List three auxiliary aids that help provide equal access to programs or activities.

5. When using a language translator, reduce content by how much to allow for translation time?

6. What's the "bottom line" when encountering a distraction during the program?

7. In the historical context, what is meant by the statement "there are many truths"?

8. What's the controversy with keeping wild animals for exhibit?

9. Which of the following are appropriate methods of publicizing programs. (Circle all that apply.) Why?

   Bulletin boards

   Personal invitations

   Media releases

   Entrance-stations handouts

References

Books

Axtell, Roger. 1991. *Gestures: The Do's and Taboos of Body Language around the World.* New York: John Wiley and Sons, Inc.

Beck, Larry and Ted T. Cable. 1998. *Interpretation for the 21st Century.* Champaign, Ill.: Sagamore Publishing.

Fazio, James and Douglas L. Gilbert. 2000. *Public Relations and Communications for Natural Resource Managers, Third Edition.* Dubuque, Iowa: Kendall/Hunt Publishing Company.

Ham, Sam H. 1992. *Environmental Interpretation: A Practical Guide for People with Big Ideas and Small Budgets.* Golden, Colo.: Fulcrum Publishing.

Knudson, Douglas, Ted T. Cable, and Larry Beck. 1995. *Interpretation of Cultural and Natural Resources.* State College, Pa.: Venture Publishing.

Porter, E. 1994. *All Visitors Welcome: Accessibility in State Park Interpretive Programs and Facilities.* Sacramento: California Department of Parks and Recreation.

Regnier, Kathleen, Michael Gross, and Ron Zimmerman. 1994. *The Interpreter's Guidebook: Techniques for Programs and Presentations, Third Edition.* Stevens Point, Wisc.: UW-SP Foundation Press.

Sharpe, Grant. 1982. *Interpreting the Environment, Second Edition.* New York: John Wiley and Sons, Inc.

Smith, Ralph W., David R. Austin, and Dan W. Kennedy. 1996. *Inclusive and Special Recreation: Opportunities for Persons with Disabilities, Third Edition.* Madison, Wisc.: Brown & Benchmark Publishers.

Stensrud, Carol Jean. 1993. *A Training Manual for Americans with Disabilities Act Compliance in Parks and Recreation Settings.* State College, Pa.: Venture Publishing.

Online

The Center for Universal Design, North Carolina State University. www.design.ncsu.edu/cud.

National Center on Accessibility, Indiana University. www.ncaonline.org.

National Park Service. Interpretive Competencies, Interpretive Development Program. www.nps.gov/idp/interp/competencies.htm.

U.S. Bureau of the Census, Population Division. www.census.gov/population.

U.S. Department of Justice, Americans with Disabilities Act Home Page. www.usdoj.gov/crt/ada/.

Pamphlet

Adaptive Environments Center, Inc. 1992. "The Americans with Disabilities Act Fact Sheet Series." Washington D.C.: National Institute on Disability and Rehabilitation Research.

Papers

Dwyer, John. 1993. "Customer Diversity and the Future Demand for Outdoor Recreation." Paper presented at the Technology Assessment and Future Analysis Working Group session at the Society of American Foresters' National Convention, Nov. 7–10, Indianapolis, Ind.

Geiger, Roy and W. Kay Ellis. 1991. "Attracting Senior Visitors to Your Programs and Facilities." In Proceedings, National Interpreters' Workshop, Vail, Colo.

Chapter 12

Multisensory Equipment: Audiovisual

Capturing a fleeting moment with a photograph allows you to share it with
visitors for years to come. Keep your camera handy. Courtesy of Alan E. Wilkinson

Employing multisensory program-
delivery devices enhances presentations,
increases understanding, facilitates
message retention, and improves
visitor enjoyment.

Main Points

Interpretive programs can be enhanced with the use of audiovisual equipment (A/V). A/V presentations range from the very basic, such as using a flip chart, to much more sophisticated computer- and projector-integrated presentations. This chapter will provide an overview of the various tools that can help

Make things as simple as possible, but not simpler.

—Albert Einstein 1879–1955

provide personal interpretive programs that appeal to the eyes and ears of your target audience. We'll discuss the advantages, disadvantages, proper operation, and maintenance of A/V equipment. We'll also briefly discuss copyright law and basic principles of photography.

Even though in our fast-paced world, technology seems to be driving much of what our visitors have come to expect, don't be misled. The program styles that Enos Mills, John Muir, and Freeman Tilden offered more than a hundred years ago are still very well received and appreciated. The same principles of interpretive delivery apply, but with A/V, we can augment our presentations to be more diverse. More than 35 years ago, Tilden said, "Gadgets don't supplant the personal contact; we accept them as valuable alternatives and supplements" (Tilden 1967, 97). Much has changed, but the principle still holds true.

While A/V equipment is designed to aid in various presentations, it certainly need not be applied in all situations. Visual aids should act as a supplement to your thematic program, not the driving force behind its creation. As we discussed in Chapter 6, visual aids add to the program, but all programs should be able to stand alone. Before incorporating A/V equipment into the program, ask if it contributes to the understanding of the theme. Do the "whistles and bells" support or detract from your message?

Once again, it is your responsibility to have an appropriate theme, know the audience, and employ suitable techniques that enhance delivery of the presentation. As is the case with any sophisticated piece of equipment, it is critical to familiarize yourself with the proper setup and operation well in advance of your actual presentation. Use of A/V technological gadgets is tempting, and most interpreters want to incorporate them into programs. With that in mind, while it is not the intent of this chapter to discuss specific brands and models of equipment, we will provide an overview of a variety of equipment and some applications in interpretive programming. Remember, the more technology used in your presentation, the more care and time you will need to invest during the preparation stages.

Equipment

Cameras

The most underutilized piece of equipment in an interpreter's arsenal is the camera; we simply don't use our cameras enough. As an interpreter, you are in a unique position to capture special interpretive moments with the camera that you can share in the future. Experience and practice will make you less preoccupied with the mechanics of the camera and more able to relate to the scene and the final picture. Experiment with the full range of controls offered by the camera, and you will soon become more comfortable and proficient at photo-composition. Let's now focus on the two most popular types of cameras: 35mm film and digital.

Traditional or Technology— Which Is Better?

This discussion has been going on for decades. Is calligraphy better than moveable type? Is a painting better than a photograph? Is the movie better than the book? Is the CD better than the live performance? And so on. With so many new technologies available, the challenge for the interpreter is to choose those tools that help connect the audience with the resource. Use the media that clarifies, reinforces, and enhances your message, not just razzamatazz with smoke and mirrors.

35mm Film

While there are many models of 35mm film cameras available, the two basic types are single-lens reflex (SLR) and compact cameras (point-and-shoot). The SLR allows you to look directly through the lens at the intended subject. With most compact cameras, the subject is seen through a viewfinder that is separate from the camera lens.

Compact cameras, which are relatively small and inexpensive, have become

Field Tips for Using 35mm Film

Film for both the SLR and compact cameras is **available in three different types:** color negative (print), color transparency (slide), and black-and-white negative (print).

Film quality measurably degrades over time, so take note of the expiration date on the packaging. In addition, film is adversely affected by extreme heat and humidity.

Unexposed film will remain good for six months to a year if stored properly.

Shoot lots of film! A *National Geographic* photographer on a short assignment will shoot as many as 400 rolls of film!

Film has different speeds or sensitivity ratings. Film with a faster speed captures action and is better in reduced-lighting situations. Film with a slower speed is good for very sharp pictures in bright light. The speed of the film is identified by the ISO (International Standards Organization) or ASA (American Standards Association) number located on the package. An ISO/ASA of 25 to 64 is considered slow, 100 to 200 medium, 400 fast, with very high-speed film at 800-plus.

Always take your camera! Make your camera a standard part of your kit bag. You never know when that perfect shot will appear. Courtesy of Alan E. Wilkinson

increasingly popular. They commonly include features such as automatic film advance and rewind, automatic exposure, automatic flash, and automatic focus. A compact 35mm camera is an excellent choice for casual photography. The point-and-shoot capability makes them

extremely convenient and requires less technological knowledge regarding focus, exposure, lens choices, and shutter speeds. In addition, because they are lightweight and compact, they are easy to pick up at a moment's notice. All of these features assist in taking pictures, but good photographic skills are still required for the best results.

Despite their more technical characteristics, SLR cameras continue to be very popular. In spite of the fact that they are larger, more expensive, and require more technical skills, they are favored for their interchangeable lenses and their ability to be fine-tuned by the operator. Those with photographic experience usually favor an SLR over a point-and-shoot camera. When focusing on an image with an SLR camera, you are actually looking at your subject through the camera's picture-taking lens. Viewing the actual image formed by the lens is important both in terms of extremely accurate viewfinding and focusing as well as allowing for

Field Tips for Storing Film

Storing film in the freezer is not recommended. While it may slow the natural aging process of the film emulsion, it won't necessarily increase the useful life. Depending on the film's ISO rating, ambient radiation can deteriorate film, and freezing does not lessen that. It is also possible that odors and fumes from food stored in the same refrigerator or freezer will contaminate the film, or vice versa.

If the film has been stored in a moisture-proof package in a cool environment (refrigerator), it may be satisfactory a year past its expiration date; however, under poor storage conditions—high temperature and/or humidity—film can degrade before it becomes outdated.

If you do store film in your freezer, leave the entire package unopened. The plastic can help protect the film from moisture damage, and the outer cardboard packaging provides valuable information that you will need when you are ready to use the film. It's a good idea to place the unopened film package inside a plastic bag for additional protection and keep it away from foods. When removing film from the freezer, do not open the sealed film package until the film has reached room temperature (about 90 minutes). If you open the moisture-resistant plastic can too soon, condensation could form on the film surface and result in spots on your pictures.

—Adapted from Eastman Kodak Company, 2002

preview of the vast effects and range of accessories available.

Digital

Outwardly, there is very little difference between a digital camera and a 35mm film camera. They come in both SRL and compact styles and have basically the same options, including automatic exposure, flash, and focus. In the 35mm film camera, light coming through the lens is recorded on film. On digital cameras, incoming colors are sensed electronically on a charge-coupled device (CCD) or complementary metal oxide semiconductor (CMOS). The data from the CCD/CMOS is written to electronic memory. In the field, instead of changing a roll of film, you change to a new memory stick or disk.

Professionals estimate that an 8.3-megapixel digital camera with a full-frame sensor would have resolution equal to 35mm film. Is cost not a factor? Full-frame 10- to 15-megapixel cameras are now available!

To ensure you have the best picture quality, you should always get as close to the subject as possible. Cropping a digital photo takes away valuable image data important to printing.

So, which camera is best? That's like asking if a knife or a pair of scissors is better. For some jobs, such as chopping carrots, the knife is better. Scissors are better for cutting cloth or clipping hair. So, too, a film-based camera is better for some jobs. Film is best for really detailed pictures, especially those you want to enlarge. A digital camera is better in other ways. Digital allows instant viewing of images, which are easy to manipulate and share electronically, and there is no cost for film or processing. Digital-camera technology is advancing so rapidly that it may soon supplant film cameras for most jobs. Currently, several factors deter digital cameras from completely replacing film cameras, including resolution, the knowledge to operate a computer with appropriate software, and cost.

Digital Photography

Photography is the process of capturing images. With film, you have slides, negatives, or prints that can be digitally scanned. With a digital camera, you have images that can be electronically transferred, printed, or made into slides. So, what are some of the advantages and disadvantages of digital photography?

Advantages	Disadvantages
Instant gratification—easily deleted photos	Longer time needed between shots
No film or processing costs	Expensive equipment and software
Easily imported into computer	Fragile in harsh environments
Increased image manipulation ability	Dependent on the computer
Easily stored and e-mailed	Generally, resolution is not as great
Resilient—won't fade, crack, or peel	Images can be accidentally deleted

So, Which Camera?

There is no "right" camera for every job. Sometimes film is the only medium that will provide the best photograph, and other times, digital will give you exactly what you need. What makes digital photography so exciting is that it opens a whole new environment to explore with opportunities that are parallel to, not substitutes for, traditional film-based photography. In this electronic age, the challenge is to learn what digital photography has to offer.

Information is "captured" when a picture is taken. An average digital camera's memory may record several million bits, or pixels, of information. The silver-halide crystals in 35mm film record hundreds of millions, even billions, of bits of information! A digital scan that captures the equivalent data or resolution of a 35mm slide will create a digital file of over 40MB (megabytes). Now that's resolution! The more details captured, the more realistic the image, and the better the ability to enlarge the photograph without losing quality.

Field Tips for Using Lenses

Opportunities for interesting photos are greater when you employ a variety of lenses. Changing from a normal to a telephoto lens brings in distant subjects. Changing to a wide-angle lens includes more of the area surrounding your subject.

A macro lens allows you to focus on objects as close as one to two inches from the camera. This is a very useful lens for photographing wildflowers, insects, and fine graphic details. It also works well for copy stand work.

Digital cameras approaching the higher film resolution are currently very expensive. Some of the more sophisticated software employed to manipulate the digital image is also very expensive. As technology continues to advance, the trend is certainly pointed toward higher resolution chips, increased memory, and lower overall costs.

Lenses

One of the most critical components of any camera is the lens. The lens plays a vital role in determining the picture quality. Developing your skills to take full advantage of the various types of lenses of the camera pays dividends in terms of better, more exciting pictures. The ability to accept interchangeable lenses is a feature that greatly adds to the versatility of many cameras.

There are four main types of lenses: normal, zoom, wide-angle, and telephoto. Each lens has its particular uses. The normal lens provides a natural perspective and an angle of view similar to the central vision of the eye (45 to 55 millimeters). A zoom lens offers all the focal lengths that fall within that particular zoom range (35 to 135 millimeters). A wide-angle lens offers a shorter focal length than the normal lens with a greater angle of view (28 to 35 millimeters). A telephoto lens provides a narrower angle of view, making distant objects appear a great deal closer (100 to 200-plus millimeters).

Copy Stands

Think of a copy stand as a specialized camera tripod that allows you to precisely photograph still objects. At the basic level, a copy stand is very simple to use and consists of few moving parts. There is a base, a column, and an attachment on the column that holds the camera. A copy stand may or may not have lights.

Use a copy stand to photograph pages from books, photographs, and other small, flat objects. If you use slide film, the photographs

Obtain written permission from the owner before photographing copyrighted material. U.S. government publications are in the public domain and do not require permission to reproduce.

can then be directly incorporated into your slide program. If you use a digital camera, images can be directly incorporated into your digital-presentation software program. Converting from digital to a slide for a slide-projector program is a time-consuming and costly process, and you may lose quality. Digitally scanning bound manuscripts, fragile, or larger items may be difficult or impossible to accomplish with the common flatbed scanner, but would be easy to photograph with a copy stand.

When using a copy stand, you need to control glare, shadows, and the level of lighting. Reflectors that fill in shadows, diffusers that soften harsh light, and lights to illuminate the subject can all assist in accomplishing this goal. While good copy work can be done with ambient light, more-consistent results are obtained by using enhanced lighting. The copy stand should be mounted on a low table so the camera controls and eyepiece are at a comfortable height. A zoom lens on your camera will allow you to frame the subject without moving the camera.

Projectors

Showing images to a large audience requires some type of projection device. Just as we've seen with cameras, there are different types of projectors. Some, such as the slide and movie projector, have been used for a long time, while others, such as the LCD (liquid crystal display), are just beginning to be employed. Overhead and opaque projectors fill special needs and are used only on particular occasions.

Slide Projectors

A slide projector is basically a piece of equipment containing a light source and lens system that focuses an image from a slide transparency mounted in a cardboard, glass, metal, or plastic frame onto a screen. Projected slides produce life-size, high-quality images that are sharp and have the brightest colors of any comparable media, for a fraction of the cost. They are portable, easy to set up, relatively inexpensive, and can project numerous individual images in a controlled sequence. Some models have features such as a built-in rear-viewing screen, reading light, high-intensity light source, random access, automatic advance, and automatic focus. Slides are contained in trays, cartridges, carousels, or drums for use

Field Tips for Using a Copy Stand

Keep the material being photographed as flat as possible. Use nonglare glass or straps to hold the page.

Have a grid on the base to help align objects.

If the whole scene is not needed, use your lens to zoom in close or lay a mask surrounding the image.

Use a remote control to release the shutter to minimize movement.

Use an 18 percent grayscale card to set the exposure. Grayscale cards are commonly available at photography stores.

Use a blue "80A" filter on your copy stand lens if you are using a regular incandescent lightbulb.

To avoid unwanted reflections, align lights at a 45-degree angle to the work being copied. Remember to turn off overhead lights.

Use your camera's built-in light meter to determine proper settings. Most modern cameras have automatic modes of operation.

> *You cannot depend on your eyes when your imagination is out of focus.*
>
> —Mark Twain, 1835–1910

in appropriately designed projectors.

In Chapter 8, we discussed how to put together a slide program. Using a single projector is straightforward, but, once again, knowing your equipment and practicing how to use it properly are the key steps to a professionally delivered program. We will discuss the use of two or more projectors with a lapse dissolve and sync recorder later in this chapter. Since the specific model of projectors vary, this chapter will focus on more-general issues and problems associated with slide projectors.

Field Tips for Automatic Focus

The automatic-focusing mechanism is very delicate and critically aligned. It can easily be thrown out of adjustment if your projector is dropped or damaged.

Automatic focus is accomplished optically using light reflected off the emulsion surface of the slide. The projector detects extremely small changes in the position of each slide. All slides must be inserted with the emulsion side facing the same direction or some slides may be slightly out of focus.

For proper automatic-focus operation, you must focus the first slide manually.

If the slides are loaded correctly, then all the other slides should focus automatically.

Does your projector even have automatic focus? On a Kodak projector, look for an "A" or "AF" in the model number. This indicates that it has automatic focus. If it has automatic focus, check that the switch is in the "on" position.

Warped or damaged slide mounts may never focus properly.

The slide projector is extremely durable and reliable. With care, periodic maintenance, and cleaning, it will serve you well. Generally, there are few problems that arise, and most can be solved easily if you are familiar with the instructions in the owner's manual. Following are several of the more common problems.

- The projector won't reverse; it only goes forward, even when repeatedly pressing the remote reverse button. You may not be holding down the reverse button long enough. Kodak slide projectors are designed in such a way that you must depress and hold the reverse button for a little while longer than the forward button. If you just tap the reverse button, the machine will go forward.

- The projector advances on its own. Check that the automatic timer is not turned on. Even if it is off, this timing device may be defective or worn out on older projectors.

- One of the most common problems is not with the projector, but with a slide jammed in the tray. There are several ways to rectify this, depending on the projector and the tray. Look for a silver latch at the center of the tray. Push it, and the tray should release. The other common method of releasing the slide tray requires using a coin. If you don't

Which Tray Is Best?

Only use an 80-slide tray. The 140-slide trays jam more often, because the slots are very close together. If you have more than 80 slides (you probably should not), it's much better to use two 80-slide trays rather than run the risk of a jam. Better yet, develop a lapse-dissolve presentation using a dissolve unit and two 80-slide trays.

see a silver latch, look for a slot in the middle of the projector in the center of the jammed slide tray. Place a coin in the slot and turn to release the tray. Once you have freed the tray, turn the tray upside down (first, make sure the locking ring is secure or the slides will fall out) and spin the metal plate so the slot lines up with the beginning notch in the tray (#0). A click sounds as these two line up. Turn the tray right side up, remove the locking ring, remove the slide from the projector, and then replace both the slide and the locking ring. Put the tray back on the projector and press down to seat it properly. Press and hold the "index" button, and spin the tray to where you left off.

The time to learn these solutions is not during a formal presentation, but during practice sessions. Although you may not jam a slide, see if you can follow these steps to rectify the situation just in case it happens during your talk. In addition, turn the tray over and make sure all the round posts on the circumference of the tray are there. If any are broken off or badly chipped, replace the tray.

Film Projectors

We will just say a few words about 16mm film projectors. Film projector use is not terribly common, but a few are still used in some locations. Historic and natural history films that are not available in other mediums, such as video and DVD, present the most likely application for a film projector. If you plan to show a movie that is appropriate to your theme, make sure the projector is working correctly and that you are thoroughly familiar with its operation.

Just before showing a film to your audience, you should test your equipment again. A good technique is to thread and advance the film through the blank film

---

Field Tips for Loading Slides

Remove the locking ring from the tray. Hold each slide up to the light. If everything is facing the correct way (i.e., words read correctly and the sky is up), then turn the slide upside down. Put it in the tray facing the lowest number. After the slides are in, project them to double-check for accuracy, correct orientation, and quality. Then, for future reference, place a mark with a marking pen across the front and top of the slides to indicate the correct loading position. Make sure you securely replace the locking ring.

---

leader prior to the start of the presentation. Preset the film to begin with the opening title or your desired starting location. This will help you ensure that the projector is operating properly, the focus is correct, and the audio levels are comfortable. After focusing the film, don't forget to secure the lens lock. Remain near the projector throughout the showing in order to be able to quickly make any necessary adjustments and to trouble-shoot.

Field Tips to Answer "Yes" before Projecting a Film

Have you read the instructions, and do you understand how to operate the projector?

Have you cleaned the aperture and optical components?

Have you threaded the film correctly?

Are both loops the correct size?

Is the film gate closed?

Is the film properly started on the take-up spool, with all the slack removed?

Is the reverse switch set at "forward"?

Is the rewind lever in the "run" position?

While the primary A/V equipment of most multimedia interpretive programs has been the slide projector, the trend is toward the computerized version of a slide program using computer-presentation software and an LCD projector.

LCD Projectors

In the ever-growing world of modern technology, the popularity of computers to generate presentations is rapidly increasing. Today's laptop computers, coupled with many of the common software packages and an LCD projector, offer another exciting tool to the interpreter. An LCD projector is a self-contained unit that combines red, green, and blue LCD panels and a light source for a computer and/or video-projection device. LCD projectors come in a wide variety of sizes and specifications.

People only see what they are prepared to see.
—Ralph Waldo Emerson, 1803–1892

LCD equipment can be expensive, depending on the features and options offered. It requires the support of a computer and appropriate technical software interfaces to work. Significant preparation is required to ensure that you are thoroughly familiar with the system and that everything is working properly.

With the advent of presentation software and the vast resources of the Internet, computer-projected images have become a popular high-tech A/V tool. Since there are literally thousands of laptop configurations, models, and resolutions, we cannot address

LCD is an acronym for liquid crystal display.

Always turn the projector on prior to starting the computer.

how each computer works with each projector. It is important to remember that changing projectors or computers results in an entirely different system. Just because the presentation worked on one computer does not necessarily mean that it will work on a different system.

Always turn on the projector before turning on the computer. Generally, the computer will detect the projector as an external monitor and will set itself up automatically. If turning on the computer first, the proper keystroke sequence is needed to get things working. Once again, know your equipment.

When projecting the program on the screen, be aware that LCD projectors have either a fixed or adjustable keystone factor. A fixed keystone projector needs to be placed at about an eight-degree angle lower than the center of the screen. Changing the vertical plane of the screen can allow some variation on placement of the projector. The adjustable feature found on some projectors allows for electronic correction of this distortion without having to worry about screen placement.

Maintenance for all A/V equipment is important; for LCD projectors it is critical. Clean or replace the filter regularly according the manufacturer's instructions, as the screen filter can quickly become dirty. A clogged

If the LCD projector won't turn on, don't panic. Check the filter door(s) to be sure they are closed. Most projectors have a safety switch associated with these doors that prevents the unit from operating unless the door is properly secured.

filter will cause the projector to overheat, shut down, and shorten lamp life. Even worse, the dust that collects on the filter will eventually make its way into the projector and deposit itself on the LCD panels. Once this happens, colored spots will develop in the image, and the projector will require expensive professional cleaning.

Overhead Projectors

An overhead projector is a device that produces an image on a screen by transmitting light through a transparency lying on the face or stage of the projector. The lens and mirror arrangement in an elevated housing make possible a bright, projected image in semidarkened or -lighted rooms. The overhead projector can be a very effective tool for school and community-service presentations and even campfire programs. While the current trend is heading toward the use of the LCD projector, the overhead projector is a viable presentation device that shouldn't be overlooked.

An overhead projector is a cost-effective presentation tool that can jazz up and add visual impact to your message. It has a number of features that give it tremendous versatility, including its ease of operation, its ability to be used in normal room lighting, and its operation from the front of the room with the interpreter visible to the audience. In addition, the low cost and ease of creating transparencies makes this an affordable option. With the overhead projector, you can write directly on the transparency as you project it. In other words, transparencies need not be entirely completed ahead of time. This allows you to disclose information in a manner that suits the message. These are key advantages that allow for audience interaction, customizing the presentation, and using a straightforward, practical projection system for visual aids.

Many consider the overhead projector only a tool for presenting text information; however, consider this medium to better

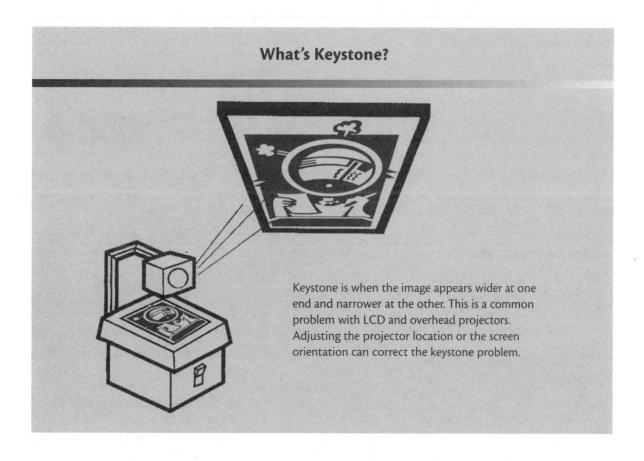

What's Keystone?

Keystone is when the image appears wider at one end and narrower at the other. This is a common problem with LCD and overhead projectors. Adjusting the projector location or the screen orientation can correct the keystone problem.

Field Tips for Making Transparencies

Blank acetate film provides a "chalkboard" for illustrating the program and spontaneously responding to audience questions and comments. More commonly, prepare your program ahead of time and make transparencies on clear film printed directly from the computer printer or made from copies on a copier.

use graphics, actively show progressions, and make connections to the audience. For example, a picture that could only be passed around or held up could be copied onto a transparency and projected. You can project a visual of an item on the screen in a less than completely dark environment while also displaying the physical item. The transparency reinforces and further clarifies the tangible, handheld object. It also allows the audience to take notes, read handout materials, and interact face-to-face with you. Being able to pick up verbal and nonverbal cues from the audience helps you to understand and update the presentation. Consider using an overhead projector for such programs as map reading and orientation discussions,

Lamp Options

Lamps are critical components of all overhead projectors and vary in type, life, wattage, and cost. Some projectors offer "high" and "low" switches. The low setting can greatly extend the life of the lamp. Some projectors also have a built-in lamp changer that allows you to switch over to another lamp if the first one fails. Know your equipment.

safety equipment demonstrations, and even sing-alongs.

Opaque Projectors

An opaque projector uses the principle of light reflection to create an image of non-transparent objects, such as printed or typed pages, stamps, coins, photographs, drawings, maps, diagrams, or flat objects in single sheets or in book form. Opaque projector images require a darkened room.

While this projector is rarely used during an audience presentation, it can be useful for preparing visual aids. By projecting and thereby enlarging items, you can then draw, trace, or examine the images more closely. Sam H. Ham discusses this as the projection method for do-it-yourself illustrations (Ham 1992, 116).

An overhead projector creates enough ambient light for the audience to see you as well as displayed handheld items, and to take notes. This semilighted environment also permits you to assess nonverbal feedback from your audience. Courtesy of Alan E. Wilkinson

Field Tips for Presenting Transparencies

Stand to the side of the overhead projector opposite your writing hand. This will make it easier to face your audience, write on the transparency, and not block the screen. Have enough room next to the projector to stack transparencies before and after you use them.

Avoid that blare of bright, projected light and cover the transparency with an opaque mask (piece of cardboard) when you are done projecting it. You may also turn the projector off, but beware: this can cause the projector bulb to burn out prematurely. Additionally, you can use a cover to progressively reveal topics one point at a time.

Have the top of the screen tilted forward toward the overhead projector (if possible) to prevent the keystone effect.

Protect transparencies to keep them clean and free of dust and scratches.

Format pages in landscape rather than portrait. This allows projection of the page a little higher on the screen and improves visibility to more of the audience.

Minimize text. Use an easy-to-read, sans-serif font, such as Arial.

Use different colors, including pen markers, for emphasis.

Write with transparency pens to illustrate, clarify, or highlight a point.

If you plan to use a transparency over again, be sure to use a water-soluble transparency pen or cover the transparencies with clear sleeves to avoid altering the original.

Screens

Projection screens are available in two basic types: front or rear screens. For most interpretive presentation purposes, a front projection screen is the obvious choice, simply because it can fit into any room without the need to build a rear-projection booth.

If you have the luxury of a rear-projection system, there are definite advantages. A rear screen permits the use of visuals in near-normal room lighting, your audience can take notes, and you can maintain eye contact. The rear-projection system allows the interpreter to walk in front of the screen without casting shadows. Locating projection equipment in a separate room minimizes noise and distractions.

The type of screen at your location is probably based on budget, need, sophistication of presentation, mobility/flexibility, and a host of other factors. In some outdoor locations, the screen is simply made of wood or a similar material covered with a flat white paint, while another location may have an electric, roll-down, beaded screen.

The in-house, constructed, painted screens, while not entirely desirable, can be repainted. Quite often, once a fabric screen is marred by graffiti, it must be replaced. Glass-beaded and rear-screen cleaning should be attempted with great care, because the beads or projected coatings can easily be damaged. Even "cleanable-surface" screens should be exposed to very light pressure using only mild soap and water. Use of chemical cleaners may destroy their reflective properties.

Lapse Dissolve and Audiovisual Sync Recorders

When presenting a slide show with one projector, there is a "blackout" between slides on the projected screen. With lapse-dissolve equipment and two slide projectors, one slide actually dissolves into the next slide without any blackout. This makes for a smoother transition from one slide to the other, presents a more professional-looking presentation, and is less disturbing to the eyes of the audience. By incorporating prerecorded music and narration, you can build on this professional presentation.

When producing a slide show that is synchronized with an audiotape, it is necessary to use a tape recorder that has at least two separate audio tracks. Audiovisual sync recorders have independent audio channels that allow for recording music or narration on one track and synchronizing signals for the dissolve control on the other track. During the performance, a tape playback unit amplifies the sound signal and transmits it through a speaker system. At the same time, the dissolve unit that controls the operation of the slide projectors detects the magnetic cues. A/V sync recorders are quite different from home stereo cassette recorders.

Three-projector multi-image programs allow for rapid-fire slides. They are especially effective in illustrating movement, change, and transformation. Courtesy of California State Parks, Cahill

Multi-Image Program

A dissolve or multi-image program will require a minimum of two projectors and a dissolve control. With these and a standard remote control, you can produce a traditional narrated program with smooth dissolves between the images.

A more advanced presentation will require the addition of a sync recorder and perhaps an additional projector. Believe it or not, a three-projector multi-image show is easier to create than a two-projector show! This is because with two projectors, one always has to wait for the dark projector to advance. This takes 1.5 seconds, during which you cannot bring up a new image. By having a third projector, there will seldom, if ever, be a time when you have to wait.

We discussed the steps for creating basic theme-based slide programs in Chapter 8. Once you have developed your program and wish to integrate it into a synchronized A/V production, you normally begin with recording the music and/or narration. Once you are satisfied with the audio portion, concentrate on integrating visuals. At this point, listen to the audio and record synchronizing signals from the lapse-dissolve control onto the second channel of the tape.

Sound Systems
The ideal sound system makes speech and music clearly and comfortably audible yet

When using a lapse dissolve, the dissolve unit and all projectors must be plugged in to a single power strip.

never draws attention to itself or its operation. Sound systems can be very basic, consisting of just a microphone, amplifier/mixer, and speakers. For larger applications, a sound system might need to be fairly complex, including a CD player, cassette recorder, amplifier/mixer, speakers, microphones, turntables, transmitters, and lots of wires. Become familiar with your particular equipment's operation, functional status, and its care and maintenance.

Microphones

The sound system begins at the microphone, where acoustic sound is converted into an electrical signal. A microphone is connected to an audio mixer, where the input signals are amplified, adjusted, and combined to produce a single output signal. From the mixer, the output signal is sent to a power amplifier. The amplifier strengthens the signal further, making it powerful enough to drive loudspeakers, which convert the microphone signals back into acoustic sound.

Microphones and the associated system amplify your voice and are useful for several reasons. They assist in not overtaxing your vocal cords, permit easier listening for the audience, and, especially when you are moving around, ensure that everyone can hear you. Microphones are available in wired and wireless versions with either handheld or clip-on capabilities.

The wireless clip-on, or lapel, microphone is preferred for its convenience and the full freedom of movement it offers. A

Whether you use one or multiple slide projectors with a lapse dissolve or an LED-projected software presentation, the mechanics for developing and presenting the program are much the same. Refer to Chapter 8 for a discussion on how to create an A/V program.

Feedback is that tortured howling that results when the output of the speakers gets fed back into the microphone and is amplified and sent back to the speakers in an endless loop. There is no complete cure for feedback. If the volume of any microphone is boosted loud enough, it will eventually cause feedback. There are a number of measures you can take to reduce feedback.

miniature clip-on microphone connects by a short cable to a small transmitter worn on the belt or elsewhere. A special receiver picks up the signal and feeds it to the mixer. Generally, a separate receiver/transmitter is needed for each microphone used.

When using a handheld microphone, sing or speak *across* it rather than directly into it to reduce the popping caused by sudden breath blasts. The microphone should be positioned in front and slightly to one side of the mouth. The user must stay within the acceptance angle of the microphone to avoid unwanted changes in

Field Tips on Controlling Feedback

Turn down the volume.

Move the microphone(s) farther away from the sound path of the speakers. Direct your microphone so that it doesn't pick up speaker output. Because it can be placed more purposefully, a microphone on a stand gives less feedback than a clip-on one.

Place speaker(s) as far forward of the performing position as possible.

Decrease gain on equalizer or tone controls.

—Adapted from
Dale A. Robbins, 1990

Field Tips for Solving Microphone Problems

No Sound?

➤ Make sure the microphone and system are both on.

➤ Check the battery.

➤ Check that "mute" is not selected.

➤ Ensure that the cord is securely plugged in the belt pack/control system.

Cuts In and Out?

➤ Make sure the belt pack antenna is hanging straight down and isn't twisted.

➤ Move the belt pack to your back.

➤ Check the battery.

➤ Avoid the location where the interruption occurred.

Feedback?

➤ Turn down the volume.

➤ Stay behind the speakers.

➤ Avoid the location where feedback occurred.

A/V technological gadgets are tempting, and most interpreters want to incorporate them into programs. Just remember, the more technology used in presentations, the more care and time needed to invest during the preparation stages.

the volume setting is the professional approach. Unusual circumstances, such as unexpected ambient noise, a larger or smaller group than normal, or employing guest speakers, may necessitate changes in volume. Ask the audience or have a partner signal when the sound is comfortable.

Other Types of Audio Equipment

There is a considerable diversity of audio equipment available to augment any sound system. Trying to address all the various components exceeds the scope of this book; however, let's take just a moment to mention equipment you may want to research. A mixer controls the audio inputs going into the sound system. It can switch between inputs, control the volume of each input, and control the outputs to which each input is sent. An equalizer fine-tunes a sound system's frequency response to a given location. Use it to adjust bass, treble, and midrange to provide the most pleasing sound and to minimize feedback. Reverb is sometimes used to provide artificial echo effects, but its real purpose is to provide extra depth and clarity to your sound. Cassette decks or record players that are "PA" (public address) capable allow you to use a microphone and the unit's amplifier and speaker (or external speakers) as a public address system. Powered speakers have a built-in amplifier. The more commonly used nonpowered speakers don't. You'll want a powered speaker for portability or to use in cases where an amplifier would be expensive or inconvenient.

volume. Using proper techniques, and perhaps an accessory windscreen, will solve most popping problems.

If you are having a guest speaker or a panel discussion, use additional microphones. Counsel your speaker(s) on how to properly use the microphones. Be aware of chains or necklaces that can hit the microphone and cause annoying disturbances.

Generally, you don't need to turn the volume up as high as you think. Preplanning

The proper location of the clip-on microphone is about six inches below the chin. Anticipate movements that may rub against or obstruct the microphone.

Digital-File Formats

TIFF (Tag Image File Format)—The most versatile, reliable, and widely supported bit-mapped format. Good for print use.

PICT—Macintosh's standard format for graphics and drawings that are cut or copied to the clipboard.

EPS (Encapsulated PostScript)—The standard format for storing high-resolution PostScript illustrations.

GIF (Graphics Interchange Format)—Intended mainly for online transmission.

JPEG (Joint Photographic Experts Group)—Data compression for images and a file type. Compression loses data. Not recommended for high-quality print uses.

PSD—Format that can only be opened and edited in PhotoShop. It can preserve layers, channels, and paths in a form that can be edited.

PDF (Portable Document Format)—Images can be saved from Photoshop as PDF files that can then be viewed using Acrobat Reader. JPEG compression can be used.

Computers are wonderful tools for developing programs that combine and manipulate text and digital photos for exciting LCD-projected presentations. Courtesy of Carolyn Widner Ward

applications can open and save in a number of file formats that can then be used to transfer images from one application to another. Some of the more common file formats include TIFF, PICT, EPS, GIF, JPEG, PSD, and PDF.

Brief notes for the presentation can be lightly written on the chart. The audience won't be able to see these notes if you use a pencil.

Computers

In the rapidly developing world of technology, the popularity of computers to generate presentations is definitely growing. Today's laptop computers coupled with common software packages offer tremendous flexibility for program design. A professional presentation can be prepared ahead of time and displayed using this exciting technology.

Computers are at the heart of the digital revolution in imaging. Be generous with memory, disk space, and monitor size. If you cut back because of cost constraints, cut back on processor speed—it's nice but not as crucial as memory. Most major graphics

Flip Charts

Don't assume that investing a lot of money in high-tech visual aids and equipment will make the presentation *better*. Remember, the purpose of using visual aids is to enhance the presentation, not upstage it. While everyone seems to be interested in creating high-tech computer-generated presentations, don't overlook the lowly flip chart. A flip chart is still an effective, portable, and useful presentation tool with many applications for interpretive programs.

Making flip charts can take a considerable amount of time. Make sure charts are prepared early enough to review them before

Flip charts are mobile and adaptable and are a simple way to help clarify your topic. Whether preprepared or spontaneous, the flip chart is an economical visual aid. Courtesy of Carolyn Widner Ward

the presentation. A poorly prepared chart can be very distracting.

Lighting

Lighting is often the last thing considered when planning a presentation, and yet it may be one of the most important elements to success.

General lighting is accomplished with flood lamps. More direct and intense lighting can be accomplished with spot lamps. Dramatic and special effects can be accomplished with theatrical stage lighting; however, this type of lighting can be very expensive, bulky, and is prone to the negative effects of weather and vandalism, especially if left outdoors for extended periods. Something as simple as a single spotlight can add dramatic effect to highlight objects, people, and focus attention. A simple alternative to the more expensive professional stage lighting is to use a slide projector with a blank black slide with a pinhole opening. Experiment with the size of the opening needed for the distance from the projector.

Lighting considerations for visitors with hearing impairment should also be recognized and provided. If these visitors have sufficient lighting, they are often able to lip-read, or they may be watching the oral or American Sign Language interpreter. If the room or area is too dark, a spotlight on you and/or the sign-language interpreter works well. Consult with an Americans with Disabilities Act (ADA) specialist. We discuss ADA needs and standards more thoroughly in Chapter 11.

Proper Operation and Maintenance of Audiovisual Equipment

Common sense, good practices, and a professional approach to proper operation and maintenance of valuable A/V equipment are essential. Many staff members rely on these expensive tools to assist in their program delivery. Equipment that does not function correctly detracts from the visitors' experiences and is certainly inconvenient for the interpreter. A/V equipment is not cheap to purchase, repair, or replace.

Flip Charts

Do not need electricity—No need to worry about the lamp burning out or needing an extension cord

Are economical—No special films or printers are necessary to produce your presentation materials

Let you add color—Flip chart markers allow creativity

Allows for spontaneity—Provide an interactive format

Are adaptable—Last-minute changes are easily accomplished

Proper operation of equipment is a key to successful A/V presentations. Knowing how the equipment functions, the safe use and storage of the equipment, and how to make repairs are all essential for program success.

Batteries

Batteries are used in all types of portable video, audio, and computer equipment. Understanding what type of batteries equipment uses and how to take care of them can make the difference between interpretive disasters or interpretive programs that succeed. There are three basic types of batteries: alkaline, nickel-cadmium, and lead-acid.

To ensure quality performance, routinely clean the battery contacts in the equipment and the charger. Use a cotton swab saturated with rubbing alcohol (isopropyl alcohol) to clean the contact points on the battery and the charger. Most charging problems are caused by dirty contacts on the battery or charger.

Portable Energy

Alkaline batteries—Usually found on drug-store counters. Alkaline batteries are not rechargeable. They are available in various sizes, such as A, AA, AAA, D, and 9V.

Nickel-cadmium (NiCad) batteries—The most widely used rechargeable battery in A/V equipment. NiCads charge quickly, last approximately 700 charge-and-discharge cycles, and perform well in cold weather. But even when unused, they can lose as much as 10 percent of their capacity each year. They should be totally drained before recharging. NiCad batteries are notorious for developing a recharge-resistant "memory."

Lead-acid batteries—Recharge immediately after use. If they are stored partially or totally discharged, they may never recharge again. Lead-acid batteries can be recharged roughly 500 times with slightly less usable power each time. Unused, they can lose up to 20 percent of their capacity each year.

Field Tips for Equipment Care

➤ Read the instruction manuals.

➤ Use the equipment for its intended purpose.

➤ Don't force controls and mechanisms.

➤ Perform periodic maintenance and safety inspections.

➤ Keep equipment clean and protect it from environmental hazards.

➤ Properly store equipment.

➤ Remove batteries from equipment when not in use.

Cleaning Lenses

Cleaning lenses is not a difficult task. It is a simple matter of using isopropyl alcohol or a photographic lens–cleaning solution along with lens-cleaning tissue. Other cleaning materials may leave lint or other residue on the glass. Blow the dust off the lens with a dry-air gun. Apply the cleaning solution to the lens-cleaning tissue. Avoid applying the solution directly to the lens surface. Wipe the lens in a spiral motion, beginning in the center of the lens and ending on the outside. If necessary, repeat the above steps until the lens is clean and free of streaks.

Changed Circumstances

If you are taking the interpretive program to a different venue, don't forget to take an extension cord supplemented with a power strip. An ungrounded plug adapter may also come in handy, because some facilities

---

Never store batteries in a refrigerator. Cold storage won't prolong the life of a battery. It may actually shorten it.

Field Tips for Using Equipment with Lamps

Moving the equipment while the lamp is on, or even shortly after turning it off, can cause premature failure. A hot lamp filament will fall apart if the machine is handled roughly.

Average lamp life means just that. On some lamps, the published life average maybe 65 hours; however, the lamp that lasts only 35 hours is not considered to be defective.

Never move a lamp changer lever (if your machine is so equipped) while the on/off switch is in the "on" position.

Excessive heat will shorten lamp life. A slow-running fan caused by lack of lubrication or a dirty motor will not cool a lamp sufficiently. Regular maintenance is required.

Don't block the airflow of the projector's cooling fan. Keep filters clean. The intake and output grills must not be obstructed or overheating will occur, shortening the lamp life.

A higher-than-normal AC line voltage will tremendously decrease lamp life. Whereas higher voltage might not affect other appliances, an increase of only two volts will shorten lamp life by as much as 20 percent, five volts as much as 58 percent!

A lamp that is not properly seated in its socket may seem burned out. The lamp may not make good enough contact to light, but it may make just enough contact to arc and burn its pins or the contacts of the socket.

When your program is over, turn the projector completely off and let the bulb cool naturally. Try not to move the projector for at least 15 minutes. Don't leave the fan running. Using the fan to cool the bulbs in modern projectors will actually shorten the life of the bulb.

—Adapted from
United Visual's Web site, 2002

still don't have three-prong grounded outlets. For everyone's safety, tape the power cord and cables to the floor to prevent tripping.

A spare backup lamp is also good insurance. Make sure you know how to change the lamp in case it burns out during your presentation. To protect yourself from burns, don't touch a hot lamp with bare fingers. Handle the new replacement lamp by the metal or porcelain base or with a handkerchief, because the oils from your hands can mar the lamp. A pair of clean cotton gloves is very useful when changing lamps.

Other Considerations

Copyright

A copyright is a form of intellectual-property protection that grants its holder the legal right to restrict the copying and use of an original expression (i.e., literary work, photograph, music, painting, software, mask work, and so on). Copyright laws do not specifically exempt making copies of other people's work, even if it is for interpretive or educational objectives; however, often the owner of copyrighted material will grant nonprofit, educational, and government agencies permission to use copies of their work. Additionally, works in the public domain do not have copyright restrictions. To further clarify the intricacy of the copyright law, the United States

To avoid copyright problems, use your own work, materials that are in the public domain, created prior to 1922, or are copyright free.

Copyright Office (2002) provides the following information. (See table 12.1.)

Photography

Producing quality photographs takes skill and practice. We encourage you to explore the discipline and the equipment options available. To improve your skills, take advantage of the hundreds of books on photographic techniques. You might also want to visit the Eastman Kodak Web site for many helpful tips. One of the best ways to improve your photography skill is to practice. Keep a record of camera settings, weather, and other conditions under which each picture was taken. After a while, you will learn what worked and what didn't by seeing the picture itself and referring to the conditions under which it was taken.

Field Tips for Good Composition

➤ Have a strong center of interest.
➤ Find the best camera angle.
➤ Frame your subject.
➤ Fill the frame.
➤ Use the "rule of thirds" for subject location.

Table 12.1—Copyright

Copyright is a form of protection provided by the laws of the United States (title 17, U.S. Code) to the authors of "original works of authorship," including literary, dramatic, musical, artistic, and certain other intellectual works. This protection is available to both published and unpublished works.

It is illegal for anyone to violate any of the rights provided by the copyright law to the owner of copyright. These rights, however, are not unlimited in scope. One major limitation is the doctrine of "fair use," which is given a statutory basis in section 107 of the 1976 Copyright Act.

Section 107 contains a list of the various purposes for which the reproduction of a particular work may be considered "fair," such as criticism, comment, news reporting, teaching, scholarship, and research. Section 107 also sets out four factors to be considered in determining whether or not a particular use is fair:

1. The purpose and character of the use, including whether such use is of commercial nature or is for nonprofit educational purposes;

2. The nature of the copyrighted work;

3. Amount and substantiality of the portion used in relation to the copyrighted work as a whole; and

4. The effect of the use upon the potential market for or value of the copyrighted work.

The distinction between "fair use" and infringement may be unclear and not easily defined. There is no specific number of words, lines, or notes that may safely be taken without permission. Acknowledging the source of the copyrighted material does not substitute for obtaining permission. The safest course is always to get permission from the copyright owner before using copyrighted material. When it is impracticable to obtain permission, use of copyrighted material should be avoided unless the doctrine of "fair use" would clearly apply to the situation.

—Adapted from the Copyright Office, 2002

Top Five Picture Tips

1. Show one subject clearly. A picture with a single dominant subject makes its point quickly and clearly. When you look through the camera's viewfinder, it is human nature that the eye and mind will see only one subject, even if there are many objects. This often results in cluttered pictures with unclear intent. When taking a picture, carefully arrange the scene so that one subject stands out.

2. Get close. Fill the picture area with a subject so it stands out and grabs the viewer's attention.

3. Simplify the background. Busy backgrounds sap pictures of their power by competing with the subject. Move the subject or yourself to position a plain background, such as grass, a wall, or sky, behind the main subject.

4. Observe the light. Harsh sunlight casts deep shadows. Cloudy daylight evenly illuminates scenes so everything is clearly visible. Low lighting reveals textures, while overhead lighting reduces textures. The best effect depends on your subject and intentions. Observe the light and change your position to get a better angle or wait for the sun to disappear behind a cloud to get better results.

5. Hold the camera steady. If you don't hold the camera steady, the results may not be disastrous, but they won't be acceptable. Your pictures will be blurry and perhaps unusable. Holding the camera steady is especially important on very cloudy days outdoors. A good technique to help with this is to pull your elbows into your sides and hold your breath right before releasing the shutter.

—Adapted from the
Eastman Kodak Company
Web site, 2002

The Rule of Thirds

A picture is more interesting if the main subject is not centered. Arrange it off to the side. Compose the picture as if there was a tic-tac-toe grid overlaying the image; each spot where the lines intersect is ideal for placing a subject. Additionally, have the subject "look" into the photo.

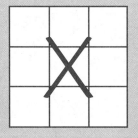

Avoid putting your subject in the center of the photo

lower left

upper right

upper left

lower right

The basic principles of composition are extremely important to achieve good photographs. Photographic composition is simply the selection and arrangement of subjects within the picture area. Become familiar with these rules of composition and practice them until they become second nature to you.

In the Next Chapter ...

Now that we have an understanding of interpretation, program types, and supporting equipment, let's turn our attention to how to evaluate whether or not we are presenting effective and informative programs.

Review

1. Incorporate A/V equipment when and where appropriate to augment and enhance presentations by auditory and/or visual means.

2. The camera is the most underutilized piece of equipment in the interpreter's arsenal of A/V tools.

3. Storage of film in the refrigerator/freezer is okay, but that is not a good location for batteries.

4. Advancements in digital camera technologies have greatly increased their popularity and use, but there continue to be opportunities for film-based photography.

5. An LCD projector coupled with a computer is rapidly becoming the preferred choice for presentations; however, the rugged, portable, and simple-to-operate slide projector still produces life-size, high-quality images that are sharp and have the brightest colors of any comparable media.

6. The 80-slide tray is the preferred standard. If your program has more than 80 slides, consider reducing the number of slides or using two trays and a lapse dissolve.

7. Keystone occurs when the projector is not on a perpendicular plane with the screen. The image appears wider at one end. Adjusting the projector location or the screen orientation can correct the keystone problem.

8. The overhead projector provides an environment for the presenter to stand in front of the audience, exhibit an object, and project information about that object in a lighted room. It allows for hands-on demonstrations while projecting an image of the finer details of the object on the screen. It also provides a lighted atmosphere where open discussion and feedback with the audience are possible.

9. When using a lapse dissolve with slide projectors, make sure that everything is plugged in to the same power strip.

10. Microphone feedback is caused when the output speakers get fed back into the microphone, amplified, and sent back to the speakers in an endless loop. Remedy this by turning down the volume, moving the microphone away from the sound path of the speakers, and decreasing gain on the equalizer or tone controls.

11. Photographic composition is the selection and arrangement of items within the picture using the "rule of thirds" for subject location.

Questions and Exercises

1. What are the advantages/disadvantages between film and digital cameras?

2. What speed of 35mm film affords the greater opportunity to capture fast action?

   64

   200

   400

   800

3. What is an LCD projector and what type of media does it project?

4. What is keystone and how do you correct it?

5. What does a lapse-dissolve unit do?

6. Name three advantages of using a flip chart over other more sophisticated presentation techniques.

7. To control feedback from a microphone you should: (Circle all that apply.)

   Turn volume up

   Move microphone away from the speakers

   Increase the tone

   Place your speakers behind you

8. Lenses can be safely cleaned with window cleaner and paper towels.

   True or false? Why?

9. Storing batteries in the refrigerator can extend their life.

   True or false?

10. What is the "rule of thirds" in photography, and why should you use it?

11. What is "fair use" of copyright materials?

12. List at least four ways to avoid copyright problems.

13. Describe when you should use A/V equipment.

References

Books

Ham, Sam H. 1992. *Environmental Interpretation: A Practical Guide for People with Big Ideas and Small Budgets.* Golden, Colo.: Fulcrum Publishing.

Heinich, Robert, Michael Molenda, James Russell, and Sharon Smaldino. 2001. *Instructional Media and Technologies for Learning, Seventh Edition.* Upper Saddle River, N.J.: Merrill.

Hooper, Jon K. 1997. *Effective Slide Presentations: A Practical Guide to More Powerful Presentations.* Golden, Colo.: Fulcrum Publishing.

McPherson, Alan and Howard Timms. 1988. *The Audio-Visual Handbook.* New York: Watson-Guptill Publications.

Rowell, Jan. 1990. *Picture Perfect: Color Output in Computer Graphics.* Beaverton, Oreg.: Tektronix, Inc.

Schroeder, Don and Gary Lare. 1989. *Audiovisual Equipment and Materials: A Basic Repair and Maintenance Manual.* Metuchen, N.J.: Scarecrow Press.

Tilden, Freeman. 1967. *Interpreting Our Heritage, Revised Edition.* Chapel Hill: University of North Carolina Press.

Online

Eastman Kodak Company, Rochester, New York. 2002. www.kodak.com.

National Park Service. 2002. Harpers Ferry Center Interpretive Media Resources. Harpers Ferry, W.Va. www.nps.gov/hfc.

Robbins, Dale A. 1990. "Understanding Church Sound Systems." Grass Valley, Calif.: Victorious Publications. www.victorious.org/soundsys.htm.

United States Copyright Office. 2002. Washington, D.C. www.copyright.gov.

United Visual, Inc. 2002. "Tech Tips." Itasca, Ill. www.unitedvisual.com.

Pamphlet

Eastman Kodak. 1989. "Kodak Sourcebook: Kodak Ektagraphic Slide Projectors." Publication No. S-74. Rochester, N.Y.

Chapter 13

Practicing Defensible Interpretation: Evaluation

All interpretive efforts should be carefully evaluated to determine if program objectives are being met. Courtesy of Humboldt State University

Defensible interpretation can be tangibly measured for effectiveness.

Main Points

Why Conduct Evaluation?
What to Evaluate?
    Interpreter
    Audience
    Program
When Should Evaluation Be Conducted?
    Before (Front-End)
    During (Formative)
    After (Summative)
Who Conducts Evaluation?
    Audience
    Supervisor
    Peer
    Expert
    Interpreter
How Should Evaluation Be Conducted?
    Traditional and Scientific Evaluation
    Objective-Based Assessment
        Cognitive Objectives
        Behavioral Objectives
        Affective Objectives
        Measuring Cost-Effectiveness
    Putting It All Together
Reporting Evaluation
Closing the Loop (Modification)

> There is much to be learned
> from evaluating interpretation,
> if we only ask the right questions.

to answer useful questions and ask the unanswerable ones. In order to understand the best use of precious economic, human, and biological resources, evaluation efforts must be an integral element of the design and delivery of interpretation. They should not be treated as an external afterthought to programming. The survival of interpretation and your programs depends on the critical examination of what is done, how it is done, and what results from it. Evaluation is the foundation of the practice of the science of interpretation.

Before addressing practical methods of evaluation, let's begin by looking at the basic concepts and theories of evaluating interpretation. The following are the guiding questions that should be used to design evaluation procedures: *Why conduct evaluation?*, *What to evaluate?*, *When should evaluation be conducted?*, *Who conducts the evaluation?*, and, finally, *How should evaluation be conducted?* The answers to these questions directly impact which methods and procedures of evaluation are appropriate. Let's review the potential answers to each of these questions and discuss the resulting impacts.

Evaluation is a critical component of all interpretation. It links many of the elements discussed in the other chapters and brings us full circle from program creation to program assessment. Evaluation is conducted because we want to know more and we want to do better. It must be applicable to the practitioner, the manager, and the public. It needs

> *Having developed the art of interpretation to a high degree, [we are] increasingly stepping back and looking at the science of evaluating interpretation.*
>
> —William Penn Mott Jr.,
> 1909–1992

Eval-u-ate (transitive verb)

: to determine or fix the value of
: to determine the significance, worth, or condition of usually by careful appraisal and study

—*Merriam-Webster's Online Dictionary*, 2006

Interpretation must be accountable to the people it serves, the agency it represents, and the resources it interprets.

Why Conduct Evaluation?

There are many purposes, and thus benefits, of conducting evaluation. Each is important and provides insight into the overall success of interpretive efforts. As a practice, evaluation is the key to the survival and development of the discipline of interpretation itself. Without tangible, defensible results from interpretive programs and services, interpretation as a service will go the way of the dinosaur. In this day and age of limited budgets, personnel, and time, only those services with discernible results will continue to be supported. Evaluation provides the glue that links our services, the interpreters, the audiences, and the managers together within the science of the practice of interpretation.

Interpretation is often considered to be a "nice to have" fringe visitor service without real tangible benefits. As a result, the profession itself is being increasingly marginalized in budgets and staffing. Despite ideas of what interpretation can or should do, a lack of "evidence" and demonstrable outcomes result in interpretation being the first to go when funding is low and the last to be considered when resource planning is conducted. Historic functions and benefits of interpretation, such as education and visitor management, are no longer demonstrably provided by interpreters, but instead are carried out by environmental educators and law enforcement officers, respectively. Both of these groups provide tangible measurable outcomes of their services and thus are being increasingly supported over interpretation.

Resources are experiencing pressure from growing numbers of visitors while managers, faced with decreasing budgets, are asked to control behavior, protect visitor experiences, and provide for recreation opportunities for everyone. Amidst this climate, the key to ensuring the survival of interpretation is through providing services that clearly meet or address visitor, resource, and management needs. Making the discipline of interpretation unexpendable is one of the roles of evaluation.

The key to defending and ensuring the survival of the profession is to critically examine what interpretation does, how it is done, and what results from it. In other words, conducting *defensible* interpretation is the key to the survival of our discipline. Evaluation is the element in the interpretive process that links all other steps and participants. It begins the planning process by allowing interpreters to identify target audiences, understand and know the resource, and establish program goals and objectives. Evaluation is also at the heart of the creative process. The design of appropriate messages that meet audience, resource, and management needs requires evaluation. Finally, evaluation provides the measurement and assessment of whether or not goals and objectives were met.

For example, evaluation sets the direction and helps establish what interpretation should do. From managers to field interpreters, it is through evaluation that appropriate goals and objectives are outlined for interpretive services. The *purpose* behind the program should always be able to be articulated within the framework of management goals and objectives. Interpretation conducted without a purpose is simply entertainment, and although we hope that our interpretive services are pleasurable and enjoyable, they are *not* simply a means to entertain visitors. "An interpretive program should exist for a reason, and the best reason is to fulfill one or more management objectives or goals" (Huggins 1986, 65).

Numerous researchers, authors, and practitioners echo this position. The National Association for Interpretation (NAI) agrees with this and has added "purposeful" to the basic qualities of good interpretation. According to NAI, "If you can't state the goals and objectives for your program, there's probably no reason to be doing it" (Brochu and Merriman 2000, 42).

Once evaluation has established what should be done, the second primary role of evaluation is to guide how best to accomplish those objectives. What messages are the most appropriate for identified target audiences? Which mediums are the most useful? Evaluation should guide the design and delivery of appropriate messages to meet audience, resource, and management needs. For example, does a hands-on program work more effectively to increase message retention than does a program without hands-on activities? Will nonpersonal or personal interpretive services work better? Evaluation and research are the keys to answering these questions and guiding our interpretive efforts and services. How we conduct interpretation should not be based on what we think works, but what we know, based on empirical evidence, works. This role of evaluation is especially valuable to field interpreters.

This leads us to the third role of evaluation: to know whether or not the interpretive services accomplished what they set out to do. There seems to be a variety of perspectives on how research and evaluation in interpretation should be conducted, ranging from rigorous scientific surveys to casual observations of visitors' behavior. There have been many debates regarding the appropriateness of each method. This is similar to the discussion of whether or not interpretation is an art or a science.

Seeing the sparkle in the eyes of visitors and sensing the enthusiasm in the audience are both traditional methods of evaluation. Seasoned interpreters often feel that they can

Why Conduct Evaluation?

➤ Increase program effectiveness
➤ Determine if visitors' needs are met
➤ Assess if program goals and objectives are met
➤ Assess interpreter's effectiveness
➤ Establish professional legitimacy
➤ Measure cost-effectiveness
➤ Provide budget justification

tell when their program when well. These traditional proponents often view scientific evaluation as minimizing the true impact and effect of interpretation to the heart and mind of the individual. After all, we are exposing the "soul of a thing" (Tilden 1957) to the heart of a person. How can this be measured, and doesn't the mere attempt to assess it degrade the spirituality of it? How can you measure and quantify art?

Although there is certainly a spiritual nature to the art of interpretation, given the current climate of accountability and limited resources, interpretation must justify the time, money, and personnel it requires. Interpretation must be accountable to the people it serves, the agency it represents, and the resources it interprets. Just as ministers or priests may be "called" to the church, they are still trying to accomplish particular goals and are periodically evaluated on their effectiveness in meeting those goals. It does not lessen their spirituality to be evaluated, but instead is an indicator of their commitment and dedication to their profession. Regardless of the specific methods used, measurement of the success of meeting the mission, goals, and objectives of the agency and the program is critical to maintaining support for interpretive services, increasing overall effectiveness, meeting audience needs, and protecting the resource and the visitor.

Evaluation is the element in the interpretive process that links all other steps. It is the first, the middle, and the last. It begins the planning process by allowing the interpreter to identify target audiences, understand and know the resource, and establish program goals and objectives. It provides the guidance and direction for the design of appropriate messages to meet audience, resource, and management needs. Evaluation is also the final step in the process. It provides the measurement and assessment of whether or not goals and objectives were met and, by doing so, helps establish future issues and goals, thus closing the loop. Evaluation links the manager and administrator to the field interpreter, the field interpreter to the visitor, the visitor to the resource, and the resources to the overall program goals and objectives.

What to Evaluate?

Deciding what should be evaluated is the next component of determining the appropriate methods for conducting assessment. There are numerous aspects of the interpretive services that can and should be evaluated, such as facilities, accessibility, interpreters, programs, information-delivery services, and so on. One of the key questions that should guide choices of what to evaluate is the perceived value of the information that would be collected. Always know why you are conducting evaluation.

There are three categories of personal interpretive services relevant to evaluation: the interpreter, the audience, and the program. Each of these elements acts and reacts with the others to create the whole of the interpretive experience. Thorough evaluations need to consider each of these elements to gain a true picture. For example, the interpreter could be a fabulous communicator and entertain the audience very well; however, without a meaningful message, the whole of the interpretive service would fall short. Conversely, the program could be technically accurate but be performed in a monotone by a lifeless interpreter. Once again, the whole of the interpretation service would be less than desired. As a result, when conducting evaluation, it is important to examine from numerous perspectives.

Interpreter

When referring to interpreter evaluation, all who deliver interpretive services to the public are included. For example, volunteers, docents (highly trained volunteers), seasonal

What Should Be Evaluated?

Interpreter	Audience	Program
Body language	Learning	Connects
Appearance	Attendance	Relevant
Enthusiasm	Satisfaction	Enjoyable
Credible	Enjoyment	Appropriate
Voice quality	Behavioral change	Thematic
Eye contact	Emotional impact	Engaging
Confidence	Attention	Structured
Grammar	Memory	Cost-effective
Passion	Provocation	Accessible

interpreters, and so on, should all be evaluated. The interpreter controls program delivery, content, and interacts directly with the audience. As such, examining the interpreter is a critical component of all evaluation of interpretive services.

Evaluations of the interpreter should include verbal and nonverbal communication techniques and skills, interpersonal interactions with the audience, and expertise in and ability to address visitor needs and meet program goals and objectives. Interpreters can be evaluated using numerous methods (surveys, observations, and so on) implemented by a variety of sources (supervisor, audience, and so on). Specific methods of evaluation will be reviewed later in the chapter.

Audience

The audience is another focus of evaluation. The audience could be a group of schoolchildren, a mixed-age audience at a campfire program, or general visitors encountered during roving. Anyone who receives interpretive services is considered the audience. Attendance, attention, satisfaction, and recall are some of the most common elements evaluated.

Care should always be taken when collecting data to ensure the information will be helpful. For example, how many people attend the program is probably one of the most common forms of data collected. It is easy to assess and gives some reflection of the program's success. It reflects attendance levels and, examined over time, could yield useful patterns in program attendance; however, although attendance level data is useful, popular programs do not necessarily equate to *effective* programs. A critical question of evaluation should be *Is the program effective?* Who better to answer that question than the audience? There are numerous ways that the audience can evaluate interpretive services. Since satisfaction, program objectives, and overall success of interpretation are

judged based on the target audience, audience evaluations are a critical component of interpretive assessment.

Program

The third target for evaluation is the program itself. Whether for a formal school-based program or an informal roving contact, evaluations must include an examination of the program. There are many elements regarding a program that can be evaluated: visitor accessibility, meeting goals and objectives, relevance, organization, and cost-effectiveness are only a few.

Each of the elements of evaluation are interrelated. For example, the interpreter delivers the program and must be considered in the program evaluation through assessment of the delivery characteristics. The program should have specific, measurable objectives that reflect careful planning. These objectives should clearly answer the questions *What is the goal of the program?* and *How should effectiveness be measured?* In other words, the objectives of the program determine the direction of the evaluation. The program is the focal point of the evaluation, but elements surrounding the effectiveness of the interpreter, the satisfaction of the audience, and meeting goals and objectives of the program should all be included in the assessment. The key is to thoughtfully consider how the audience, the interpreter, and the program evaluations impact each other.

When Should Evaluation Be Conducted?

Deciding when to conduct evaluation is another question that must be answered in order to identify the best methods for evaluation. There are three basic times to conduct evaluation: before, during, and after the program (Diamond 1999; DeGraaf, Jordan, and DeGraaf 1999; Roggenbuck and Propst 1981). The best strategy will include examination of effectiveness throughout the planning, delivery, and feedback phases of program development.

Before (Front-End)

Evaluation conducted before the program is called front-end and typically occurs during the planning stages. Evaluation conducted at this stage involves the planning and selection of the topic, theme, target audience, method of delivery, and the goals/objectives of the program. Front-end evaluation is similar to a needs assessment, where the target audiences' needs, wants, and goals are examined and programs are matched accordingly (DeGraaf, Jordan, and DeGraaf 1999). These aspects of evaluation were covered in detail in Chapter 4. This stage of the process is critical for successful and meaningful evaluation of the program in the later stages. It is in this front-end planning stage that the direction, goals, and objectives for the program are established. These goals and objectives, written in WAMS style (page 64), are the very indicators used to evaluate effectiveness in the later stages of evaluation.

During (Formative)

Formative evaluation occurs during the program and is often used by interpreters to ascertain if the program is going well. This type of evaluation was discussed in Chapter 3 when we reviewed the steps of the communication process. Formative evaluation occurs naturally when communicating by watching body language, facial expressions, and other cues to know if communication is effective. For example, we may watch visitors' eye contact as an indicator of our ability to hold their attention. Although these are not very scientific, they are classic examples of assessing interpretation during the program.

After (Summative)

Depending on your perspective, summative evaluation occurs at the end of an individual

Conducting evaluation during an interpretive program provides critical insight into overall effectiveness. Courtesy of Alan E. Wilkinson

program or at the end of an entire interpretive season. For example, a manager might consider all evaluations occurring during the season to be formative and only end-of-the-year, cumulative assessments to be summative.

Summative evaluation conducted at the end of an individual program is beneficial for discovering the impact of a program. At the end of the interpretive season, summative evaluation is beneficial for indicating the overall success of interpretive programming. Impact assessment (product evaluation) is considered one of the most important forms of assessment (Diamond 1999; DeGraaf, Jordan, and DeGraaf 1999). Program effectiveness can be partially judged based on whether or not the outcomes matched the objectives of the program. If the answer is no, modifications to the objectives, the target audience, the interpreter, or the program are in order. Thorough evaluation will make it clear which should be modified.

Who Conducts Evaluation?

The person or group providing the evaluation clearly impacts how the process is conducted.

Putting It All Together—An Example

Front-End (Before)

➤ Goals and objectives for a program are outlined in the planning process.

➤ A target audience for the program is determined based on research.

➤ Messages and themes are identified to meet audience needs and fulfill goals and objectives.

Formative (During)

➤ Interpreter communication characteristics during the program are assessed.

➤ Audience reactions to the program are examined.

➤ Messages and themes are analyzed to determine if appropriate for audience needs.

Summative (After)

➤ Message retention and recall by the audience are examined.

➤ Interpreter self-assessments are conducted.

➤ Behavioral impact of the program is assessed.

➤ Cost-effectiveness is determined.

Closing the loop (Modification)

➤ Modifications to programs, delivery, and assessment methods are made.

➤ Program goals and objectives are reevaluated.

The audience, supervisor, peer, expert, and the interpreter are all potential sources for conducting the evaluation. Each of these evaluators may use different methods and strategies of assessment. The following section provides an overview of these sources of evaluation.

Audience

The audience is a critical group performing evaluation. From their informal feedback during a program (body language, eye contact, and so on) to more formal written evaluations, the audience is especially effective at telling us if program goals and objectives are met, if their needs are addressed, if the program itself is effective, and what their overall satisfaction level is. This feedback is usually initiated and facilitated by someone other than the audience, such as the interpreter, supervisor, expert evaluator, and so on. Although anyone can initiate evaluations, it is your responsibility as the interpreter to ensure that evaluation occurs.

Supervisor

Assessment conducted by a supervisor or manager is very beneficial. This type of evaluation can provide insights into the program's effectiveness, the interpreter's skills and abilities, audience reactions, and how well the program meets agency and program goals and objectives. Much of what supervisory evaluations are geared toward is helping to coach you through the developmental stages of your interpretive careers. The National Park Service has a well-developed coaching program (Module 330) and focuses on providing the feedback necessary to develop personal skills. The feedback and coaching received from supervisors should be used to help improve your interpretive techniques, skills, and abilities.

Peer

Peer evaluation occurs when a colleague conducts the evaluation. These evaluations are useful on many levels and highly recommended. They can be very helpful in increasing overall effectiveness, building

Every performance, every summer season, every service, and the entire program merits some kind of serious, systematic, open, fair analysis …

—Douglas Knudson, Ted T. Cable, and Larry Beck, 1995

collegiality, enhancing comprehensive knowledge of the resource, and providing nonthreatening feedback. It's important that the parameters of the evaluation are predetermined. Discuss ahead of time what you expect, establish a game plan, and decide whether you would like oral and/or written comments. Peers can also attend the program as members of the general audience and observe visitor reactions and comments throughout the program. This unsolicited audience feedback can provide very authentic insight into program and interpreter effectiveness.

Expert

A professional evaluator, researcher, or statistician performs expert evaluation. This is one of the most objective forms of evaluation. Expert evaluators have the advantage of being neutral and, as such, are often more able to recognize problems or issues that may be overlooked by peers or supervisors. Expert evaluation is very beneficial for providing rigorous objective results that are free of the bias that in-house evaluations may have. There are many methods and strategies for expert evaluation, including in-depth interviews, focus groups, observations, and surveys. Expert evaluations are typically more costly and time-consuming than other types of evaluation; however, the precision and quality of the information is often worth the cost.

Interpreter

Interpreters themselves must also initiate evaluations. As the interpreter, you have the primary responsibility to evaluate your

programs yourself and audience reactions to and satisfaction with the interpretation. Evaluations conducted by interpreters themselves are called self-evaluation. Douglas Knudson, Ted T. Cable, and Larry Beck said this is the "most efficient and least threatening method of evaluation" (1995, 448). The remaining sections of this chapter review and discuss practical and effective methods that you can implement in order to evaluate the effectiveness of personal interpretive services. There are disadvantages *and* advantages of evaluating your own programs. We'll review and discuss these as we examine the various methods for conducting evaluation.

How Should Evaluation Be Conducted?

Traditional and Scientific Evaluation

The quality of feedback is only as good as the methods used to collect it. There are numerous methods for how evaluation should be conducted, ranging from rigorous scientific surveys to casual observations of visitors' behavior. In fact, most authors in the literature make two classic distinctions of assessment methods: traditional and scientific. There have been many debates regarding the appropriateness of scientific assessment versus the more traditional, gut-level impressions about

Hiring an expert researcher is a useful strategy to provide much-needed information on the users in your resource. Courtesy of Carolyn Widner Ward

> *Since an objective of any park administration is to improve the quality of park use, the effectiveness of our interpretive program is a major concern of all administrators.*
>
> —George Hartzog, 1920–present

programs; however, as discussed previously, scientific evaluation provides defensible results with tangible outcomes as opposed to the more traditional methods of assessment. For example, a gut-level feeling about your program is not easily demonstrated to a supervisor, nor is it an adequate justification for an increase in budget. Traditional evaluations are often based on biased questions, selective perception, and result in inaccurate conclusions (Nardi 2003).

There are clearly merits to each evaluative approach and a time and place for each method. As you move between the two ends of the continuum, you trade off between

precision of measurement and cost. Scientific evaluation measures are typically much more precise and accurate but at a cost of time, finances, and effort. *Both* methods can be used to gain an accurate, total picture of the effectiveness. The most appropriate methods for conducting evaluation depend on the answer to many questions, such as *Who is conducting the evaluation?*, *What is being evaluated?*, and *When will the evaluation take place?* They also depend on other issues, such as money, time, and the expertise available.

Let's proceed with the practical realization that you, as an interpreter, have no money, probably know very little about evaluation, and are already feeling overwhelmed with the amount of work you have to do. So, how can you possibly conduct defensible interpretation and thus quality evaluation with your very first program?

Objective-Based Assessment

Before beginning a discussion of specific

Evaluations

Scientific Evaluation

Pros	Cons
➢ Generates definitive evidence of effectiveness	➢ Requires money, time, and expertise
➢ Respected by researchers and administrators	➢ Difficult to collect, tabulate, and analyze
➢ Often results in quantifiable data	➢ Reduces intangibles to tangible numbers
➢ Allows for precise measurement of interpretive services	➢ Field application of results is often difficult

Traditional Evaluation

Pros	Cons
➢ Provides immediate feedback	➢ Often inaccurate and unreliable
➢ Easy to implement	➢ Biased
➢ Requires little training	➢ Based on emotion and feeling
➢ Based on intuition and gut feeling of interpreter	➢ Provides no distinction between entertainment and interpretation
➢ Cheap/inexpensive	

Cognitive Objective Assessment Techniques

Quizzes and games—Learning can be easily assessed before, during, or after a program by having a quiz or game to assess knowledge. Games and quizzes provide enjoyment, hands-on participation, social interaction, and allow for assessment. Divide visitors into teams or have them participate as individuals. Quizzes may involve answers to questions, identification of objects, smells, etc. Use your imagination to make the evaluation part of the program fun.

Pre- and postassessment written responses—A very useful method to assess cognitive objectives is a measure of knowledge before and after the program. There are many ways in which this knowledge can be measured. The following is one example. Have two colors (for our example, yellow and green) of 3 x 5 index cards and hand out one card of each color and a pencil to each individual at the start of the program. After your introduction, ask visitors to put their birth date in the top left corner of both cards. This is so you can match the two cards later. Have them write the answer to a question you ask at the start of the program on the green card and collect them. Conduct the program as planned and repeat the question at the end

of the program. Have them record their responses on the other card. After the program, the cards can be matched to assess any increase in knowledge. Note: If there are children in the group too young to meaningfully answer, let them participate by drawing a picture of something from the program before and after.

Review questions—Similar to the above methods is the use of review questions during and after the program. Ask questions to assess visitors' knowledge levels of information presented during the program. These can be conducted formally or informally as the program proceeds. For example, on the return after a guided walk, ask visitors questions about information covered during the walk.

Comment cards—Comment cards are similar to the pre- and postresponses described above, but are typically used after the program. They can be used to assess both knowledge and affective objectives. They are easy, convenient, and effective measures that first-time interpreters can implement.

evaluative methods, we need to establish a framework through which to review them. For example, in discussing surveys, we could focus on who conducts the survey (audience, supervisor, peer, and so on), when it is conducted (front-end, formative, and so on), and/or what it will examine (interpreter, program effectiveness, meeting goals and objectives, and so on). Since each of the guiding questions introduced at the start of this chapter impacts and affects the others, let's return to one of the guiding issues underlying all interpretation: *What is the objective of the program?* As discussed in Chapter 4, all programs should have clearly stated objectives. Methods of evaluation,

regardless of when, by whom, or where they are conducted, should be based upon assessments of what you were trying to accomplish with programs (Knudson, Cable, and Beck 1995; Diamond 1999). This idea brings us full circle back to the original guiding discussions in Chapter 2 about why we conduct interpretation in the first place.

The purpose behind the program should always guide evaluation. In addition, good objectives should demonstrate the connection between front-end, formative, and summative assessment. As reviewed in Chapter 4, there are three basic types of objectives for interpretive programs: cognitive, behavioral, and affective. Closing the

Comment Card—An Example

Hungry Mother State Park
You can help us improve the quality of our interpretation.

1. What was the main point or message of the program?

2. How did you find out about the program?

3. What did you enjoy most about the program?

4. What did you enjoy least?

5. Name two reasons it is important to protect the Yellow Lady Slipper.

Thank you for your time!

Field Tips for Cognitive Objective Assessment

Randomly survey the population—For example, asking every fifth person produces results more reflective of the entire population of users than allowing them to take one if they wish. Keep it simple. Don't ask too many questions—no more than five. Too much data will be difficult to tabulate and analyze. In addition, visitors are generally on vacation and should not be extensively disrupted from their recreational experience.

If written, keep it small—Keep the actual written surface small and unimposing. This also forces you to carefully select the questions.

If oral, have a method of recording—Have a coworker or friend available to discreetly record answers to any oral methods of assessment. If that is not possible, placeholders can be used to serve as hatch marks of answers. For example, move coins from one pocket to another in between stops on a walk to signify the number of correct responses.

Multiple methods of return—Provide multiple drop-off points for any written data. Make it easy and anonymous for visitors to return the information.

Assess throughout the season—Conduct evaluations throughout the interpretive season. This information can be used very effectively to show patterns and changes. For example, if you conduct 15 wildflower programs throughout the season, randomly sampling five of them will yield a good picture of the entire season.

Pre- and postassessment (change)—Incorporate before and after assessment methods to determine the cognitive impact of programs.

loop with our planning discussions, let's use these objectives to guide our understanding of the associated methods of assessment for each type of objective.

Cognitive Objectives

Cognitive objectives involve the understanding, information transfer, and/or learning that occurs based on the program. An example of this would be, *During a quiz at the end of the program, 80 percent of randomly selected visitors will correctly identify two adaptations of desert life.* One of the classic methods of measuring cognitive objectives is through pre- and postassessment. Knowledge is measured before *and* after exposure to a program to determine if a difference exists. If the evaluations are conducted appropriately, the increase in knowledge after exposure to the program can be attributed to the program. This information can be used to assess whether or not program objectives were met. This is one of the most common forms of assessment, primarily due to the ease of data collection and the tangible results produced.

Behavioral Objectives

Behavioral objectives focus on the physical activities of visitors. For example, *50 percent of visitors will take a brochure on tide pool*

A Special Note about Survey Data Collection

➤ Always check with your agency for any rules and criteria that regulate data-collection methods or procedures.

➤ If you work for a federal agency, conduct programs on federal land, or use federal dollars to conduct programs, then the Office of Management and Budget also regulates data-collection procedures.

protection is a behavioral objective. One of the classic methods of measuring this type of objective is by observing actual behavior. The key for implementing and measuring behavioral objectives is to ensure that observation is easy, practical, discreet, and can reveal the targeted behavior. For example, if the desired behavior is to protect the resource, then what behaviors will you tangibly measure? Objectives must be stated in terms of observable phenomena. One of the most common problems with using behavioral objectives to measure program success is that objectives often attempt to assess behaviors that are not

Behavioral Objective Assessments—An Example

If the behavioral objective in your program is to change visitors' behavior regarding picking up litter, then observing visitors' responses to a planted piece of garbage may be indicative of program success. For example, before the program, observe random visitors in the parking lot and their response to a "planted" piece of trash. How many visitors walk by the trash before someone picks it up? If 40 visitors walk by before someone picks it up, this could be a general average for this behavior (i.e., one out of 40 visitors will pick up trash), but repeat this several times to get an average for the behavior. After the

program, count how many visitors walk by before someone picks up the same type of planted trash. If only 10 program attendees walk by the garbage before someone picks it up, then the program may have reduced the average to one out of 10 visitors. This produces a tangible behavioral result from the program.

Keep in mind that this is not statistically defensible data; however, it does yield practical results that, if found repeatedly or averaged over time, produce meaningful, practical, defensible results of our interpretive efforts.

Field Tips for Behavioral Objective Assessment

Conduct random observations of visitors— Randomly choose times, places, and visitors to observe. This produces results more reflective of the general population of users.

Implement pre- and postobservations— Observations of random visitors can be compared to random observations of visitors exposed to the program to determine a difference due to exposure.

Target only specific observations— Keep observations very specific and manageable. Don't conduct observations of resource protection. These observations are often too general to be very useful. Instead, determine what specific behaviors reflect resource protection.

Assess behavior during the program— Conduct observations during or immediately after the program. Assessments should be linked as closely as possible to the time of exposure to the program.

Observe evidence of behavior— Sometimes it is easier and more discreet to observe the *evidence* of the behavior. For example, instead of watching visitors pick up trash, count the number of pieces of planted litter along a trail before and then after the program.

Be sure the behavior is observable— If the desired behavior is to provoke visitors to want to learn more, then you must be able to observe and assess that behavior.

easily observed or connected with program exposure.

Affective Objectives

Affective objectives focus on the emotional impact of programs. The goal is for visitors to care, to support, to feel, and to be changed by the emotional impact of the resource and our programs. This is one of the most powerful types of program objectives, but also one

of the most difficult to assess. *Randomly surveyed visitors before the program compared to those surveyed after will demonstrate a 20 percent increase in positive feelings that tide pools should be protected* is an example of an affective objective. One of the classic methods of measuring this type of an objective is a self-report of emotion. In other words, ask the visitors how they feel about something.

Observations can also be used to measure targeted affective objectives. For example, the number of visitors purchasing books or taking brochures about the program's topic after exposure could assess visitors caring about the topic. Keep it simple and be sure that observations or self-report measures reflect the targeted emotions. Tips and techniques for conducting this type of evaluation are similar to the strategies we reviewed for cognitive and behavioral objectives. For example, if using self-report measures of emotions or feelings, then follow the tips for measuring cognitive objectives, but if using behavior to measure effectiveness, then the tips for measuring behavioral objectives will be helpful.

Measuring Cost-Effectiveness

Another useful element to include is a measure of cost-effectiveness. Although cost-effectiveness should not be the primary focus for determining the program's effectiveness, it is useful information to include in reports providing a review of the overall effectiveness of a program. As with all evaluation, there are varying degrees of assessment. As a first-time interpreter, you can calculate a rudimentary assessment of the cost-effectiveness of your programs.

Like it or not, budgets drive much of the practical ability to conduct interpretation. Determining cost-effectiveness can be a significant contributor for providing budget justifications (Machlis 1986; Roggenbuck and Propst 1981); however, assigning a dollar figure to the "worth" of

Measuring Cost-Effectiveness—An Example

Input measures
Staff
        Program design—5 hours
        Program length—1 hour
        Total number of programs—10
        Total staff time—15 hours
        Staff cost—$15 per hour
        Total staffing cost—$225

Materials
        $5 per program
        Total season cost—$50

Total input cost—$225 (staff) + $50 (materials) = $275

Output Measures
        300 total people attended throughout the season
        Cost/person of the program = 0.92 cents
        10 percent reduction in litter due to program
        10 hours staffing time saved to clean up this litter
        $150 maintenance salary savings
        10 percent increase in book sales regarding recycling due to program attendance
        $55 book-sales increase

Total output benefits—300 people served + $150 salary savings + $55 in book sales increase

Cost-Effectiveness Overview
    Recycling program
        Total cost—$275 ($0.92 per person contacted)
        Total benefit—$205 ($150 maintenance salary savings + $55 book-sales increase)

Overall cost-benefit analysis = $70 cost (0.23 per person contacted)

interpretation is a double-edged sword. Although it often provides a tangible measure, many would argue that you cannot place a dollar value on intangibles, such as inspiration or provocation. Although we agree, you can place a value on *some* of the outputs. For example, cost-effectiveness can be measured in the reduction of litter after a program and the budgetary savings of reduced clean-up hours spent by personnel. In addition, book-sale increases after a program on the same topic can provide good measures of cost-benefit.

In addition to measuring output, the cost-effectiveness of a program can also be evaluated by assessing input. For example, the hours spent preparing and delivering a program can be converted into the equivalent amount of salary ($P) and then divided by the total number of people contacted in the program (N) to ascertain the cost per individual visitor ($P/N) of the program. This measure, coupled with any discernible outputs in dollar figures, can provide a compelling picture of the cost-effectiveness of a program.

Evaluation Strategy—An Example

Let's look at one way this program could be evaluated.

This outline provides a strategy for evaluating the program that reflects many different points of view, times throughout the season, and purposes for the evaluation. By conducting evaluation that relies on more than one method, you gain greater insight into the true success of your program. No one method is perfect, but taken together, many different ones can yield a more complete picture of the effectiveness of the interpretive services you provide.

Program: Afternoon tide pool walk

Theme: Tide pool life strives to survive with each changing tide

Goals:

➢ Increase visitor satisfaction with the experience of exploring tide pools

➢ Promote tide pool protection

➢ Increase visitor knowledge about the fragile nature of tide pools

Objectives:

➢ Visitors surveyed randomly before and then again after the program will demonstrate a 20 percent increase in positive feelings that tide pools should be protected.

➢ Seventy percent of randomly surveyed visitors using a comment card will indicate positive satisfaction levels with the program.

➢ Eighty percent of visitors asked will correctly identify two reasons to protect tide pools.

Implementation: The following methods would not all be implemented at once, but instead throughout the entire season.

Audience

➢ Have randomly selected visitors complete comment cards regarding tide pool objectives.

➢ Conduct visitor satisfaction surveys.

Supervisor

➢ Invite supervisors to your program early in the season, the middle, and, finally, near the end so they can see the improvements made based on their feedback.

Interpreter

➢ Observe visitor behavior at the tide pools before and after your programs.

➢ Collect attendance levels at all programs.

Putting It All Together

The best solution for increasing the overall effectiveness of evaluation is to use several methods. Since each method has strengths and weaknesses, evaluation through multiple strategies will produce a more accurate assessment of program effectiveness. This is called triangulation. Triangulation increases overall accuracy. For example, if three separate methods are implemented to assess accomplishing program objectives and all three produce similar results, this is a more accurate measure than if only one method were used. Methods discussed in this chapter are often not as rigorous as the scientific methods used by researchers or expert evaluators. Different methods can be used within one program or across the season of the program to produce a summative evaluation more accurate than the results from any single method.

Reporting Evaluation

Another aspect of conducting evaluation is documenting the results. Reporting should be simple, brief, and related directly to the gathered information. A primary use of this information is to help you, the interpreter, increase effectiveness. Additionally, the documentation should assist supervisors and

Incorporating evaluation measures into the program as an activity, coupled with outside observers' assessments, result in an effective strategy to measure program effectiveness. Courtesy of Humboldt State University

administrators to recognize your efforts and justify additional support for interpretive efforts. Reporting should include program summaries, outlines, objectives, attendance levels, and summaries of assessment measures used.

Be sure to keep a copy of all your reports and reporting procedures for your own records. Don't forget to place a copy of the reports in the individual program folders created in the planning stage. This information will be very useful for future interpreters.

Evaluation is an extremely useful tool to indicate program effectiveness, encourage interpreter development and growth, and further the mission of the department. When asked why you are conducting an interpretive program, you should now be able to answer and clearly demonstrate your effectiveness in meeting those objectives.

Closing the Loop (Modification)

Modification to the original program, if warranted, is the next step of evaluation. This highlights one of the key aspects of evaluation, namely, that it is a *process* and should always influence and inform subsequent steps. Reflecting back to Chapter 4, you'll recall that we discussed how monitoring and evaluations are an integral part of the creation process for interpretive programs. A report produced from the evaluation is not the *final* step; instead, it is part of a cyclical process. Evaluations can suggest program modifications, give statistical summaries, and provide information for year-end reports regarding the products, successes, and satisfactions with interpretive efforts.

In the Next Chapter ...

We have completed our journey in understanding what interpretation is, how to conduct various program types, and, finally, how to evaluate the success of our efforts. We now turn to the profession and its future. What does it mean to be an interpreter? What are the responsibilities of the profession, and what role do interpreters play to ensure further development of the discipline? In Chapter 14, we'll discuss these and other issues facing the developing profession of interpretation.

Review

1. Evaluation is the key to conducting defensible interpretation.

2. Evaluation provides a critical examination of what interpretation does, how it is done, and what results from it.

3. Evaluation should be guided by the objectives set forth in the planning process of program design.

4. The three primary elements that should be evaluated involve the characteristics inherent to the interpreter, the program itself, and the audience.

5. Ideally, evaluation should be conducted before, during, and after the actual program.

6. Evaluation carried out before the program is called front-end evaluation and typically occurs during the planning process.

7. Formative evaluation occurs during the actual program and usually incorporates the traditional forms of audience feedback, such as eye contact and body language.

8. Summative evaluation at the end of the program or an entire season is also known as impact assessment.

9. Evaluation can be conducted by the audience, the interpreter, a peer, a supervisor, or an expert. Regardless of how evaluation is conducted, results should be discernable and demonstrable.

10. Scientific evaluation methods include surveys, interviews, and focus groups and are more rigorous assessment methods.

11. Traditional evaluation methods include causal observations of visitor behavior, comment cards, and gut-level assessments of program success.

12. Scientific and traditional types of evaluation represent the two ends of the continuum of assessment methods, trading off between precision of measurement and cost of assessment.

13. Objective-based assessment provides an opportunity for first-time interpreters to conduct meaningful evaluation.

14. Objective-based assessment is driven by program objectives and the assessment of whether or not the program met and addressed those needs.

15. Cognitive objective assessment techniques include quizzes and games, pre- and postwritten responses to questions, comment cards, and review questions.

16. Behavioral objective assessment techniques primarily involve observations of observable targeted behavior.

17. Affective objectives can be evaluated by observation and survey methods.

18. Tips for successful objective-based assessment include randomly surveying or observing the population, designing questions or observations of phenomenon that will clearly address the objective in question, conducting evaluation with a minimal amount of questions or criteria to observe, and having a discernable method of tabulating the collected data.

19. Cost-effectiveness is another method of assessing program effectiveness and can be done relatively easily by comparing input costs to output benefits.

20. The best evaluation strategies will include several methods of assessment.

21. Evaluation is not the end of the process, but instead links directly back to the initial planning stages and program modification.

Questions and Exercises

1. List four reasons why we should conduct evaluation of interpretive programs.

2. Name two positive characteristics of expert evaluation.

3. Describe one method of assessing learning based on program objectives.

4. To save time, you should only distribute surveys to visitors you think will fill them out.

   True or false? Why?

5. Describe how you could successfully measure the emotional impact of an interpretive program.

6. A common goal for interpretation is to change long-term behavior. Describe one way you can observe and measure this behavior.

References

Articles

National Park Service. 1997. "Interpretation as Communication." *Trends* 34 (4).

Roggenbuck, Joseph and Dennis Propst. 1981. "Evaluation of Interpretation." *Journal of Interpretation* 6 (1): 13–23.

Books

Babbie, E. 1992. *The Practice of Social Science Research, Sixth Edition.* Belmont, Calif.: Wadsworth Publishing Company.

Brochu, Lisa and Tim. Merriman. 2000. *Interpretive Guide Training Workbook.* Fort Collins, Colo.: National Association for Interpretation.

———. 2002. *Personal Interpretation.* Fort Collins, Colo.: National Association for Interpretation.

DeGraaf, Donald G., Debra J. Jordan, and Kathy H. DeGraaf. 1999. *Programming for Parks, Recreation, and Leisure Services: A Servant Leadership Approach.* State College, Pa.: Venture Publishing.

Diamond, Judy. 1999. *Practical Evaluation Guide: Tools for Museums & Other Informal Educational Settings.* Walnut Creek, Calif.: Alta Mira Press.

Hart, Diane. 1994. *Authentic Assessment: A Handbook for Educators.* Menlo Park, Calif.: Addison-Wesley Publishing Co.

Henderson, Karla A. 1991. *Dimensions of Choice: A Qualitative Approach to Recreation, Parks, and Leisure Research.* State College, Pa.: Venture Publishing.

Huggins, Robert. 1986. "Going for the Gold." In Gary E. Machlis, ed., *Interpretive Views: Opinions on Evaluating Interpretation in the National Park Service.* Washington, D.C.: National Parks and Conservation Association.

Knudson, Douglas, Ted T. Cable, and Larry Beck. 1995. *Interpretation of Cultural and Natural Resources.* State College, Pa.: Venture Publishing.

Lewis, William. 1986. "Evaluation of Interpretation." In Gary E. Machlis, ed., *Interpretive Views: Opinions on Evaluating Interpretation in the National Park Service.* Washington, D.C.: National Parks and Conservation Association.

Loomis, Ross J. 1987. *Museum Visitor Evaluation: New Tools for Management.* Nashville, Tenn.: American Association for State and Local History.

Machlis, Gary E. 1986. *Interpretive Views: Opinions on Evaluating Interpretation in the National Park Service.* Washington, D.C.: National Parks and Conservation Association.

Mitra, Amanda and Sam Lankford. 1999. *Research Methods in Park, Recreation, and Leisure Services.* Champaign, Ill.: Sagamore Publishing.

Nardi, Peter M. 2003. *Doing Survey Research: A Guide to Quantitative Methods.* Boston, Mass.: Allyn and Bacon.

Sharpe, Grant and Wenonah Sharpe. 1986. "Evaluating the Role of Interpretation." In Gary E. Machlis, ed., *Interpretive Views: Opinions on Evaluating Interpretation in the National Park Service.* Washington, D.C.: National Parks and Conservation Association.

Tilden, Freeman. 1957. *Interpreting Our Heritage.* Chapel Hill: University of North Carolina Press.

Online

Merriam-Webster Online Dictionary. 2005. www.m-w.com/netdict.htm.

Chapter 14

Growing from a Tradition: Professionalism

There is an art and science to the profession of interpretation.
Courtesy of Steve Martin

The future of the profession involves
developing the science of high-quality
standards for the practice, the trainings,
and the evaluation of the art of interpretation.

Main Points

- Profession: *n.* a calling requiring specialized knowledge and often long and intensive academic preparation
- Professional: *n.* characterized by or conforming to the technical or ethical standards of a profession
- Professionalism: *n.* the conduct, aims, or qualities that characterize or mark a profession or a professional person
    —*Merriam-Webster*
    Online Dictionary, 2005

Now that we have uncovered the history, purposes, theories, and skills of practicing interpretation, we turn to a more philosophical discussion about the profession itself. Is interpretation a profession? And what does it mean to be a professional interpreter? We know what it means to practice the art and science of interpretation, but what is it to *be* an interpreter?

We have an ethical responsibility when we practice interpretation. We have a responsibility to fairly and appropriately represent the resource, the agency, and to act in the best interest of the public, ourselves, and the discipline itself. These responsibilities and standards of practice combine to form the foundation of much of the profession of interpretation. This chapter will introduce and propose issues and ideas for contemplation. Keep them in mind as you develop and grow as an interpreter.

What Is a Profession?

Before we begin a discussion of whether or not interpretation is or should be a profession, we must understand what a profession is.

Ere long may nature guiding be an occupation of honor and distinction. May the tribe increase!

—Enos Mills, 1920

There are numerous definitions of profession, professional, and professionalism. It is important to remember that when we try to define something, we typically do so in order to distinguish it from something else. In this case, the effort is to distinguish the professional from the amateur or the untrained. For example, all of the definitions of a professional seem to converge on the ideas of formal training, education, and standardized practices.

When love and skill work together, expect a masterpiece.

—John Ruskin, 1819–1900

In the field of interpretation, discussions of professionalism abound. From the early calls of Enos Mills (1920) to develop the profession to the current directions by the National Association for Interpretation (NAI) (2002) to pursue and improve the profession, most assert the desire for interpretation to be considered a "true profession." So, what is a profession? Let's begin by examining some basic characteristics and see how interpretation measures up.

There are some basic characteristics of a profession on which most agree (Baseman 1998; Beck and Cable 2002; Brochu and

Merriman 2002; Knudson, Cable, and Beck 1995; Sontag and Haraden 1988). One of the central tenets is that a profession must have a knowledge base, a collection of information, theories, and ideas that form the philosophy, framework, and foundation of the field. Freeman Tilden (1957) and Mills (1920) outlined much of the original philosophy of interpretation. Authors and practitioners such as Sam H. Ham, Douglas Knudson, Ted T. Cable, Larry Beck, John Veverka, Grant Sharpe, and others expanded upon the early work. These later publications didn't serve to replace the articulated philosophy of Mills and Tilden, but instead contributed to a living and evolving philosophy. In terms of this first characteristic, interpretation does indeed seem to be a profession.

A second characteristic of a profession is accepted standards of practice. In order for interpretation to be considered a true profession, it must assert and maintain a standard code of ethics and practice. In order for this to occur, there must typically be one organization that speaks for the body of practitioners. In other words, in a profession, there should not be different rules, standards, and practices for different individuals, organizations, or agencies. For example, the American Medical Association speaks for the medical profession. In interpretation, we do have a central organization, the NAI; however, they are not the licensing organization, nor are practitioners of interpretation required to belong or ascribe to the standards asserted by this organization in order to practice interpretation. In addition, there are different standards of practice depending upon the organization or supervisor for whom you work. This characteristic of a profession, although constantly changing and evolving, is not strongly or consistently demonstrated in interpretation.

Closely linked with the idea of standards of practice is the issue of accreditation and licensing. Peer recognition, standards of practice, codes of ethics, and many of the other qualities of a profession are often driven and controlled by a licensing organization to which members give the power to provide oversight and control. The Bar Association and the American Medical Association are just a couple of examples. Until recently, there has not been a single organization that licensed or certified interpreters. This lack of professional certification was an indication of the members' inability to determine what standards *should* be prescribed. This lack of certification changed in 1998 when NAI began offering certifications in four categories. This was done in order to "support the organization's mission of advancing interpretation as a profession" (Brochu and Merriman 2002, 5). The National Park Service has also fostered the successful Interpretive Development Program, designed to increase the overall professionalism of interpretation practiced in the national parks. The program has training modules allowing interpreters to progress through skill development and demonstrate interpretation at a national standard.

> *It is probable that nature guiding will become a nation-wide and distinct profession, and, though different, ranks with the occupations of authors and lecturers.*
>
> —Enos Mills, 1920

A fourth characteristic of a profession is quality control, oversight, and measurement of the application of standards. Research, evaluation, and monitoring are critical to professional development. Methods of increasing the knowledge base, developing understanding, and examining the successes and failures of the standards of practice must exist. This is essentially the research-and-development arm of the discipline. Over the years, standardized practices of research and evaluation have been increasing and contributing to the development of the

> Training is part of an interpreter's journey
> to becoming a professional.

discipline. Conferences and other networking opportunities are also available to develop and disseminate the knowledge generated through research. In fact, our effectiveness "depends upon a regular nourishment by well-directed and discriminating research" (Tilden 1977, 5). Although research and critical examinations are increasing, there is always room for improvement.

The fifth characteristic or quality of a profession is that it provides opportunities for training, education, and development. Ideally, this training and education should be based on documented and defensible results from research about what works, when, and for whom. Mills (1920) recognized early the need for training and development of interpreters when he said, "While I have trained a few nature guides there appears to be a need for a State University or a Foundation regularly to develop nature guides" (139). Today, there are numerous training, educational, and development opportunities provided by private, state, national, and international resource-management agencies, universities, and NAI. These trainings serve to further the development and growth of the individual, which promotes the overall success of the profession. There are "many avenues [that] contribute to our professional growth. As we continue to work at a particular site, we grow in our knowledge of the place, we grow in our experience there, and we grow to love the place" (Beck and Cable 2002, 115). This practical site experience, combined with special training and education, helps further the development of the profession.

Interpretation is beginning to demonstrate the necessary basic qualities and characteristics of a profession. It is in its

infancy, and the initial stages of growing from a practice to a profession are not without turmoil. Now let's turn to a discussion of the difference between the *practice* and the profession of interpretation.

Characteristics of a Profession

> ➤ Knowledge-based
> ➤ Standards of practice
> ➤ Accreditation
> ➤ Quality control
> ➤ Continuing educational opportunities

From Practice to Profession

As a discipline, interpretation is evolving from individuals practicing a craft to a cohesive group building and participating in a profession. Interpretation as a practice is as old as the ancient art of storytelling. Interpretation, in this sense of the word, was used to convey meaning, history, and tradition and was practiced by many. Interpretation as a profession with the associated characteristics previously discussed is a much younger phenomenon. Let's explore the distinctions between the practice of interpretation and the profession of interpretation.

Interpretation is a developing discipline. Although there are many of the qualities and characteristics of a profession throughout the practice of interpretation, the consistency of their application is lacking. In addition, there are thousands of volunteers, or "happy amateurs," as Tilden called them, and novice practitioners of interpretation throughout the country. In fact, Tim Merriman, executive director of the NAI, estimates that there are more than 250,000 individuals volunteering in the field of interpretation. Many of these individuals have little to no interpretive training yet practice interpretation daily. These individuals are sometimes critical to the overall accomplishment of the mission in various resource locations; however, they are not professionals practicing the discipline of interpretation. Because so many novice, untrained individuals practice interpretation, many feel that interpretation may never be a *true* profession. For example, would the public ever accept a novice practicing medicine or would they demand that he/she be a trained, licensed professional? Since it is commonly accepted that volunteers with little to no training work as interpreters, then how could interpretation ever be elevated to a true profession, and should it be?

These issues prompt us to make a distinction between the *practice* of interpreting and the *profession* of interpretation. This distinction is not meant to assert judgment about the rightness or the quality of the service, merely to allow for a critical discussion of interpretation as a profession.

Many in the field become very uncomfortable discussing professionalism. They feel they were "called" to be interpreters and categories and titles of *professional* only minimize the spiritual aspects of what they do. Some wonder if the path to professionalism will result in a "path of standardized and sanitized mediocrity" (Basman 1998, 6). The profession is a noble one that is not easily captured by titles, categories, or certifications. The art of practicing interpretation is not easily conveyed in trainings or in technical

Academic training, accreditation, and certification are several methods moving interpretation from a practice to a profession. Courtesy of Carolyn Widner Ward

classes. Passion, enthusiasm, and love for the art of interpretation cannot be taught. Further, the attempt to teach the techniques to those without the love results in meaningless and emotionless education-driven programs. These sentiments are not without merit. The dry, information-laden programs performed by the uninspired interpreter are certainly not models of *good* interpretation.

> *Our struggle to be recognized as an integral service will come only when we are recognized as professional.*
>
> —Cem Basman, 1998

The other side of this debate recognizes the importance and value of training and education in the development of a profession. Although training can't replace or teach innate passion, the hope is that practitioners possess the passion and learn the techniques to better carry out the mission. Even ministers and priests who were "called" to the church undergo education, training, and certification processes. This is not to degrade or minimize the spiritual nature of their calling, but instead to elevate the seriousness of their

> *Perhaps the real challenge is to come up with a code of ethics that all interpreters can subscribe to and leave it at that.*
>
> —Wil LaPage, 1998

mission by adopting, scrutinizing, and promoting set standards and practices. There are no absolute answers to these issues, only the need to have discussion and continue the evolutionary development of interpretation.

Responsibilities

Now that we have an understanding of what constitutes a profession and the tenuous journey of interpretation to become a profession, let's turn to a discussion of the responsibilities of an interpreter. As a *professional* interpreter, you have a responsibility to the science of interpretation that you practice, the agency for whom you work, the audience you serve, and the resources with which you work. In addition, one of the most critical responsibilities is to yourself. Each of these areas interacts with the others to weave a tapestry of what it means to be an interpreter. Although we will discuss each separately, they are all interrelated. These responsibilities help us to distinguish the mere *practice* of interpretation from the *profession*.

The Discipline of Interpretation

Every interpreter has a responsibility to know, understand, and apply the best practices of interpretation. It is the collective group that makes up the profession.

> No one can question the importance of professionally certifying teachers to ensure a standardized level of competence. We must be sure of the credentials of those who influence our children. Conversely, no one can logically question the impossibility of institutionalizing the creativity of artists (although some have tried). Our challenge is to embrace both of these components of our trade and incorporate them into how we define excellence in our diverse (and sometimes eclectic) profession.
>
> —Cem Basman, 1998

> We have professional responsibility to accurately tell the interpretive stories.

"Interpreters, as individuals, must protect the dignity and value of the profession in the careful handling of every activity" (Brochu and Merriman 2002, 4). Every time an interpreter interacts with the public, he or she represents the field as a whole. The collective reputation of the profession, especially in its infancy, is only as strong as its weakest link. Administrators, managers, and visitors form opinions about the field of interpretation based on personal experiences with individual practitioners. The key responsibility to the discipline of interpretation is to know how to conduct quality interpretation. It is the individual's responsibility to stay current in the literature, to learn new skills and strategies, to contribute to the discipline through articles, research, and so on, and to participate in trainings and conferences. Networking is a critical component of improving and growing the profession of interpretation. The profession is only as strong as the members creating and adhering to it.

Organization

As an interpreter, you have responsibility to represent the organization for which you work in an appropriate and ethical manner. In the field of interpretation, you work for the public you serve, the resource you represent, and the organization that writes your check. You have a responsibility to positively represent your organization, promote its mission, increase public support, and conduct ethical action in the organization's best interest. Hopefully, you are working for an organization with which your personal values and perspectives agree. Life is short. Be sure you are doing something you

Every interpreter has a personal responsibility to research carefully the messages being conveyed, to represent their organizations faithfully, and to handle the facts, artifacts, and stories of culture and science ethically.

—Lisa Brochu and
Tim Merriman, 2002

The audience looks to you to speak for the resource, the past, and the agency you represent. Help your resource come to life for visitors. Courtesy of Carolyn Widner Ward

love. In the field of interpretation especially, the love and passion for what you do plays a tremendous role in the success with which you perform your job. Visitors can see the innate interest, passion, and care you have for your resource and your programs. This can't be taught through trainings, books, or manuals. It is *you* who must bring the belief and support of the mission of the employer for whom you work to the public you serve. This is not to say that you should blindly follow or agree with all decisions or policies. You have other responsibilities as well.

Promote the interpretive mission
in all endeavors.

Audience

It is your responsibility to serve your clients in the most appropriate and ethical manner possible. The audience depends on you to convey accurate, fair, and meaningful information. We serve as the conduits of information, history, and meaning to the individual. As such, most visitors do not approach our programs and messages with skepticism. Therefore, you have an ethical responsibility to ensure that the information and messages you share with the public are conveyed with the utmost quality, discretion, and honesty. Balancing the needs and mission of your employer with the demand to accu-

rately represent the resource is your responsibility. The audience deserves the "truth" of the science, the place, the people, and so on, and it is your job as a professional to provide this as ethically as possible.

Resource

You must represent the resource to the public in such a manner as to ensure its protection, promote visitors' respect and support, and encourage the development of future resource stewards. For many visitors, interpreters serve as the link between the resource and the meanings ascribed to it. In addition, for many locations, the interpreters are the ones most familiar with the resource and the

The audience and even the organization may not know when the interpreter fails to act ethically. Interpreters, as individuals, must protect the dignity and value of the profession in the careful handling of every action.

—Lisa Brochu and
Tim Merriman, 2002

impacts that occur because of visitor use. You have a responsibility to promote resource knowledge, understanding, and protection through your carefully planned programs. We "speak for the trees," and in this role, we must be able to know what they would say (Seuss 1971). Research, research, and research are the keys to fulfilling our responsibility to the resource. There is no substitute for field experience, for walking the halls of the historic building, for being in the resource, and for knowing the place. As a professional, it is your responsibility to the resource to know it so well that you may accurately and appropriately translate its voice.

> Any fire, even one of the spirit,
> must be tended or it will soon smolder and die.

Interpreter

The final responsibility you have is to yourself. In order to be an effective and happy interpreter, you have to feel it, to believe in it, and to sincerely care about what you are doing. You must fuel your enthusiasm, your innate interest, and your passion. During the first weeks on the job, excitement permeates everything you do. As the interpretive season wears on, you become more comfortable with your programs, the public, and your resource. After the 50th time you give that same program, … well, it is easy to become

> Do not burn yourselves out. Be as I am—a reluctant enthusiast … a part-time crusader, a half-hearted fanatic. Save the other half of yourselves and your lives for pleasure and adventure. It is not enough to fight for the land; it is even more important to enjoy it.
>
> —Edward Abbey, 1927–1989

Interpreter's Creed

As an interpreter, I shall endeavor to:

➤ Be approachable, kind, and respectful to visitors and colleagues.

➤ Know, understand, and apply the "best practices" of interpretation.

➤ Conduct evaluation of my programs and myself.

➤ Stay current in the literature, techniques, and skills of interpretation.

➤ Conduct meaningful thematic interpretation based on thorough research.

➤ Keep in touch with visitors' needs, goals, and desires.

➤ Make all of my presentations, programs, and displays relevant, enjoyable, and accessible.

➤ Be a role model for environmental responsibility.

➤ Be a resource, mentor, and professional colleague to others.

➤ Continually refresh my interest and love of the resource.

complacent. The other responsibilities of a professional interpreter that we have discussed will all be affected if you become bored, tired, or too comfortable. Keep your programs fresh; add new information, modify, read, learn, and always try to remember, it is the first time visitors will hear it. Most importantly, keep yourself fresh and renewed. The number-one way to do this is to repeatedly get out in the resource. Walk the trails and the historic sites and remember why you entered this field in the first place.

The Future

These responsibilities coupled with the basic qualities and characteristics of a profession, paint *one* possible picture of the development and growth of interpretation as a profession. The directional development of the discipline should not and will not proceed without division, controversy, and debate. This developmental process should bring about lively discussions regarding quality, quantity, management, standards, oversight, evaluation, and certification among other topics. It is only through intellectual discussions and debates that the profession will evolve and grow. The participation of the practicing members of the profession is necessary for the critical questions to be asked and answered. Where is the profession heading? What direction should it be going? What is the role of individual members? These are the questions we should be asking ourselves.

The future of the profession is up to *you*, the practicing interpreter. The role you play in the development of the discipline is significant. We all determine what the profession is, how it will be managed, and what the accepted standards will be. How you develop and grow as an interpreter is largely up to you. There are many paths to an

Don't forget to stay in touch with why you became an interpreter. Enjoy the resource, smell the flowers, and go fishing. Courtesy of Carolyn Widner Ward

The National Association for Interpretation— Joining the Profession

In an effort to link numerous individuals across the country participating in and practicing the art and science of interpretation, the National Association for Interpretation (NAI) was established in 1988. NAI was formed when the Association of Interpretive Naturalists joined with the Western Interpreters Association. This, for the first time in the history of interpretation, created one voice to speak for the discipline. Although the organization is still young and evolving, it does help meet one of the qualities of a profession by uniting practicing individuals into one group. Joining NAI is easy and provides many useful benefits.

end, and which road you choose to follow is up to you. The profession of interpretation is a noble and distinguished one, deserving the dedication and participation of its members. *That is you!* Ask questions, contribute, grow, change, challenge, and discover. The profession begins to die when the members become complacent and stop learning.

Our mission is one of distinction and importance. "It is a worth-while life work and one that will add immeasurably to the general welfare of the nation" (Mills 1920, 140). Especially in this day and age of dissolution, environmental degradation, terrorism, fear, and general unease, our natural and cultural resources and our connections to them are critical. Not only is connecting the public to natural and cultural resources important to the overall health of the world, but interpretation of the critical issues facing the world and its people is important. Who better than an interpreter to

The future of interpretation
is up to each of you.

help make sense of the critical issues we face? Isn't that our job, to translate the science, link people to the places, and speak for the issues? We cannot and should not restrict ourselves to just the simple topics. Instead, we should tackle those that are difficult, complex, and unclear. These critical managerial, political, and emotional issues are the worlds we should help illuminate for the public and for ourselves.

What's Next?

You now have the theories, tools, skills, and techniques of an interpreter and are ready to begin practicing the art and science of interpretation. There will be many new opportunities and experiences that will teach you more about the essence of interpretation than could ever be imparted in a book. Learn, grow, and teach others. As an interpreter, you wield enormous strength, influence, and responsibility … use them well.

Review

1. Professionalism requires standardized practices, trainings, and the rigorous evaluation of the art of interpretation.

2. The key qualities of a profession are that it has a theoretical base, standards of practice, licensing or accreditation, research and development, and continued opportunities for training and education.

3. As an interpreter, you have a responsibility to the organization for which you work, the resources you represent, the audiences you serve, the disciplines you practice, and to your own internal values and beliefs.

Questions and Exercises

1. What do you consider to be the primary quality of a profession? Why?

2. Do you think interpretation should be a profession? Why?

3. What steps can you take to assist in your own professional development?

References

Articles

Basman, Cem. 1997. "On Defining Professionalism." *Legacy* Nov./Dec.

———. 1998. "The Soul of Interpretation." *Legacy* May/June.

LaPage, Wil. 1998. "The Power of Professionalism." *Legacy* May/June.

Lee, Cassandra. 1998. *Bibliography of Interpretive Resources*. Fort Collins, Colo.: National Association for Interpretation.

National Park Service. 1997. "Interpretation as Communication." *Trends* 34 (4).

Books

Beck, Larry and Ted T. Cable. 2002. *Interpretation for the 21st Century, Second Edition*. Champaign, Ill.: Sagamore Publishing.

Brochu, Lisa and Tim Merriman. 2002. *Personal Interpretation*. Fort Collins, Colo.: InterpPress.

Ham, Sam H. 1992. *Environmental Interpretation: A Practical Guide for People with Big Ideas and Small Budgets*. Golden, Colo.: Fulcrum Publishing.

Jordan, Debra Jean. 2001. *Leadership in Leisure Services: Making a Difference, Second Edition*. State College, Pa.: Venture Publishing.

Knudson, Douglas, Ted T. Cable, and Larry Beck. 1995. *Interpretation of Cultural and Natural Resources*. State College, Pa.: Venture Publishing.

Machlis, Gary E. and Donald R. Field, eds. 1992. *On Interpretation: Sociology for Interpreters of Natural and Cultural History, Revised Edition*. Corvallis: Oregon State University Press.

Mills, Enos. 1920. *Adventures of a Nature Guide*. Garden City, N.Y.: Doubleday, Page, & Company.

Nyberg, K. 1977. "Some Radical Comments on Interpretation: A Little Heresy Is Good for the Soul." In Gary E. Machlis and Donald R. Field, eds., *On Interpretation: Sociology for Interpreters of Natural and Cultural History, Revised Edition*. 1992. Corvallis: Oregon State University Press.

Seuss, Dr. T. 1971. *The Lorax*. New York: Random House.

Sharpe, Grant. 1982. *Interpreting the Environment, Second Edition*. New York: John Wiley and Sons, Inc.

Tilden, Freeman. 1957. *Interpreting Our Heritage*. Chapel Hill: University of North Carolina Press.

———. 1977. *Interpreting Our Heritage, Third Edition*. Chapel Hill: University of North Carolina Press.

Veverka, John A. 1994. *Interpretive Master Planning*. Helena, Mont.: Falcon Press.

Online

Merriam-Webster Online Dictionary. 2005. www.m-w.com/netdict.htm.

Paper

Sontag, William and Tom Haraden. 1988. "Gotta Move! We've Outgrown the House." In *Proceedings, National Interpreter's Workshop*, National Association for Interpretation, Oct. 24–28, San Diego, Calif.

Index